FLY DRESSERS' GUIDE

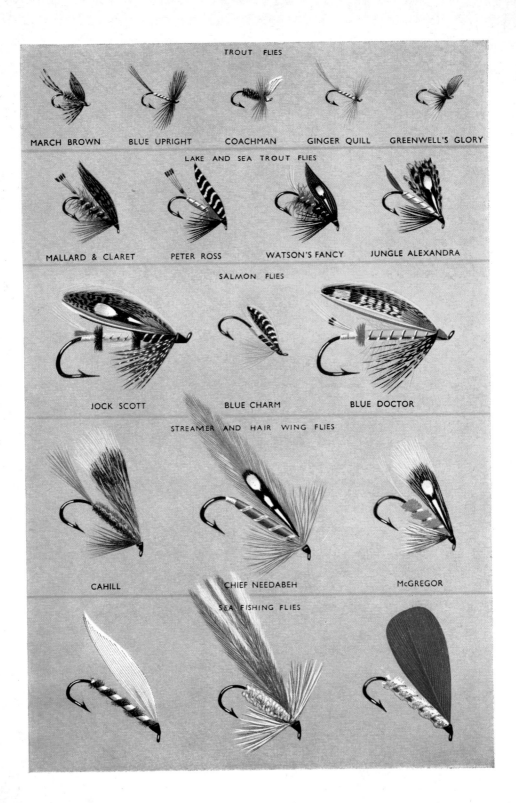

TROUT FLIES

MARCH BROWN   BLUE UPRIGHT   COACHMAN   GINGER QUILL   GREENWELL'S GLORY

LAKE AND SEA TROUT FLIES

MALLARD & CLARET   PETER ROSS   WATSON'S FANCY   JUNGLE ALEXANDRA

SALMON FLIES

JOCK SCOTT   BLUE CHARM   BLUE DOCTOR

STREAMER AND HAIR WING FLIES

CAHILL   CHIEF NEEDABEH   McGREGOR

SEA FISHING FLIES

FLY DRESSERS' GUIDE

John Veniard

ADAM & CHARLES BLACK : LONDON

First published 1952

Reprinted 1953, 1957, 1960 and 1964

Second edition 1966

Third edition 1968

Fourth edition 1970

Reprinted 1972, 1973

A. & C. BLACK LTD

4, 5 & 6 SOHO SQUARE LONDON W.1

© 1966, 1968, 1970 JOHN VENIARD

ISBN 0 7136 1185 5

Printed in Great Britain by
Redwood Press Limited
Trowbridge, Wiltshire

DEDICATION

To my brothers, Ernest and Frank, whose long
experience and assistance have helped to make
this book possible
And to the memory of
my father
ERNEST VENIARD

ACKNOWLEDGEMENTS

The production of this book was only made possible by the help and encouragement I have received from many sources.

Mr. Maurice Riesco was especially helpful. Besides his keen interest, he also supplied many of the patterns of trout flies tied by past masters.

Thanks must also go to R. Bergman (U.S.A.), J. C. Arseneault (Canada), A. Dalberg (Sweden), P. Curry, T. J. Hanna and M. Garnett (Ireland), Roger Woolley, E. C. Coombes and A. Martin for their examples of the art of fly-tying, and to Mr. H. George, who tied the salmon flies illustrated facing page 188. Also to Mr. P. Deane, Mr. A. S. Rooke, Mr. J. Harris, Mr. M. A. Wardle, and Mr. A. Wanless, whose "wrinkles" will be found in these pages.

I also wish to thank all those authors of books on fly-tying who made the work of research and reference so much simpler.

A special mention must be made of Mr. Eric Cumberland Owen, the artist, who devoted so much painstaking care on the coloured illustrations, Peter Dakin, and Donald Downs who assisted with many of the black and white drawings.

JOHN VENIARD

CONTENTS

ILLUSTRATIONS

In Colour

ILLUSTRATIONS

Black and White Photographs

ILLUSTRATIONS

Drawings

PREFACE

When Mr. Veniard originally invited me to write a foreword to his book on fly-dressing, my chief worry was whether I could do justice to the subject, but, after reading the proofs, I feel a heavier responsibility: that of doing justice to the excellence of this particular book.

I have known the writer for many years and, during that period, we have spent long hours discussing fly-dressing and the necessary materials; so, when he said he thought of writing a book on the subject, I did all I could to encourage him, knowing he proposed explaining in simple language and with diagrams all those stages of the process which are so often taken for granted.

I have read most of the books issued on the subject and I may say that I have gleaned something from nearly all of them, but I still remember the difficulty I experienced in tying in the wings of a dry fly and also in marrying the various feathers that go to make some of the salmon wings. If, however, he will read Mr. Veniard's explanations, I think the novice will find little difficulty in following the various processes.

Every fly-dresser has some little idiosyncrasies which have been worked out over many years and which are found good by him. Personally, I never use wax, which I find messy and quite unnecessary; I also tie in my hackle first in a trout fly, and I like to make sure that there is plenty of room at the head to take the cast. But these are things which come after long practice, and they do not detract from the value of a good orthodox grounding of the kind given in this book.

The illustrations are excellent and the diagrams of the various sequences are extremely lucid; there is also a first-class list of dressings.

Altogether, I feel that this is a work which will appeal to every fly-dresser, whether a complete novice or a proficient amateur, and that the professional will do well to add it to his library for reference.

MAURICE RIESCO

"But there is one thing more
I will teach him; he must
learn to tie his own flies."

COOMBE RICHARDS

INTRODUCTION

Fly-tying goes back for at least five centuries in this country, but only during the past hundred years has there been such a keen interest in the art as there is today.

During the leisurely period of the last half of the nineteenth century and the early years of the present one, many famous fishermen contributed with their knowledge and experience to make fly-fishing the grand sport we know it to be.

Such men as F. M. Halford, G. E. M. Skues, H. G. McClelland, T. Gordon, Dr. V. Baigent, J. W. Dunne, Major J. H. Hale, A. Courtney Williams, L. West and many others, have all played their part, and the good work is still being carried on by those who have followed in their footsteps. Special mention should be made of T. E. Pryce-Tannatt, Major Sir Gerald Burrard, E. Taverner, T. R. Henn, R. L. Marston, Editor of *The Fishing Gazette*, E. Marshall Hardy, Editor of *Angling*, and those fine professionals, Roger Woolley, T. J. Hanna, Ray Bergman, and W. Lunn. To all these, and many others, together with famous fishing tackle firms such as Hardy's, Allcock's, Milward's, Farlow's, etc., who gave them encouragement, we owe the pleasure of the infinite variety we have today.

Although intended primarily as a textbook and book of reference for the amateur fly-tyer, it is hoped that fly-tyers of all kinds will find something of instruction or interest in its pages.

Instructions will be found to cover practically every known type of fly, both trout and salmon, etc., I say practically, because to include every type would not only be a monumental task, but the book would never be up to date. New materials and ideas are always cropping up, and it is this constant interest, and the search for new ideas and materials, which makes fly-tying the fascinating and absorbing pastime which many of us know it to be.

The emphasis will be on materials and fly-tying, as the entomological side of the subject has been dealt with successfully by others more versed in this than myself. Two of the most up to date entomological works, both of outstanding merit, are *An Anglers' Entomology* by J. R. Harris, and *Trout Fly Recognition* by John Goddard. Both give graphic details of those natural insects which are important to fly-fishing, and both have helpful coloured plates of the larval, nymphal and adult stages of these insects.

The imitation of the natural fly and the patterns required for specific waters, must be left to the ingenuity and knowledge of the fly-tyer himself, but these cannot be applied unless he has the ability to tie his flies, and the necessary materials at his disposal. I hope this book will simplify this part of his work. Much of the information contained herein has already been dealt with by other authors, but no book of this kind would be complete without it.

I can think of no better conclusion for this introduction than to continue the quotation from the pen of Coombe Richards which is on the fly-leaf of this book— "Fishing, to my mind, is incomplete until the angler does that, be they for Salmon, Sea, or Brown Trout, for each one brings with its fashioning a wealth of pleasure, anticipation, and delight."

JOHN VENIARD

In 1964 a companion volume to this book was published, entitled *A Further Guide to Fly Dressing*. This was found necessary to encompass the many developments in fly dressing and patterns during the years following the publication of the *Guide* in 1952.

JOHN VENIARD

CHAPTER ONE

TOOLS

THE TOOLS REQUIRED by the fly-tyer are few, although there are several ingenious accessories which he will find of great assistance.

The basic items are—

A vice to hold the hook (*see* illustrations, pages 20 to 23).

A pair of hackle pliers.

A pair of scissors, with short sharp blades.

A dubbing needle.

It is quite difficult to mass-produce hackle pliers and ensure that the jaws of every pair will have a perfect fit. To counteract any deficiency of this nature, a

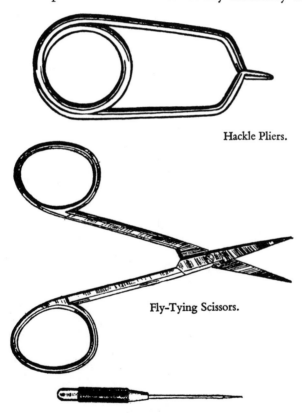

Hackle Pliers.

Fly-Tying Scissors.

Dubbing Needle.

small piece of cycle valve rubber is all that is necessary. This is slipped over only one of the jaws, and will give the pliers a non-slipping grip, and prevent the breaking of hackle tips in those pliers which might have sharp edges.

Under the heading of accessories we have—

Tweezers—For plucking hackles from the skin, and picking up feathers from the work bench. Also very useful for holding flies when the head is being varnished.

Bobbin Holder—To hold the spool of silk during the tying operations. In my opinion this is the most useful of the accessories, as it dispenses with the need of a silk retaining button on the vice, and eliminates the necessity of numerous knots and half hitches at the end of each stage of the tying. Its weight alone is sufficient to hold any materials that have been tied in, and its shape enables it to be held in the palm of the hand, leaving the thumb and forefinger free to wind the silk.

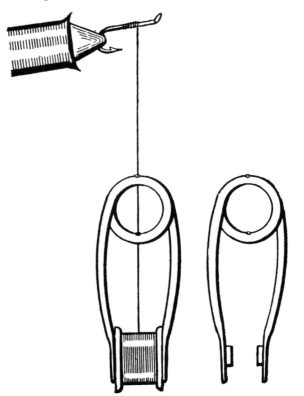

To wax the silk it is only necessary to draw off about a foot or so, wax it, and rewind it back on to the spool.

Whip Finish Tool—This ingenious little tool is of American origin, and while it is not an essential item, it will be found most helpful when it comes to finishing off a fly neatly. It imparts a neat "whip finish" which is practically invisible on small dry flies, and is just as useful for wet or salmon flies.

At first glance its manipulation may seem rather involved, but after the rudiments of the operation have been mastered, ten minutes' practice is all that is necessary.

Having completed the tying of the fly with the exception of the whip finish, take the tool in the right hand, as shown in Fig. 1, and place the silk behind the spring retainer A. Bring the end of the silk back in line with the fly, and with the nose-hook of the tool pick up the strand of silk between the fly and A (Fig. 2). Keeping the end of the silk in the left hand in line with the fly, and the tool also in line with it, place the nose of the tool as close to the hook as possible. In fact the hook can rest in the curve at the base of the nose-hook. Now rotate the tool in a clockwise direction *round* the hook shank, and this will cause the silk held in the nose-hook to be laid over that which returns along the body. The latter *must* be held in line with the fly and close up to it.

With practice it will be found that the tool can be rotated round the hook at a distance (Fig. 3), and in this manner it is possible to place the turns of silk exactly where one wants to. This illustration also shows clearly the principle of the tool's working.

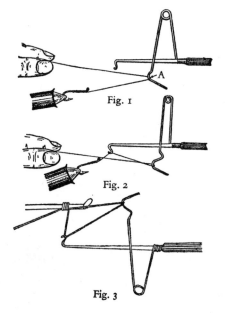

Fig. 1

Fig. 2

Fig. 3

When sufficient turns have been made, slip the nose-hook from its loop, and pull the silk held in the left hand until the spring retainer is drawn almost up to the hook. Slip the spring retainer from its loop, and then with a slight pull of the left hand to draw the silk tight, the whip finish is complete.

The spring retainer must not be pulled too near the nose of the tool at the commencement, as it is the length of silk between the nose and the spring which provides the whip finish. Practise on a large bare hook before attempting to finish a completed fly. Use well waxed silk for this purpose. The tool must be rotated round the hook shank, and not just on its own axis.

These tools and accessories are all that the fly-tyer should ever require, although if he or she is unable to work during the hours of daylight, a good adjustable table lamp is to be recommended. Personal comfort goes a long way to make this fascinating pastime a real pleasure.

FLY-TYING VICES

The perfect all-round fly-tying vice has yet to be invented. By all-round, I mean suitable for both salmon and trout flies. It is fairly easy to get a good one for one or the other, but it is combining the best qualities of the two that presents difficulty. When it is realised that hook sizes range from over 3 in. down to less than $\frac{1}{4}$ in. with corresponding differences in thickness, the reason for these difficulties will be readily understood.

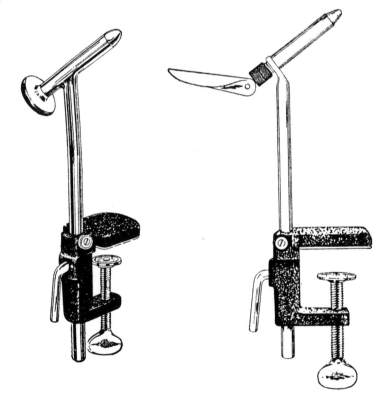

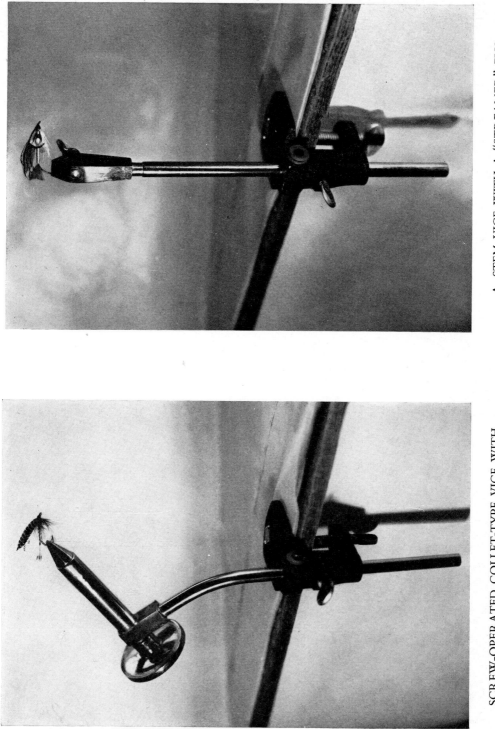

A STEM VICE WITH A "STREAMER" FLY

SCREW-OPERATED COLLET-TYPE VICE WITH "PETER ROSS" FLY

PEACOCK SWORD FIBRES AND "ALEXANDRA" FLY

If a very small dry fly is to be tied comfortably and well, there must be no bulk of metal to interfere with the manipulation of the fingers. Therefore, a vice with a pointed nose, set at an upward angle is the best type to use.

For a salmon fly, however, it is necessary to have plenty of gripping surface, and also sufficient area of metal to cover the point of the hook.

The best design of vice for combining these two qualities is the collet type, as the two vices illustrated on page 20. The one on this page is similar, but was designed specifically for salmon flies.

The only difference between the two shown is that the jaws are operated in one instance by a rotating screw, and in the other by a lever. Both will take the smallest of hooks, and if larger or salmon size hooks are used they can be inserted further into the jaws so that the points are concealed. They also have the advantage of being able to be rotated a full 360 degrees, so that the far side of the fly can be observed during any stage of the tying, and are adjustable to any height.

Any vice should have a good broad clamp to ensure a sound fixture to the work bench.

The original model of the vice below was produced by a skilled engineer, the late Francis Bontor, who was also a very keen fly-tyer.

It incorporates several new features, plus those which have always been useful to the fly-tyer who produces a wide range of flies, trout or salmon.

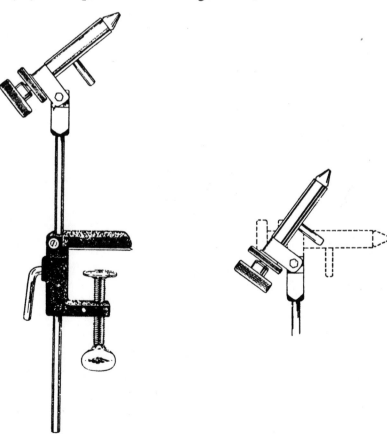

1. The head is adjustable to any angle, as shown in the illustration, and therefore can be set to suit individual preference.

2. The jaws themselves can also be set at any angle, which enables double hooks to be tied on a level plane.

3. The head can be rotated during the tying of the fly, which facilitates the winding on of the floss silk and flat tinsel bodies, especially on large salmon flies. It also enables the tyer to view the fly in all its aspects during the tying. The larger knurled screw at the rear tightens the jaws, and the smaller one fixes or releases the head as desired. The added projection on the barrel simplifies the control of these screws, making the manipulation of the vice a very simple operation.

The solid pillar gives both radial and vertical adjustment, both now accepted as standard on all good fly-tying vices, and the lever type screw set in the clamp ensures a firm fixture. Another standard fitting is the rubber button for anchoring the silk.

The chuck type of vice such as the "A" illustrated here is suitable for trout flies, and will also take salmon hooks in the smaller sizes. It has a very simple,

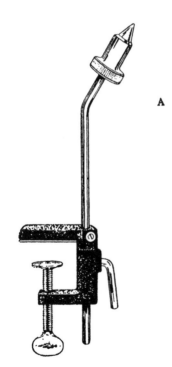

A

B

quick action, and has the advantage of not being quite so expensive as the collet type of vice.

The vice as "B" is of entirely different design to those already mentioned, and although used by many professionals for both trout and salmon flies, it is more suitable for the latter. The jaws are opened and closed by a winged nut, and the stem is adjustable for height and rotation.

The "Aird" Vice Adaptor—This simple but multi-purpose Vice Adaptor was devised by Mr. R. H. E. Aird, of Muir of Ord, Ross-shire, and it is a most useful addition to any fly tying bench. As the illustrations show, it is an excellent device for holding tying equipment and reels of floss silk, and when placed in the vice clamp instead of the vice, the latter can be adjusted to take double hooks and bring them on to an even plane for easier tying. Furthermore, if the jaws of the vice are set absolutely upright, this will facilitate fly tying on very small hooks, as in this position it leaves very little metal for the fingers to encompass when tying on wings and tails.

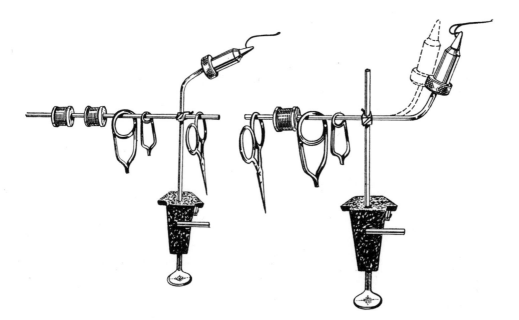

CHAPTER TWO

HOOKS

GOOD QUALITY HOOKS are not as easily available as they were before the Second World War, owing to the loss of many craftsmen to other industries during and after. The scarcity is felt most in the smaller light wire dry fly hooks, light wire (low water) salmon hooks, and small doubles.

The better-quality hooks are still made by the older craftsmen; consequently the output is limited. The manufacturers are, for the most part, confining themselves to the more popular patterns, and do their best to deliver a regular supply of these in the most needed sizes.

Most manufacturing fishing tackle firms had their own "speciality" nearly all of which had something to recommend them. Many became world famous, such as the "Model Perfect" made by Messrs. Allcock of Redditch, and Messrs. Hardy Brothers' "Oval Wire" salmon hooks.

I have given on the following pages, scales of all the hooks the fly-tyer is likely to need. "New Numbers" came into being with the advent of eyed hooks, the "Old Numbers" being in use during the days of eyeless hooks. As all the numbers now have their corresponding size given in inches, much of the confusion which can arise from these two scales is no longer justified.

It is generally accepted that a turned-up eye hook is the best for dry flies, although there are many fishermen who claim that this is of little importance. There is no doubt that a dry fly tied on an up eye hook looks more attractive. That a down eye hook is not essential for wet flies is proved by the fact that nearly all salmon flies are tied on up eye hooks, regardless of size or type.

In addition to the standard trout fly hook patterns as illustrated there are other patterns that are either shorter or longer in the shank for the same gape; the "gape" being the distance between the hook point and the shank vertically. For instance, a Limerick No. 10X Short is one size shorter in the shank than the standard pattern, while a Limerick No. 10X Long is one size longer than the standard pattern. A No. 10XX Long would be two sizes longer, and so on. The smaller sizes of these long-shank hooks are used mainly for May flies and the larger sizes for streamer flies.

"Wide Gape" Trout Hooks—This is one of the few hooks that can be obtained with both up and down eyes nowadays. They are light in the wire, and very suitable for dry flies. They have a very slight reversed sneck, i.e. the point of the hook is set at an angle to the shank.

"Round Bend" Trout Hooks—These are used mostly for wet flies, but many anglers like to tie their small dry flies on them. They have good hooking qualities, and the round bend ensures that no weakness is imparted during the manufacture.

"Limerick" Trout Hooks—Probably the most universally known of all the hook shapes. They are usually made in stout wire, and are very suitable for tying wet flies of the lake- and sea-trout variety.

"Sneck" Trout Hooks—This is a hook with an angular bend and a slight sneck.

N.B. The outpoint of "sneck" hooks turns to the right, holding the eye of the hook towards you, while the outpoint of "reversed" hooks turns to the left.

That a fly-tyer should use only the best-quality hooks is readily understandable. It is very exasperating to have the hook point break off in the vice during the

STANDARD PATTERNS

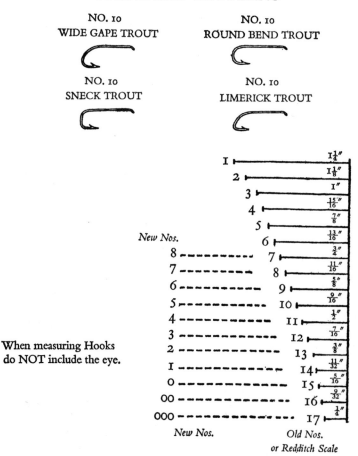

NO. 10
WIDE GAPE TROUT

NO. 10
ROUND BEND TROUT

NO. 10
SNECK TROUT

NO. 10
LIMERICK TROUT

When measuring Hooks
do NOT include the eye.

New Nos.

*Old Nos.
or Redditch Scale*

last operation of tying the fly. It is even more exasperating if the same thing happens when a fish is hooked.

"Ordinary Forged" Salmon Hooks—This pattern is the stand-by of the salmon fly-tyer, and is used for all the standard types of fly. They are obtainable in a large range of sizes from about $2\frac{1}{2}$ in. to $\frac{1}{2}$ in. Double hooks in this style are not quite so easy to obtain but fortunately the need for these is not so great.

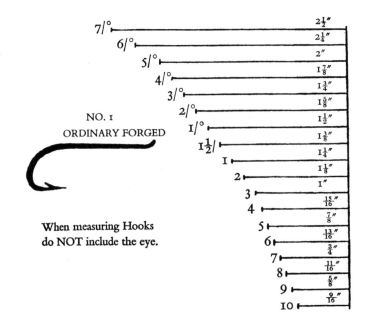

NO. 1
ORDINARY FORGED

When measuring Hooks
do NOT include the eye.

"Limerick" Salmon Hooks—This pattern is used by tyers who prefer a down eyed hook, and it also differs from the "Ordinary Forged" in that it is finished in bronze instead of black enamel. The scale of sizes is the same.

NO. 1
LIMERICK

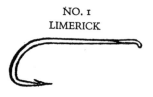

When measuring Hooks
do NOT include the eye.

"Wilson" Dry Fly Salmon Hooks—This is a very fine quality light wire hook specially designed for the type of salmon dry flies described on pages 240 and 241. They are slightly longer in the shank than standard patterns of the same gape, so can be utilised to make very attractive Low Water flies.

Their strength, coupled with extreme lightness, are two features which should not be overlooked if one is making dapping flies for trout.

Size No. 4

WILSON DRY FLY SALMON HOOK

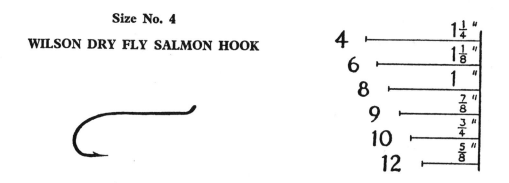

"Low Water" Salmon Hooks—These are made in finer wire than the other patterns and are used for tying the lightly dressed summer or "Low Water" flies. They are about two sizes longer in the shank than "Ordinary Forged" for the same width of "gape".

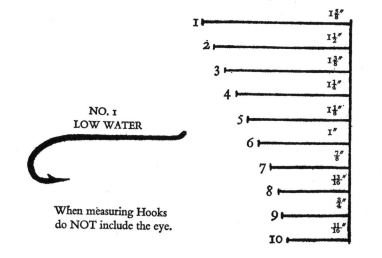

NO. 1
LOW WATER

When measuring Hooks
do NOT include the eye.

There were a number of articles in the angling press during the latter months of 1951 advocating a radical change in the type of hooks used for salmon fishing.

The main theme was that a round bend hook with a sneck had greater hooking powers than the orthodox flat salmon hook with a Limerick bend.

The theories propounded are very sound, and it is at times like this that the difficulty of getting special hooks made is felt very keenly.

The nearest approach to the type of hook described is Allcock's "Model Perfect" forged trout hook. It has an almost round bend and a prominent reversed sneck and, although it has a tapered eye (not a loop eye like a salmon hook) and is used primarily as a trout fly hook, it is very strong and could be used for salmon flies up to size No. 1. This type of hook is obtainable from this size, down to the smallest size on the scale given below, and in my opinion it is one of the best types of hook manufactured today.

They have never been as popular as other types of hooks for fly-tying, and the only reason for this, as far as I can make out, is the fact that flies tied on them seem to lack the appearance of those tied on other patterns.

No. 10

When measuring Hooks do NOT include the eye.

No.	Length
1	$1\frac{1}{8}''$
2	$1''$
3	$\frac{15}{16}''$
4	$\frac{7}{8}''$
5	$\frac{13}{16}''$
6	$\frac{3}{4}''$
7	$\frac{11}{16}''$
8	$\frac{5}{8}''$
9	$\frac{9}{16}''$
10	$\frac{17}{32}''$
11	$\frac{1}{2}''$
12	$\frac{15}{32}''$
13	$\frac{7}{16}''$
14	$\frac{13}{32}''$
15	$\frac{3}{8}''$
16	$\frac{11}{32}''$
17	$\frac{5}{16}''$
18	$\frac{9}{32}''$

WING QUILL FIBRES READY FOR TYING ON A WET FLY

A "PALMERED" HACKLE

CHAPTER THREE

SILKS

FOR MANY YEARS the firm of Pearsall, established in the eighteenth century, have been manufacturing silk for the fly-tyer and their "Gossamer" tying silk and Stout Floss body silk are world famous.

A good quality tying silk is essential to the fly-tyer, and should be as strong and fine as possible. The two silks now in general use are—

Gossamer—suitable for all trout flies and also for the lightly dressed "Low Water" salmon flies.

Naples—suitable for tying large trout and sea-trout flies, etc., and salmon flies. It is slightly thicker than "Gossamer". Both these silks are sold on spools.

They can be obtained in the following colours—

No.	Colour	No.	Colour	No.	Colour
1	White	7	Blue	13	Crimson
2	Straw	8	Purple	14	Claret
3	Primrose	9	Black	15	Dark Claret
4	Light Yellow	9a	Grey	16	Olive
5	Yellow	10	Ash	17	Brown
6	Amber	11	Golden Olive	18	Green
6a	Orange	11a	Scarlet	19	Hot Orange
6b	Red Spinner	12	Cardinal	20	Light Olive

When finishing off a trout or salmon fly, the best-known method for securing the tying silk is the "whip finish". Details of how this operation is performed, together with illustrations, will be found on page 66 (*see also* page 19, Whip Finish Tool).

For the silk bodies of flies, real silk is the best to use, as Rayon becomes transparent when wet, and the hook shows through. This naturally darkens the original colour of the silk. Pearsall's manufacture two kinds of body Silk, and these also are supplied on spools. They are—

Marabou Floss—This is a two-strand silk, and when cut in short lengths the two strands are very easily separated. The resulting single strands are suitable for all sizes of trout flies, and the smaller sizes of salmon flies. It holds its colour very well when exposed to oil or water, and can be obtained in the following colours: primrose, yellow, orange, red, white, black, blue, claret, light olive, olive, green, purple, brown, grey, dun and hot orange.

Stout Floss—This is a very fine silk of much heavier gauge than "Marabou" and suitable for all sizes of salmon flies. It is obtainable in the following colours· orange, red, light blue, blue, green, claret, olive, black, purple, brown, white, primrose, golden yellow and deep yellow.

Cellulite Floss Body Silk—This is a Rayon silk and was produced by Messrs. Wardle & Davenport for the Dunne's series of flies. It becomes transparent when oiled, and should only be used on hooks with white painted shanks. The white hook shank shows through after the silk is oiled, imparting a translucent effect that is most unique. The formulae for these flies was laid down in J. W. Dunne's book, "Sunshine and the Dry Fly".

Chenille—A "bushy" silk very suitable for the bodies of nymphs, streamer flies, lures, etc. It sinks very easily once it has become saturated.

Fluorescent Material—The use of fluorescent materials for fly-tying was first thought of by Mr. Eugine Burns of America, during the Second World War. Since then they have been produced for this purpose in the United States, and are now being manufactured in England. They consist of specially treated fibres, and usually take the following three forms—

1. **Thin Floss.**
2. **Wool Yarn.**
3. **Chenille.**

In theory, these materials are attractive to fish because they are sensitive to ultra-violet rays, and it is assumed that the vision of fish is confined to the ultra-violet end of the spectrum. They are effective only while ultra-violet rays are present—during the hours of daylight, and lose their fluorescent qualities during the hours of darkness.

Much has been written in the angling press during 1952/3 concerning fluorescents, but in my opinion they are still very much in the experimental stage as far as fly-tying is concerned.

For instance, I have read in articles that fish would only take flies that incorporated fluorescent materials in the body or wings, on certain days, and colours such as "dark olive" and "claret" were quoted. I have even heard "black" mentioned in connection with fluorescent body material. From experiments I carried out during the production of the English materials, I know that it is only pastel shades of the primary colours that can be imparted to the materials. The colours are white, blue, yellow (lemon and golden), orange, scarlet, pink and light grey. Darker colours went black under the fluoroscope. To put it simply, the imparting of a dark colour to a fluorescent material is the equivalent of giving a coat of paint to a piece of strip lighting, and very opaque paint at that. The darker the shade, the more it masks the fluorescence.

Inks of a similar nature are now being used extensively for advertisement hoardings, and on the advertisements one sees on the sides of buses and vans. It will be observed that the lettering of these advertisements is made up from the colours I have listed.

I have had varying reports on the results obtained while fishing with flies using fluorescent materials, but there is no doubt that their judicious use under certain conditions will produce fish when other flies have failed.

A brief summing up of results of which I have actual knowledge should be helpful to the fly-tyer who wishes to experiment with these new materials—

1. A black bodied fly with a wing formed of several fibres of thin fluorescent floss took trout in the late evening after a blank day with orthodox flies. Conditions —water fairly thick.

2. Lake flies tied with fluorescent wool bodies took fish late at the end of a poor day.

3. A Black Gnat with a hackle fibre wing in which fibres of red, blue, white and yellow floss were very sparingly intermingled, took fish but would only kill in bright sunshine.

4. Flies tied with bodies consisting of the usual fur required for the dressing mixed with chopped fibres of fluorescent wool or floss, attracted and took more fish than flies of the same type tied without the fluorescent mixture. Conditions were good and the fish were taking quite well.

The best "killer" of the example last mentioned, was a "Hare's Ear", the body of which consisted of the usual fur from the hare's ear mixed with finely chopped fibres of fluorescent wool—red, blue, yellow and white. The proportion was about four of fur to one of the fluorescent mixture, and the usual gold wire rib was also incorporated. The final mixture did not look very much different to the original hare fur, but when carefully inspected it was seen to contain many points of brilliance not contained in the hare fur hitherto. When viewed under the fluoroscope, the hare fur vanished into blackness and the particles of fluorescent material were left floating in nothing as it were.

Briefly then, it would seem that fluorescent materials may be the answer to many of the problems that have always confronted the fly-tyer, providing they are put to the right purpose. Overcoming the problem of thick water, for instance, the imparting of iridiscence to wings, bodies, and hackles; and perhaps we shall at last be able to give to our artificials the translucent effect that nature has given to the natural insects we try to imitate.

Also, these materials must be the answer to many a salmon fisherman's prayers, as they can be blended with the plumages, silks, seal's fur and tinsel used in his flies, even more successfully than with the materials used for trout flies. This will tend to reduce the blank days due to thick and heavy water, and if method No. 4 is used, he can control the amount of brilliance he wishes his flies to emit.

Much more experimental work must be carried out before definite conclusions can be reached, but nevertheless we must welcome this new material which will add to the interest and variety we have come to expect from the already absorbing pastimes of fly-tying and fly-fishing.

Since writing the foregoing, much experimental work has been done, and we have covered this in our complementary volume *A Further Guide to Fly Dressing*.

AN UPRIGHT DOUBLE SPLIT-WING FLY IN A VICE WITH A COLLET-TYPE CHUCK

TWO TYPES OF ROLLED WING—SINGLE AND SPLIT

CHAPTER FOUR

TINSELS

TINSELS ARE USED extensively by the fly-tyer for all types of flies, from the smallest dry flies to the largest Salmon Flies. They fulfil a dual role in that they add durability to other body materials that may be used, as well as that of their main purpose which is to make the fly more attractive to the fish.

There are various kinds of tinsel, all of which can be obtained in Silver or Gilt. They are as follows:

Flat—This is a flat metal ribbon. It is sometimes used for ribbing trout and salmon flies, but is more often used when the whole of the hook shank has to be covered with tinsel. It varies in widths from about 1/80th of an inch to 1/10th of an inch.

Embossed—This is also a flat ribbon, with the addition of the embossing. The embossing is supposed to impart extra "flash" to the tinsel, but for some reason it has never been as popular as the plain flat tinsel.

Oval—This is flat tinsel that has been wound round a centre core of silk, and then flattened. It is used as ribbing for all types of flies, especially lake trout, sea trout, and salmon. Sizes vary from about 1/50th of an inch to 1/12th.

Round—This also is very fine flat tinsel wound round a silk core, but not flattened like "Oval". Its main use is for the "tag" on salmon flies, but it is sometimes used as ribbing. Obtainable in only two thicknesses of about 1/100th of an inch and slightly less.

Twist—A heavy tinsel consisting of two or three strands of "round" tinsel twisted together. It is used for ribbing some of the larger salmon flies such as the "Akroyd", and larger sizes of some standard patterns such as the "Jock Scott".

Wire—This is ordinary plain drawn wire, and used mainly for ribbing the smaller trout flies.

"Lurex"—This is the trade name for a plastic material which has the appearance of tinsel in some instances, and which also has the advantage of being untarnishable. It can be procured in the following metallic colours: Silver, Gold, Copper, Scarlet, Orange, Chartreuse, Royal Blue, Peacock Blue, Emerald Green, and also in Black, White and Pink.

It is not as strong as tinsel, however, and a wire or oval tinsel ribbing should be incorporated when using Lurex as a body covering.

When a pattern calls for a flat tinsel body, an even foundation of silk should be wound on to the hook shank. This makes the laying on of the tinsel much easier, preventing unsightly unevenness. On large salmon flies a base of floss silk is to be recommended.

CHAPTER FIVE

DYEING

ALTHOUGH ALL DYED feathers, furs, etc., can now be obtained ready for immediate use, there are many fly-tyers who "like to do the whole job" themselves. It is quite an interesting part of the many complex operations that go into tying a fly, and although some tyers think it is a messy and unprofitable business, this need not be the case.

The old-fashioned methods, although quite effective, were very complicated, but the aniline dyes now procurable have greatly simplified matters.

These dyes can be bought from any fishing tackle shop that stocks fly-tying materials, or from the firms specialising in the sale of these items. The range of colours, some two score in number, covers all needs, and as these dyes have not been adulterated like most shop sold dyes they are very economical to use.

The only utensils necessary for small quantities are a small aluminium milk saucepan and another slightly larger. The small saucepan is first perforated with small holes over the sides and bottom with an awl until it becomes like a collander. This is for holding the material to be dyed and will stand inside the larger utensil. This "collander" will take quite a quantity of small feathers and any fur to be dyed. Larger feathers may be cut to fit the receptacle.

The object of the perforated saucepan (or collander) is for the easy control of the dyeing process and inspection of the material while dyeing. Also, it is a very clean method as the hands need not come in contact with the dye solution.

While furs do not need any preparation, feathers must be treated before dyeing. The process is quite simple. Make a solution of soapsuds in the larger saucepan by dissolving good quality soapflakes or soap powder in hot water. Place your feathers in the "collander" and immerse this in the soapy water for a few minutes. The feathers of wildfowl require to be immersed for a longer period, say half an hour. The feathers must now be well rinsed. This is quite simple with the "collander". Just lift it out of the larger saucepan and place in a bowl of clean warm water, repeating this until all trace of soap is removed. Held under a hot tap, the process is even more simple.

Now fill the larger saucepan with water a little more than half full and stand over a gentle heat. Add your dye powder, about as much as can be taken up on the point of a penknife, and allow the solution to come to boiling point. Add cold water to reduce the temperature (*feathers must not be boiled*), and immerse the "collander" in the dye solution.

Leave the material in the solution for some minutes and, having removed the "collander", add about a tablespoonful of vinegar (acetic acid). This will quickly "fix" the colour and care must be taken in order to get the right shade. The "collander" makes this quite simple. To inspect the material being dyed you lift the "collander" out of the large saucepan containing the dye solution. The water runs out through the holes, leaving the material at the bottom for inspection. It must be remembered that the material will be a lighter shade when dry and it may be necessary to add more dye to get the deeper shades. This is again quite simple with the "collander", as it can be lifted and more dye added to the solution without coming in contact with the material being dyed. You can get a very good idea of what the shade of feathers will be by watching the quill or holding up a single feather before the light.

Shades or red, yellow, blue, etc., are quite straightforward, but a little experience is required to obtain the delicate shades of olives and duns, etc. The tendency is to use too much dye. It is much better to start with a little and add as necessary.

Having obtained the desired shade, remove the "collander" from the dye solution and put under a cold water tap until all surplus dye is removed. Press the material between cloth or paper to absorb most of the moisture, and allow to dry naturally, or over, or before, a gentle heat.

The range of shades of any particular colour is infinite, and doing one's own dyeing enables one to test ideas with results that would not otherwise be obtainable.

Rhode Island Red Hackles will dye claret, purple, fiery brown, dark olive, or black, and to obtain honey dun or rusty dun shades use a white Hackle with a honey or red edge to the fibres. These hackles are freaks, but are sometimes obtainable.

Points to remember: (a) Remove all trace of soap from feathers before putting them in the dye bath. (b) Never allow the material being dyed to boil, as this takes all the life out of it. (c) Always remove the material before adding more dye, as otherwise there is a danger of "spotting". (d) Do not use a stronger dye bath than necessary. (e) Rinse well after dyeing. (f) Never dry before a fierce heat, as it will take all the life out of the material. If you follow these simple rules all your efforts should be successful.

When dyeing any materials black, at least twice the quantity of dye should be used, and they should also be left in the dye solution for several hours, the temperature of which should be maintained as high as possible without boiling.

Although white materials can be dyed black under the above conditions, quicker results can be obtained by using those which have a darker natural colour, i.e. red or brown hackles, and brown turkey tails, etc.

To bring back hackles and other feathers to their natural brilliance, they should be placed in a cardboard tray or lid and shaken over a gas ring. It does not matter how fierce the heat is so long as the feathers are kept continually in motion. It is important that the feathers still be slightly damp, as it is the combination of steam and hot air which brings about the desired effect.

CHAPTER SIX

MATERIALS FOR TROUT FLIES

A GENERAL SURVEY

THE COLLECTION OF materials is a much less haphazard business than it used to be. In the old days the fly-tyer had to obtain his materials from many sources, but today he can get everything he wants from business houses that cater for the fly-tyer only. By everything, I mean from the vice that holds the hook to the varnish that seals off the last turn of the tying silk.

He can also obtain complete dressings of hundreds of different patterns, and if he has a particular "Fancy", the materials can usually be duplicated exactly.

Many items, of course, are much easier to come by than others. The most difficult now are (and always have been) good quality hackles for dry flies. The demand for these far exceeds the supply, especially as most cockerels are killed off long before their hackles reach the necessary standard of maturity.

Most other items are fairly easy go get, with the exception of one or two of the exotic feathers used in dressing salmon flies; such items as Blue Chatterer, Toucan, Indian (red) Crow, and Macaw. Here again, however, it will be found that, if the materials supplier is unable to supply them, he usually has some substitute for these feathers.

When ordering materials it is always a good idea to state what size of fly is being tied. This gives a good guide to whoever is selecting the materials—usually an expert fly-tyer.

As the initial collection of one's materials can be a rather expensive business, care should be taken to keep moth and other parasites away from them. Airtight tins and boxes with a pinch of flake carbon (naphthalene) in each, will keep even the most persistent away.

A mistake some beginners make is in trying to do too much at the start. It is better to form one's collection with only one or two patterns in view, and then build up as one's experience increases.

Here is a list of items which could form the base of a dry fly-tyer's collection—

1. A vice with a small head to take small hooks.
2. A pair of hackle pliers for winding the hackle.
3. A pair of sharp-pointed scissors.
4. A dubbing needle for picking out fur bodies.
5. Solid wax for waxing the tying silk.

6. A bottle of thin clear varnish for finishing off.
7. A selection of tying silks (black, yellow, olive, red, claret).
8. Thin gold wire for ribbing.
9. A pair of hares' ears for fur bodies.
10. A natural Heron's Wing Quill and one dyed olive, for herls.
11. A peacock's "eye" tail. (This gives a two-colour rib simulating the bodies of many flies).
12. Strands of bronze peacock herl. (Also obtained from the peacock "eye" tail.)
13. A mole skin for fur bodies.
14. A pair of starling wings.
15. A pair of coot wings.
16. A pair of waterhen wings.
17. Plain brown and speckled brown hen quills for the wings of Alders and Sedges.
18. Red cock hackles, several shades of dun (blue dun, iron blue, etc.). One or two shades of olive, and black.
19. Brown partridge hackles.
20. Larger sizes of the above hackles to supply whisks for tails.

Other types of hackles or body materials could be used instead of the above, according to the types of flies one wishes to tie.

The tyer of Wet Flies would need a similar selection of tools, etc., but is more fortunately placed in that he does not require the scarce stiff cock hackles. He can use softer cock hackles or hen hackles, and there are many other feathers at his disposal for use as hackles. Such feathers as come from the fronts of certain wings (coot, snipe, woodcock, etc.) and the body feathers of the starling, partridge, pheasant, snipe, etc. All these feathers are fairly plentiful.

For lake- or sea-trout flies, the following extra materials would be needed—

For Wings
Woodcock wing quills.
Teal duck flank.
Brown (or bronze) mallard shoulder feathers.
Grouse tails.

For Bodies
Seal's fur, dyed various colours.
Flat tinsels and oval tinsels for ribbing.

For Hackles
Cock or hen poultry hackles, dyed various colours.

For Tails

Golden pheasant crest and tippet feathers.

Red Ibis, or substitute.

HACKLES

Without any doubt, hackles form the most important and essential part of the trout fly-tyer's collection. Not only do they have to represent the wings or legs of the fly, but in the case of dry flies they are the medium by which the fly is kept afloat.

Many feathers are used as hackles, but those that adapt themselves most suitably are those from the necks of domestic cocks and hens. Unfortunately this suitability makes the demand for them exceed the supply, especially those that come from the rarer breeds.

The most difficult of all to obtain are good quality cocks hackles for dry flies, the reason being that most cockerels are killed off long before their plumage reaches the necessary standard of maturity. A perfect hackle can be obtained only from a bird that is at least two years old, and most birds are killed off when they are about nine months old. They are worth as much to the poultry keeper at that age as they will ever be, and from then on they are just a feeding expense. Add to that the shortage of feeding stuffs in Britain and the disastrous outbreak of fowl pest in 1950, and the reason for the scarcity of these hackles will be readily understood.

The hackles most in demand are those required for the "Duns" and "Olives" and the breed of birds which supplies them (Andalusians) is practically extinct. Fortunately very good dyed imitations can be obtained, but once again the shortage of good, small, stiff white cock hackles is also a problem.

The supply of good hackles comes from old thoroughbred birds as they are killed off periodically, and although the fly-tyer may have to go on a "waiting list", a cape of hackles from one of these birds is well worth waiting for.

The following list of hackles names and their description will enable him to identify any that come his way.

Grizzle	alternate bars of black and white usually from Plymouth Rock poultry.
Cree	Plymouth Rock/Rhode Island Red cross.
Reds (Browns)	from Rhode Island Red poultry.
Red Game	from Old English Game poultry.
Badger	black centre with white outer fibres, sometimes with black tips.
Furnace	black centre with red outer fibres.
Coch-Y-Bondhu	as Furnace but with the edges of the fibres tipped with black.
Greenwell	black centre with ginger outer fibres.

Blue Dun	Slate grey.
Iron Blue	very dark slate grey.
Dun	mouse colour.
Honey Dun & Honey Blue Dun	These have honey tipped fibres.
Rusty Dun & Rusty Blue Dun	These have rusty tipped fibres.

White/ Black/ Buff/ Ginger/ Honey/ etc./ are self-descriptive.

It becomes more obvious every year that the supply of special hackles such as Badger (white/black), Furnace (red/black), and Greenwell (ginger/black) will never be able to cope with the demand. Not only are these very scarce, but very often the smaller feathers on a neck fail to run true to type. Thus the smaller hackles of a Furnace neck can be either all black or all red. Sometimes the top half is red and the bottom half black, or vice versa. The same colour variation can happen with a Badger or Greenwell neck.

I have carried out several experiments with this in mind. The most obvious was to use two hackles—a small black one to represent the black centre of these hackles, which is wound over a larger one of white, red or ginger as required.

The result was fairly good, but the difficulty was getting black hackles short enough in the fibre with sufficient length for two or three turns to be made round the hook shank.

Another method, and the one which I find gives the best results, not only from the tying angle, but also when fishing, is to use a strand of black ostrich herl to obtain the black centre. A strand that has fairly long "flue" is necessary for flies up to size 12 (New No. 3), but this is not so important for the smaller sizes.

My method of tying a hackled "Greenwell" is as follows—

Form tail, body and rib, leaving plenty of room at the eye end of the hook. Tie in the strand of ostrich herl close up to the body, and continue winding the silk until the eye is nearly reached. Tie in the ginger hackle. Wind silk back to ostrich herl, wind the hackle up to the ostrich herl, tie in the tip and cut off the surplus. Wind the tying silk back through the hackle as described on page 71. Now wind the herl through the hackle to the eye, tie it in and cut off the surplus. Finish off with the usual whip finish.

The amount of black centre is, of course, governed by the number of turns given to the herl, and I found that, for a lightly-dressed fly, one turn at the back, one through the hackle, and one in the front was all that was necessary.

The procedure can, of course, be reversed, and the hackle wound over the herl, but I find this tends to bind down too much of the "flue" on the herl, spoiling the symmetry of the black centre.

Flies requiring a Badger or Furnace hackle are tied the same, using a white or red hackle.

Wet flies can be tied in exactly the same way with hen hackles.

The fly-tyer should also endeavour to obtain a selection of large stiff cock hackles, and fortunately these are much easier to get. Two or three fibres from one of these make an excellent tail for a dry fly, and there are several dressings which require them as hackles, such as the Varients. They are also used to form "hackle fibre" wings, a description of which will be found on page 86.

It will often happen that one finds that one's collection of hackles does not contain a feather small enough to tie some particularly small pattern. In my opinion, a little judicious cutting does not come amiss at times like this. A cut hackle may not improve the appearance of the fly, but it certainly will not detract from its floating qualities.

The following list of hackle sizes is given merely as a guide. The length of hackle required depends entirely upon the length of the fibres on the hackle. I have had hackles of such excellent quality and maturity that I have been able to use one two inches in length on a No. o hook. A hackle from an old bird will have much shorter fibres in comparison to its length than will that of a hackle from a young bird.

HACKLE SIZE CHART
(Hen hackles should be about $\frac{1}{2}$ in. smaller)

HOOK SIZES		COCK HACKLES	
New Nos.	Old Nos.	Hackle Flies—(TROUT)—Winged Flies	
000	17		
00	16	1 in.–1$\frac{1}{4}$ in.	$\frac{1}{2}$ in.–1 in.
0	15		
1	14		
2	13	1$\frac{1}{4}$ in.–1$\frac{1}{2}$ in.	1 in.–1$\frac{1}{4}$ in.
3	12		
4	11	Sea Trout and Lake Trout Flies	
5	10	1$\frac{1}{2}$ in.–1$\frac{3}{4}$ in.	1$\frac{1}{4}$ in.–1$\frac{1}{2}$ in.
6	9		
7	8		
8	7	1$\frac{3}{4}$ in.–2$\frac{1}{4}$ in.	1$\frac{1}{2}$ in.–2 in.
9	6		

The tyer of wet flies is much more easily supplied, as he does not require the stiff cock's hackles. The softer hen's hackles, which are much more plentiful than their male counterpart, make for easier entry of the fly into the water, although a not too stiff cock's hackle should be used if more "life" is required, especially in fast water.

There are also many patterns of flies that call for feathers for use as hackles from birds other than poultry, and it is rarely that any difficulty is experienced in obtaining these. The following list should cover the requirements of the most exacting collector.

Starling Body Feathers—For the hackle of "Black Gnat" and midges.

Lapwing Rump Feathers—For the hackle of "Cowdung". These feathers are used as a substitute for the very rare Landrail.

Partridge Brown Back Feathers—A very useful feather, providing the hackle of the "March Brown", "Partridge and Orange", whisks for tails, hackles of nymphs and spiders, and also for several patterns of May flies. Illustrated, facing page 50.

Partridge Grey Breast Feathers—A very similar feather to the above, used for the hackle of the "Partridge and Yellow" and for the hackles of May flies. It is used dyed and undyed for the latter, yellow being the most popular colour when it is dyed.

French Partridge Breast Feathers—This is a smoky-blue feather, barred at its tip. It is only used for May flies. It is used dyed and undyed, and when dyed yellow is also a good feather for the Green Drake. It is very popular in Ireland, usually dyed green, a large bushy fly being tied, with plenty of body and hackle. Illustrated, facing page 50.

Snipe Rump Feathers—Used as hackles for the "Snipe" series of flies, the most well-known being the "Snipe and Purple". Illustrated, facing page 50.

Cock Pheasant Neck Feathers—Used for the hackle of the "Bracken Clock".

Hen Pheasant Neck Feathers—There are one or two patterns of wet May flies that use this feather, but it has few other uses.

Hen Pheasant Flank Feathers—This is rarely used in Great Britain, but often in New Zealand where it is used as a substitute for Bittern. It forms the hackle of the "Matuka", which is probably one of the best-known flies in that part of the world.

Grouse Poult Feathers—These are under-coverts from the wing, and can be obtained only from very young Grouse. They form the hackle of the "Poult Bloa".

Guinea Fowl (Gallena) Neck Feathers—Used mainly as the whisks of nymphs. They are obtainable in two colours, smoky-blue and plain white. The latter are dyed various shades of olive for some patterns.

Grey Mallard Duck Breast and Flank Feathers (Grey Drake)—These are obtainable in a large range of sizes varying from about 1 in. in length to 4 in. The smallest sizes are used for fan-wings on May flies, and the larger for the hackles of wet May flies. They are obtainable dyed and undyed, and here also the natural colouration lends itself to the imitation of the Green Drake. They are also dyed to provide substitutes for the rare Summer Duck, Egyptian Goose, and Mandarin Duck feathers. Illustrated, facing page 50.

Egyptian Goose Breast Feathers—These are lightly barred feathers, varying in colour from pale buff to brown. They are used for the wings and hackles of some patterns of May flies.

Summer Duck (Carolina Wood-Duck) Flank Feathers—These are also lightly barred brown feathers, but of a richer colour than the Egyptian goose. They are also used as hackles for May flies, and many American patterns.

Mandarin Duck Flank Feathers—Almost an exact duplicate of Summer Duck, and extensively used as a substitute for them. Although not in plentiful supply, they are easier to get than Summer Duck.

Woodcock Body Feathers, and lesser coverts from Wings—Used as hackles for May flies and nymphs, etc., and for the hackled patterns of the "Woodcock" series of flies; "Woodcock and Yellow", etc. Illustrated, facing page 50.

Grouse Body Feathers, and lesser coverts from Wings—Also used for May flies and nymphs, etc., and for the hackled patterns of the "Grouse" series of Lake and Sea-trout flies; "Grouse and Claret", etc. Illustrated, facing page 50.

Jay Wing Blue lesser coverts—These are used as hackles for many well-known patterns of Lake, Sea-trout and Salmon flies such as the "Invicta", "Connemara Black", "Thunder and Lightning", etc. Being stiff feathers they are rather difficult to use as hackles. The quill part has to be stripped as thinly as possible to enable them to be tied and wound properly (*see* page 186).

Other hackles can also be obtained from the wings of other birds, and it is the under coverts and marginal coverts that are used. Coot, Waterhen, Starling, Cock and Hen Pheasant, Partridge, Lapwing are but a few that can be utilised.

BODY MATERIALS

In addition to silks and tinsels, the fly-tyer has many other body materials at his disposal. The main ones are fur, "Quills", and "Herls", which are fibres from various feathers. These can be sub-divided as follows—

FUR

Seal's Fur—This is the best all-round fur for flies; dry, wet or salmon. Only fur from very young seals is used, which is cream coloured in its natural state. The individual fibres are bright and shiny, and they lose nothing of this brightness when dyed. It does not get matted or lose its colour when wet, which is to be expected of the fur from an animal that spends most of its time in water. It can be dyed any colour, whether it be for the imitations of natural flies (Blue Dun, Olive, etc.), or the bright colours required for salmon and sea trout flies.

Ram's Wool—This is the pink wool used when dressing "Tup's Indispensable". A little natural seal's fur should be added to give it the required creaminess.

Mohair—This is softer than seal's fur, but the individual fibres are very long, enabling it to be wound on like floss silk. This also can be obtained in any colour.

Rabbit Fur—This gives a wide range of natural colours, the most useful being the blue under fur which is suitable for the bodies of "Blue Dun".

Mole—A deep smoky-blue fur that is ideal for the bodies of the "Blue Dun" and "Iron Blue".

Hare—A most useful fur from which one can obtain a wide range of usable material from one skin, ranging from pale ginger to grizzled black/brown. The grizzled fur from the ears and poll supplies the body material for the "Hare's Ear" while the longer body fibres of similar colouration provide the hackle. It also supplies the body for many nymphs, and also that of the "March Brown".

The above are the most useful to the fly-tyer, and other furs used are from the water rat, grey squirrel, brown squirrel, etc.

HERLS

The term herl is applied to strands taken from whole feathers, and are in actual fact lengths of quill with very short fibres or "flue" on them. When the "herls" are wound round the hook shank, the short fibres stand out at right-angles thus forming a body through which light can penetrate. The most used come from the following birds:

Heron—From both wings quills and the large hackles. Two or three strands from either of these, natural or dyed, make an excellent body, especially if a wire rib is incorporated. Very good for all the "Olives".

Swan—From the large soft shoulder feathers. Being white originally, a larger range of dyed effects can be obtained than is possible with the Heron, which is a smoky blue-grey.

Goose—Also from the shoulder, very similar to the Swan feathers but finer.

Ostrich—These come from the large plumes and have a fairly long "flue" on them. These are also obtainable in any colour.

Turkey—The tail feathers of this bird supply many colours of "herls" the most used being the Brown or Cinnamon for Sedges, as they range from a deep brown to a pale buff.

Condor—A very useful and very durable material is obtained from the wing quills, and they can be dyed any colour. The "flue" is sometimes stripped, but its removal is difficult.

Cock Pheasant—The "herls" in this instance are taken from the tailfeathers, two or three with a wire rib forming the body of the "Pheasant Tail" fly, hence its name. They should be tied in by the tip and not the butt, so as to incorporate the reddish tinted fibres which do not reach as far as the root end.

Magpie Tails—These are black with a greenish sheen, and are ideal for making the wing-cases of beetles.

Peacock (*see* Illustration, page 45)—No doubt the most useful of all. The "herls" come from the long "eye" and "sword" tails, and vary in colour from bright green to deep bronze. The bronze "herl" is used in many well-known patterns such as the "Coachman", "Coch-y-Bondhu", "Alder", etc.

QUILLS

The "herls" that go to make up the actual bright coloured "eye" part of the Peacock tail deserve special mention. When stripped of their flue they have a double colour, the part from which the flue is stripped being brown, and the remainder of the quill being a lighter colour of beige or grey. The lightness of this colour varies in the quills, and the "eyes" should be inspected at the back to ensure that they are light in colour. When wound round the hook shank, this double marked quill gives a very life-like imitation of the rib markings of many natural insects, and forms the body material of well-known patterns such as the "Red Quill", "Blue Upright", "Rusty Varient", "Ginger Quill", etc. The quills need to be dyed for some of these patterns. *See* Illustration, page 45 and Instructions for Stripping, this page.

The supply of plain quills is practically limitless as they can be obtained from any quill feathers in the fly-tyer's possession. They are pared from the shiny outer face of the quill with a sharp knife, and any pith adhering to the back can be scraped off with a finger nail.

Other body materials can be obtained from raffia grass, thin sheet cork and plastic, and they are mainly used for May flies. The plastic is used in thin stripes, and many natural translucent effects can be obtained by using it in conjunction with an under-wrapping of coloured silk.

STRIPPING PEACOCK "EYE" QUILLS FOR "QUILL BODIES"

The double marked quills from the "eye" tail start at the greenish yellow triangle. All the quills below this point are one colour only.

The quills are very delicate and unless treated with care will break very easily.

One method of stripping them is as follows—

Hold the quill in the left forefinger and thumb, leaving about half-an-inch of the root end projecting to the right (Fig. 4). Now scrape it from A-B between the right thumb and the ball of the right forefinger, and at intervals, between the

Fig. 4

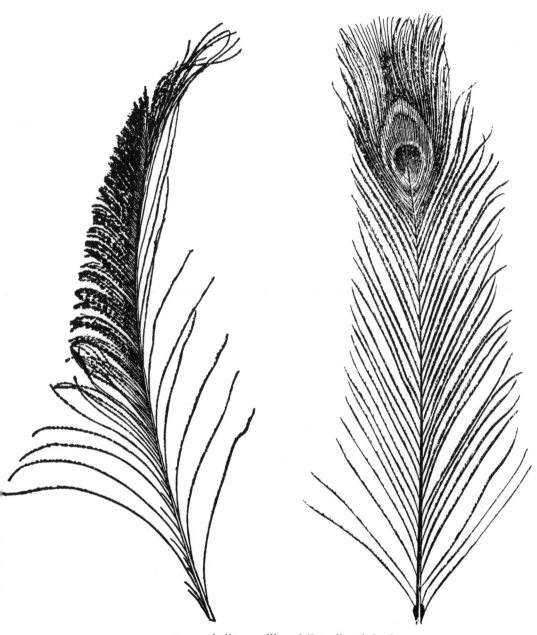

Peacock "Sword" and "Eye" tail feathers.

right forefinger nail and the ball of the right thumb. This will ensure that both sides of the quill are treated in the same manner. Extend the quill to the right a little more, and carry out the same process until about 1 in. has been cleaned. This will be sufficient for bodies on hooks up to size 3.

Another method which may be found more satisfactory is as follows—

Place the quill on a small sheet of glass or any other smooth or glossy surface, and hold it in position with the left forefinger. An old razor blade is now used for the scraping, and the quill must be turned over so that both sides are cleaned. The blade should slope slightly to the right so that its edge does not bite into the quill and split it.

The second method will be found the quicker of the two, although the finger nail may have to be brought into play for any odd fibre that proves stubborn.

There are always many breakages when one starts to strip peacock quills, but they become less as one's experience increases. The thing to remember is not to strip too much at a time, and this applies more to the finger nail method than it does to the razor blade method.

MATERIALS FOR WINGS

Most trout fly wings, especially those used on patterns that are imitations of the natural fly, are made from the wing and tail feathers of various birds. Other patterns, of course, use entirely different materials from different parts of the same birds. It is here that a certain amount of confusion can arise. For instance the Teal supplies us with wing quills for winging (grey), and also the black and white barred flank feathers for winging such flies as the "Peter Ross", "Teal and Green", etc.

The same applies to the feathers from the mallard duck, whose wings supply us with feathers for the wings of many patterns of flies, and who also supplies the brown speckled shoulder feathers for the wings of the "Mallard" series of patterns.

One or two of the feathers required for some patterns are not plentiful, but a substitute can usually be obtained. In the following list I have given both the original and substitute.

WING QUILLS—Both Secondaries and Primaries (*see* illustration on page 48) are used for winging. In many instances these are the same colour, but in others the Secondaries are an entirely different colour to the Primaries. The teal and mallard wings are excellent examples of this type. They both have grey primaries, but in the case of the teal the secondaries are a shiny green, and the mallard are a shiny blue.

Blackbird—The hen bird is lighter in colour than the cock, and its wings supplies the materials for "Greenwell's Glory". The darker cock's wings are used for the "Iron Blue".

Capercailzie—The secondaries and coverts of these wings provide a speckled feather for the wings of "Alders". They are not very plentiful, however, and the best substitute is the speckled hen wing, which is obtained from the game hen.

Coot—A smoky-blue quill feather suitable for "Blue Winged Olive", "Blue Dun", etc.

Crow—Shiny black, suitable for the "Butcher" and "Watson's Fancy".

Grouse—The Secondaries, if well marked, are used for the "Grouse" series of flies ("Grouse and Claret", etc.), but the tail feather from this bird is generally considered better for this purpose as it has more pronounced markings and pairs of wings can be obtained from single tails. This is clearly illustrated, facing page 36.

Jay—The blue coverts from these wings have alternate light and dark blue bars, and although they are used primarily as hackles for sea-trout and salmon flies, they are also used for wings in one or two patterns. Just the tips of the feathers are used and one of these patterns, the "Blue Jay", is illustrated in the coloured plate facing page 124. The larger primaries are used for winging also, the "Saltoun" and the "Hawthorn" being two patterns on which they are found.

Mavis Thrush—A pinkish brown feather, sometimes used for "Greenwell's Glory" and also as a substitute for Landrail which is now rare.

Tawny Owl and Barn Owl—These are used when tying moths, and also for the wings of the "Brown Owl" and "Cinnamon".

Partridge—Used for the wings of the "Grannom" and also on very small patterns that would normally call for a cock or hen pheasant wing.

Cock Pheasant—For the "Artful Dodger" and "Nobbler", etc.

Hen Pheasant—Both secondaries and primaries are used, and they supply the wings for many popular patterns: "March Brown", "Caperer", "August Dun", "Governor", etc. Illustrated, facing page 50.

Plover (Lapwing)—Not an extremely popular winging material but sometimes used for the "Iron Blue", and "Butcher".

Rook—Similar to the crow but smaller, and also suitable for the "Butcher" and "Watson's Fancy".

Snipe—For the "Blue Dun", "Seth Green", etc., in fact for numerous flies that call for a grey wing.

Starling—This is without doubt the most used of all the wings. Both secondaries and primaries can be used, and they provide the wings for all "Duns", "Olives" and many other patterns such as the "Hare's Ear", "Ginger Quill" varients, etc. In fact any pattern that calls for a grey wing.

Teal Duck—As previously mentioned, the primaries and secondaries differ in colour. The grey primaries can be used as are those from the snipe and starling, but as they are coarser in texture they are only used on larger sizes of these patterns.

The secondaries have a bright green sheen on them and are used for sea and lake trout patterns. The "Delius" is one of these.

Waterhen (Moorhen)—These are brownish-grey quills, suitable for the "Olive Dun" and other patterns that call for a dun-coloured wing.

Wild Duck (Mallard)—The grey primaries from these wings are used for several well-known patterns requiring a wing of that colour, the "Wickham" being perhaps the best known. They can be used for fairly small patterns if only two or three fibres are used, but they usually form the wings of the larger patterns of wet flies. They are used a great deal in America and New Zealand on large wet flies, many of which are based on the patterns used in this country. I have seen them used as the wing material for a "Greenwell" tied on a No. 8 hook. Illustrated, facing page 50.

Underside of Wing

Front of Wing

SEDGE FLY WITH SINGLE ROLLED WING

MAYFLY WITH HACKLE-FIBRE WING

FAN-WINGED MAYFLY

The secondaries which have a bright blue sheen on one side make admirable wings for the "Butcher", while the white undercoverts are quite useful for tying small "Coachman". The tips of the blue secondary feathers are white, and this part can be used when small patterns of flies such as the "Jock Scott" and "McGinty" are needed. They also form the wings of the "Heckham" patterns. Illustrated, facing page 50.

Woodcock—These quills supply the wings for the "Woodcock" series of flies ("Woodcock and Green", etc.), and also for "Hardies Favourite", "Gravelbed" and "Mole".

Speckled Game Hen—These quills are the ones most used for the wings of the "Alder" and also for some of the darker patterns of "Sedges". The lighter shades can be used as a substitute for Grouse tail and wing feathers when tying the "Grouse" series of flies ("Grouse & Green", etc.). Illustrated, facing page 50.

Plain Hen (Buff Orpington, Rhode Island Red, etc.)—Used for the rolled wings of sedges, and for "Autumn Dun" and "Welshman's Button". They vary in colour from a pale buff to a deep red-brown, and some of the intermediate shades are a suitable substitute for Landrail. Illustrated, facing page 50.

White Duck—Used for the wings of the "Coachman" and "Parmachene Belle" and when dyed they can be used for the wings of sea-trout flies such as "The King" and "The Queen". The fibres "marry" very well, so that various colours can be mixed to give the wings of small salmon and sea-trout flies. The "Parson" is a good illustration of the latter. Illustrated, facing page 50.

White Goose—These are similar to the white duck quills but much larger. They are suitable for making wings of bass flies and flies for sea fishing.

TAIL FEATHERS—Tail feathers, with the exception of grouse, are not so popular for winging as are wing quills. The reason for this is the fact that the fibres on the tails do not stay together so well as those on the wing quills. For large patterns, however, it is sometimes necessary to use the tails as the fibres on these are much longer. A good instance of this is the "March Brown". Hen pheasant tail is almost invariably used on the larger patterns of this fly.

Speckled Partridge Tail Feathers—Used for the wings of sedges, and for the whisks of the "March Brown". Illustrated, facing page 50.

Plain Brown Partridge Tail Feathers—Substitute for landrail wing, for the "Cow-Dung", etc.

Hen Pheasant Tail Feathers—For the wings of the "Invicta" and the larger patterns of the "March Brown". Illustrated, facing page 50.

Speckled Grouse Tail Feathers—The best feather to use when winging the "Grouse" series of flies—"Grouse and Claret", etc. Illustrated, facing page 50.

White Tip Turkey Rump Feathers—These are used for fairly large flies that require a feather with a white tip, such as the "McGinty".

SPECKLED HEN WING QUILL

Wings of "Alder", "Dark Sedge", etc.

PLAIN BROWN HEN WING QUILL

Wings of Sedges, etc. The colour of these quills varies from a pale buff to a deep cinnamon.

HEN PHEASANT QUILL

Wings of "August Dun", "Governor", "March Brown", "Stone Fly", "Caperer", etc. Cock pheasant quills are used similarly.

WHITE DUCK WING QUILL

Wings of "Coachman". Also, dyed various colours, for wings of sea and lake trout flies, "Cardinal", "Parson", etc.

MALLARD GREY DUCK WING QUILL

Wings of "Wickham", "Blae and Black", etc. A useful feather as it may be used for the very smallest as well as the larger patterns.

MALLARD WHITE TIP BLUE QUILL

Wings of "Butcher", "Heckham", "Jock", etc.

HEN PHEASANT TAIL

Wings of "Invicta" and the larger patterns of "March Brown", etc.

SPECKLED PARTRIDGE TAIL

Rolled wings of some Sedges, wings and tails of "March Brown", etc.

SPECKLED GROUSE TAIL

Wings of "Grouse" series of sea and lake trout flies, i.e. "Grouse and Yellow", "Grouse and Green", etc.

GREY DRAKE BREAST

Hackle and wings of Mayflies, etc.

FRENCH PARTRIDGE HACKLE

Hackle of Mayflies.

BROWN PARTRIDGE HACKLE

Hackle of "March Brown", "Partridge and Orange", Mayflies, spiders, etc.

WOODCOCK HACKLE

Hackles of north country wet flies, "Woodcock and orange", etc., and for hackles of spiders and nymphs.

GROUSE HACKLE

Hackle of "Grouse Hackle" and hackled patterns of the "Grouse" series of sea and lake trout flies.

SNIPE HACKLE

Hackle of "Snipe and Purple", etc.

The illustrations are of full size sections of the original feathers.

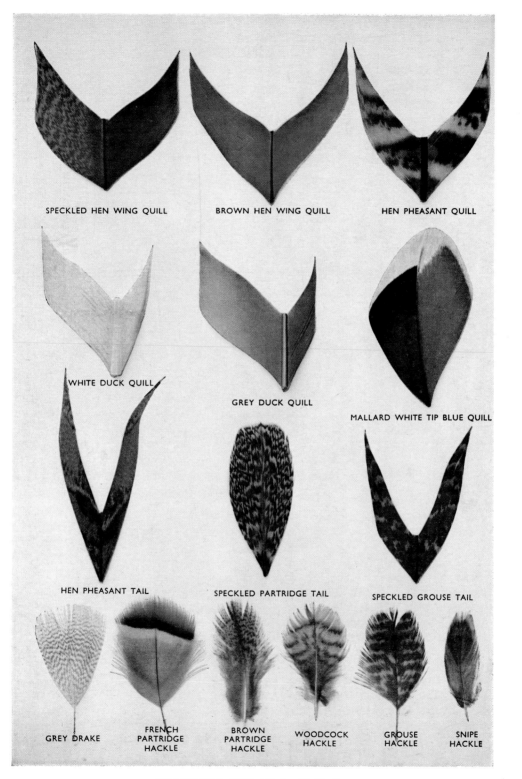

SPECKLED HEN WING QUILL   BROWN HEN WING QUILL   HEN PHEASANT QUILL

WHITE DUCK QUILL

GREY DUCK QUILL

MALLARD WHITE TIP BLUE QUILL

HEN PHEASANT TAIL   SPECKLED PARTRIDGE TAIL   SPECKLED GROUSE TAIL

GREY DRAKE   FRENCH PARTRIDGE HACKLE   BROWN PARTRIDGE HACKLE   WOODCOCK HACKLE   GROUSE HACKLE   SNIPE HACKLE

FEATHERS FOR TROUT FLIES

BREAST AND FLANK FEATHERS, ETC.

These feathers are used mainly for winging sea and lake trout flies. They are rather more difficult to handle than quill or tail feathers, being much softer in texture. This difficulty, however, can be overcome with practice. They are used in exactly the same manner, in that left and right feathers are used for left and right wings.

Brown (or Bronze) Mallard Shoulder Feathers—This forms the wings of many well-known patterns of flies, especially the "Mallard" series such as the "Mallard and Claret". Other patterns are "Connemara Black", "Fiery Brown", "Golden Olive", "Black and Orange", etc. Illustrated in Chapter XVIII, Materials—Salmon Flies, facing page 170.

Teal Flank Feathers—This is a black and white barred feather and is also used mainly for lake and sea trout flies. Perhaps the best known of these is the "Peter Ross" an illustration of which, with the feather itself, is given here. Other well-known patterns using the teal flank wings are the "Teal" series, such as the "Teal and Green", "Teal and Claret", "Teal, Blue and Silver", "Parson", etc. In many patterns a few fibres are used as "cheeks" on some other wing feather, the "Don" being one of these. Illustrated in Chapter XVIII, Materials—Salmon Flies, facing page 170.

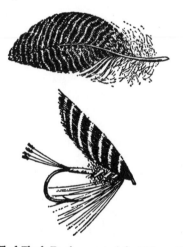

Teal Flank Feather as used for Wing of
"Peter Ross" Sea Trout Fly.

Grey Mallard (Drake) Breast and Flank Feathers—These feathers are used similarly to the brown mallard and teal feathers, but they are more popular in America than in the United Kingdom. Some of the American patterns are the "Rube Wood", "Laramie", "Grizzly King", "Queen of Waters", and "Professor". A well-known English pattern is the "John Spencer". They are also used for the wings of May flies, dyed and undyed. Illustrated, facing page 50.

Summer Duck Flank Feathers—This is very similar to brown mallard but lighter in colour. It is also more popular in America than it is here mainly because it is indigenous to that country. The most well-known fly that uses this feather for its wings is the "Cahill" a pattern that is almost synonymous with fly fishing in America. Others are the "Hoskins" and the "Gordon". It is also used on many dry flies. The fibres are tied in "bunch" fashion as it is termed in America. We use a similar type in this country on our "hackle fibre" wings the dressing of which is dealt with later in this book. Two illustrations of "bunch" wings will be found on the coloured plate of Dry Flies, facing page 96. They are the "Dark Hendrikson" and the "Light Cahill" tied by Mr. Ray Bergman.

Mandarin Duck Flank Feathers—The feathers from the mandarin duck are almost an exact duplicate of those of the summer duck. Consequently they can be used as substitutes when summer duck feathers are hard to get. The fibres are a little "stringier" so do not stay "married" quite so well as those of the summer duck, but this can be an asset when "bunch" wings are being tied.

Summer Duck and Mandarin Duck White Breast Feathers—These are round spade-shaped feathers, and their natural contour makes them ideal for "fan" wings.

Widgeon Shoulder Feathers—These are grey speckled feathers, ideally suited for sea and lake trout flies such as the "Teal Blue & Silver," "Peter Ross," etc. They are more distinctively marked than Gray Mallard Flank feathers, but not so heavily barred as Teal Flank. Their fibres stay together better than do those of most wildfowl body feathers, consequently they are much easier to tie in.

HERL WINGS—There are not many patterns of flies that use separate "herls" for wings, but the one that comes to the mind immediately is the "Alexandra". For this the "herls" from the green Peacock Sword tails are used. Illustrated, page 45.

Another pattern is the "Ilen Blue" which uses "herls" from the blue neck feathers of the peacock.

WHOLE FEATHER WINGS—This type of wing is usually tied with the extreme tip of a whole feather, or two of them back to back. The most used are—

Blue Kingfisher Feathers—These are the electric blue feathers from the body of the kingfisher. Two of them, back to back, form the wings of the "Blue Kingfisher". Illustrated, facing page 124.

Blue Jay Feathers—These are the dark and light blue barred coverts, and these also are used back to back.

Jungle Cock Feathers—These feathers come from the cape of the jungle cock, and are in fact its hackles. They are rather unique as each one has a white or cream "eye" which appears to have been enamelled on. Two of these, back to back, form the wings of the "Demon" and "Jungle Cock" flies. They are also used as cheeks or shoulders on many patterns such as "Watson's Fancy", "Jungle Alexandra", and

"Corrie Fly" (illustrated in Chapter XVIII, Materials—Salmon—Flies, facing page 170).

HACKLE WINGS—Hackles for wings are used in several ways. The tips are usually utilised for spinners, or the hackle can be wound in the usual way and then all the fibres are "bunched". The fibres can be at right-angles to the hook shank for spinners, or upright for patterns requiring a normal wing. Used in this fashion they make a very durable and attractive wing. The instructions for tying these wings will be found on pages 83 to 87.

A single hackle tip, usually a spade hackle, can be used when tying the down-winged type of fly such as the sedge (*see* pages 85 and 86).

VARNISHES, WAX, ETC.

Before commencing to tie a fly, the tying silk should be well waxed. For this a solid wax is generally used. This is obtainable either clear, black or brown, the clear being the most popular.

When dubbing or fur bodies are required, a little liquid wax on the silk is sometimes an asset.

To prevent the tying silk coming unwound, the last few turns should be sealed off with thin celluloid varnish. This can be obtained in small bottles and can be applied with the point of a needle. If it is a wet fly that is to be finished off, and a dark shiny head is required, the application of a little spirit varnish will do the job.

For the "Dunne's" series of patterns, a white lacquer should be applied to the hook shank before the fly is tied. After the fly is tied, the silk is saturated with medicinal paraffin. This makes it semi-transparent, causing the white shank to show through.

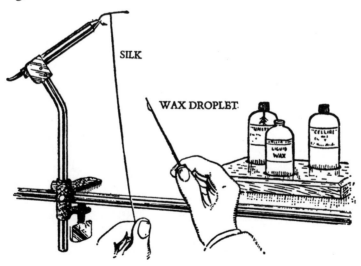

A very sound asset is a workmanlike stand in which to keep one's bottles of varnish and wax. Not only does it make for ease in use, but it also ensures that an opened bottle will not be knocked over amongst expensive materials or on completed flies.

Mr. Peter Deane, the well-known fly-tyer of Hemyock, Devonshire, evolved the stand that bears his name, and it should meet all requirements. The one illustrated on page 53 has accommodation for three bottles. The bottles are supplied with special caps for applying the wax and varnish, and the illustration shows one of these in use. *See also* page 172.

INDEX OF FEATHERS FOR TROUT FLIES

BIRD	FEATHER	USE IN FLY-TYING
Bittern	Flank	Hackle of "Matuka"
Blackbird	Wing	Wings ("Iron Blue Dun", etc.)
Capercailzie	Wing	Wings ("Alder")
Condor	Wing	Herls for Bodies
Coot	Wing	Wings ("Blue Wing Olive")
Crow	Wing	Wings ("Butcher", etc.)
Corncrake (*see* Landrail)	Wing	Wings ("Cinnamon Sedge", etc.)
,,	Breast	Hackles ("Cowdung", etc.)
Duck, White	Wing	Wings ("Coachman", etc.)
Egyptian Goose	Breast	Wings and hackles of May flies, etc.
French Partridge (*see* Red Leg)		
Golden Pheasant	Crest (head)	Tails of lake and sea trout flies
,, ,,	Tippet (neck)	,, ,, ,, ,,
Grouse	Neck	Hackles ("Grouse Hackle", etc.)
,,	Tail	Wings ("Grouse and Claret", etc.)
,,	Wing (covert)	Wings ("Indian Yellow", etc.)
,,	Under coverts	Hackles ("Poult Bloa", etc.)
Guinea Fowl	Neck (blue or white)	Hackles and whisks for nymphs
Heron	Breast (grey)	Herls for bodies
,,	Wing	Herls for bodies
Ibis	Breast	Tails of sea trout and lake trout flies
Jay	Lesser coverts (blue)	Throat hackles, etc.

BIRD	FEATHER	USE IN FLY-TYING
Jungle Cock	Neck	Sides and wings of sea trout flies
Kingfisher	Back	Wings ("Blue Kingfisher")
Landrail	Wing	Wings ("Cinnamon Sedge", etc.)
Lapwing (substitute for Landrail)	Rump (brown)	Hackles ("Cowdung", etc.)
Lapwing	Wing	Wings ("Iron Blue Dun", etc.)
Magpie	Tail	Wing cases of beetles
Mallard Duck (Drake)	Grey breast and grey flank	Wings ("Rube Wood", etc.) and Wings and hackles of May flies
" " "	Wing quill (blue with white tip)	Wings ("Butcher", "Heckham", etc.)
" " "	Wing quill (grey)	Wings ("Wickham", etc.)
" " "	Shoulder (brown)	Wings ("Mallard and Claret", etc.)
" " "	Underwing coverts (white)	Wings ("Coachman")
Mandarin Duck	Flank (brown)	Wings ("Cahill", etc.)
" "	Breast (white)	Wings of Fan-Wing flies
Mavis Thrush (substitute for Landrail)	Wing	Wings ("Greenwell's Glory", etc.)
Moorhen (see Waterhen)	—	—
Owl (brown)	Wing	Wings ("Brown Owl", etc.)
Owl (light)	Wing	Wings ("Owl", etc.)
Ostrich	Wing and tail	Herls for bodies
Partridge	Back (brown)	Hackle ("March Brown", etc.)
"	Breast (grey)	Hackle ("Hardies Favourite")
"	Wing	Wings ("Grannom", etc.)
"	Tail (speckled and brown)	Wings ("Cinnamon Sedge", etc.)
Peacock	Tail (eye)	Quill and herl bodies
"	Quills (from eye tail)	Bodies ("Blue Quill", etc.)
"	Bronze herl (from stem of eye tail)	Bodies ("Coch-y-Bondhu", etc.)
"	Sword tail (green herl)	Wings of sea trout flies ("Alexandra", etc.)
Peewit (see Lapwing)	—	—
Pheasant-Cock	Neck (red-brown)	Hackle ("Bracken Clock")

BIRD	FEATHER	USE IN FLY-TYING
Pheasant-Cock	Wing	Wings ("Nobbler", etc.)
„ „	Tail	Tails of May flies, etc., and herls ("Pheasant Tail")
Pheasant-Hen (substitute for Bittern)	Flank	Hackle of "Matuka"
Pheasant-Hen	Wing	Wings ("March Brown", etc.)
„ „	Tail	Wings ("Invicta", etc.)
Plover (see Lapwing)	—	—
Poultry (chicken) Cock	Neck hackles	Hackles
„ „	Saddle hackles	Wings of streamer flies, etc.
„ Hen	Neck hackles	Hackles
„ „	Lesser coverts	Wings ("February Red", etc.)
„ „	Wing quill (speckled)	Wings ("Alder", etc.)
„ „	Wing quill (plain)	Wings ("Sedges", etc.)
Red Leg Patridge (French Patridge)	Breast	Hackle of May flies
Rook	Wing	Wings ("Butcher")
Rouen Drake	Breast	For fan wing May flies
Snipe	Back	Hackles ("Snipe and Purple")
„	Wing	Wings ("Blue Dun", etc.)
Starling	Breast and back	Hackles ("Black Gnat", etc.)
„	Wing	Wings ("Olive Quill", etc.)
Swan	Shoulder	Herls for bodies
Summer Duck	Flank (brown)	Wings ("Cahill", etc.)
„ „	Breast (white)	Wings of fan wing flies
Teal Duck	Breast	Fan wing flies ("Grizzly King", etc.)
„	Breast and flank	Wings ("Peter Ross", etc.)
„	Wing quill (green)	Wings ("Delius", etc.)
„	Wing quill (grey)	Wings ("Wickham", etc.)
Turkey	Tail (Cinnamon)	Herls for bodies
Waterhen	Wing	Wings and hackles (Waterhen Bloa, etc.)
Widgeon Duck	Shoulder	Wings of sea-trout flies
Woodock	Breast	Hackles ("Woodcock and Claret", etc.)
„	Wing	Wings ("Woodcock and Green", etc.)

BIRD	FEATHER	USE IN FLY-TYING
Wood Duck (*see* Summer Duck)	—	—
Wild Duck (*see* Mallard Duck)	—	—

STORING MATERIALS

The best method for storing one's materials, if funds will allow, is a specially-designed cabinet with sectioned drawers to take all the tools, accessories, feathers, etc. If this is not possible, old cigar boxes and airtight tins should be utilised.

Whatever method is used, all compartments, boxes and packets should be liberally sprinkled with some form of moth deterrent. The best of these is flake carbon (or naphthalene). It will keep the most persistent parasites at bay. This is most important where feathers are concerned.

CHAPTER SEVEN

DRESSING FLIES FOR TROUT FISHING

A GENERAL SURVEY

IN THE FOLLOWING CHAPTERS I will endeavour to give as clearly as possible, the methods of dressing most of the well-known types of flies.

Fly-tying is one of the few arts that can be learned from a book and, except perhaps for the putting on of wings, the beginner should have little difficulty in picking up the rudiments. Of course, a few minutes of practical demonstration are always far more effective than the written word, and if it is possible for him to get someone to show him one or two of the more difficult operations, so much the better.

I will deal with dry flies first, and no doubt the reader will find the lists of dressings, together with the coloured illustrations, a helpful adjunct to the instructions.

Many of the patterns in the lists of dry fly dressings can also be tied as wet flies by using softer hackles and the wet style of winging. Conversely, of course, many of the wet fly patterns can be tied as dry flies by using stiffer hackles and the dry style of winging.

It must be borne in mind that none of the instructions are hard and fast rules. For instance, very few fly-tyers tie in their hackles in exactly the same fashion. Some tie in by the tip of the hackle, others by the butt. Some incorporate the butt into the body of the fly, which is quite a good method as it ensures that the hackle will not be pulled out during the winding.

The beginner should not be discouraged if his first few attempts look hopeless. The most perfect fly-tyer had to make a start sometime, and you may rest assured

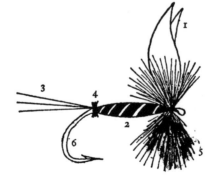

1. Wings.
2. Body.
3. Tail.
4. Butt.
5. Hackle.
6. Hook.

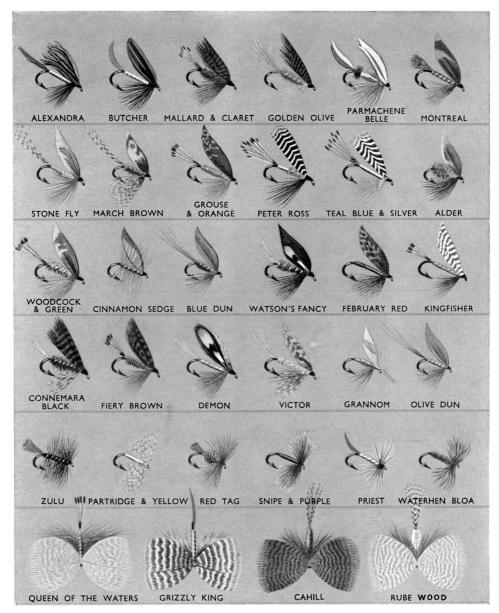

ALEXANDRA	BUTCHER	MALLARD & CLARET	GOLDEN OLIVE	PARMACHENE BELLE	MONTREAL
STONE FLY	MARCH BROWN	GROUSE & ORANGE	PETER ROSS	TEAL BLUE & SILVER	ALDER
WOODCOCK & GREEN	CINNAMON SEDGE	BLUE DUN	WATSON'S FANCY	FEBRUARY RED	KINGFISHER
CONNEMARA BLACK	FIERY BROWN	DEMON	VICTOR	GRANNOM	OLIVE DUN
ZULU	PARTRIDGE & YELLOW	RED TAG	SNIPE & PURPLE	PRIEST	WATERHEN BLOA
QUEEN OF THE WATERS	GRIZZLY KING		CAHILL		RUBE WOOD

TROUT FLIES

ADVANCE WING DRY FLY

UPRIGHT WING
DRY FLY

HACKLE POINT
WING SPINNER

HACKLE DRY FLY

WINGED WET FLY

HACKLE WET FLY

SEA TROUT FLY

FAN-WING MAY FLY

HACKLE MAY FLY

SPENT MAY FLY

A General Survey.

(a) Preparing Feathers for Wings.

(b) How to form a Dubbing Body.

(c) Making detached bodies for May Flies, etc.

(d) The Whip Finish Knot.

(e) The Figure of Eight Tying.

that his first flies looked exactly the same. Patience is the main factor, and practice the second.

If one finds that one operation is proving more difficult than any other, concentrate on that operation to the exclusion of others. If it is putting on wings, for instance, this operation can be practiced without making a complete fly each time. All that is necessary is that a "bed" of silk is wound on the hook shank. Never try to tie wings on to the bare shank. By this method the beginner should soon learn to master this most enjoyable pastime, and with just a few hints on tying the different patterns, there is no limit to the different types of fly he can tie, including unorthodox patterns of his own design.

PREPARING QUILL-FEATHERS AND TAIL-FEATHERS FOR WINGS

As winging is the most difficult part of tying a fly, I think that the preparation of the wings deserves a section of its own.

One of the first snags a beginner comes up against is "split" wings before and during the tying in, so I hope the following few points, with the illustrations, will ease this difficulty.

The first thing to do is get the quills from the wings, one from a left-hand wing, and one from a right-hand. The feather part of the quill should be one smooth plane, and if this is not the case, it is fairly easy to stroke the fibres until this smoothness is achieved.

It is not chance which causes each fibre to cling to its neighbour, and it is up to us to take full advantage of the device used by nature to achieve this object.

Along each edge of every fibre are rows of claw-like hairs, *see* Fig. 5, which act very similarly to the claws of the modern zip fastener. If this point is borne in mind it will greatly facilitate the "marrying" of split fibres. It always helps to know what one is trying to do, and does away with a lot of haphazard stroking.

To remove a section of the feather from the quill, the procedure is as follows—

1. Tear off the soft fibres at the base of the quill.
2. Hold base of quill in right hand.
3. Run the point of the scissors or dubbing needle through the fibres at the desired width, leaving the quill as at Fig. 6.
4. Grasp the fibres of the section at their extreme tips and pull them down, and at the same time pulling them slightly to the left. After a time you will find that the section will appear as Fig. 7 every time you perform the operation.

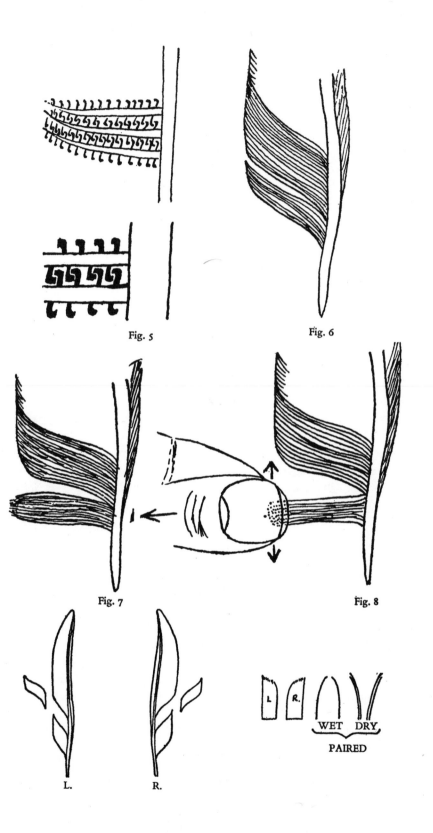

Fig. 5

Fig. 6

Fig. 7

Fig. 8

L.

R.

WET DRY

PAIRED

If the fibres split when they are pulled down, they can be re-married as follows—

1. Grasp the extreme tips again, at the same time pulling them slightly to the left.
2. Keep the pressure leftwards and move the fingers up and down (Fig. 8). This will cause the claws on the fibres to interlock.
3. Stroke the tips together.

When all the fibres are married, grasp them tightly at a point near the quill and cut or tear them off. Lay the section aside and carry out a similar procedure with the other wing quill, turning it over to bring the fibres to the left.

For a "Double Split-Wing" dry fly two sections from each of the matched wing quills will be required; two for the left-hand wing and two for the right-hand wing.

To make it easier to pick up the sections of wings when they have been removed from the quills, they should be placed on top of a small box, a matchbox will do, with their tips projecting slightly over the edge. They can then be held in place with a finger of the right hand and picked up with the left hand, ready for tying in.

HOW TO FORM A DUBBING BODY—FIRST METHOD

The dressings in some of the following chapters call for fur bodies, so before we start on the actual fly-tying instructions, the procedure for spinning the fur onto the tying silk should be studied.

To wax the tying silk with solid wax, it is necessary to draw the silk across the wax very rapidly. The friction caused by this action melts the wax immediately surrounding the silk, and it is only necessary to do this a couple of times. There should be no pause during the action, otherwise the wax sets immediately, and the silk sticks. This will either cause it to snap or strain it so that it snaps when being used during the tying.

The above should always be carried out before starting to tie a fly of any description, and will be found quite sufficient for small patterns with fur bodies. If larger flies are being tied, the addition of a little liquid wax to the silk will be found helpful.

A dubbing body consists of wool or fur spun on to the tying silk which is then wound round the shank of the hook from tail to shoulder.

The secret of successful dubbing lies in the use of very small quantities of fur, and ample waxing of the tying silk.

The procedure is as follows—

Hold the silk taut in the right hand, at a right-angle to the hook shank, towards the body.

Select a minute pinch of the necessary fur and place it on the ball of the left forefinger. Bring the taut silk down on to the fur. Now lower the second finger down on to the ball of the thumb, and roll the silk and fur in a clock-wise direction. This action will wrap the fur round the silk, and should be repeated with additional fur until a sufficient length of silk has been covered. The finger and thumb should be parted at the end of each "roll" when the silk will untwist without disturbing the "barrel" of fur that surrounds it. Roll in one direction only.

The silk is then wound to the shoulder, and the spacing judged to give the desired thickness and shape to the body. *See* below for illustrations of the main stages of the operation, Figs. 9 to 12.

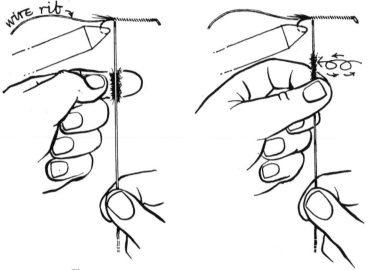

Fig. 9

Fig. 10

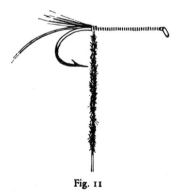

Fig. 11

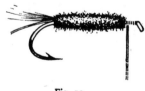

Fig. 12

HOW TO FORM A DUBBING BODY—SECOND METHOD

Another interesting method, passed on to me by Mr. J. Harris, the well-known Dublin fisherman and entomologist, is as follows—

A pin is fixed securely to the edge of the work bench, and a length of fine wire about 18 in. long is twisted round it at its centre so that two equal ends hang down. A pair of hackle pliers are then attached to each end of the wire. The two strands are then given a thin coat of liquid wax. Small quantities of the fur to be used are then dropped on to the waxed wire. When most of the two lengths are covered, the two hackle pliers are spun round each other so that the two strands twist tightly together.

The length of the wires may be varied, of course, according to the number of flies being tied. A couple of inches or so are cut off as required, tied in at the tail, and, when wound to the shoulder, give a good dubbing body with the wire rib already incorporated.

This is a good method for tying the "Gold Ribbed Hare's Ear" which requires a hackle of hare's flax. The longer fibres of the back of the hare should be used for this purpose, as when they are wound they stand out like the fibres of a hackle.

MAKING DETACHED BODIES FOR MAY FLIES, ETC.

Flies with detached bodies have fallen away in popularity during the last few years. The main reason for this is the difficulty entailed in the tying of them.

Now that long shanked, fine wire hooks can be obtained, the necessity for detached bodies is also reduced.

The best type of detached body is made from unvulcanised rubber, which can be made "tacky" by rolling it in the finger tips which have first been moistened by turpentine.

A thin needle is then placed in the vice, the tails whisks are held in position by a wedge of cork which has been split transversely (Fig. 13) and the rubber is then

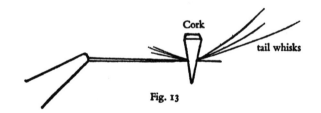

Fig. 13

wound as though one was forming a body on a normal hook shank. The tension of the turns of rubber can be varied to give the body shape.

A good length of the rubber should extend to the left at the commencement of the winding, so that, when the body is finished, there will be two short ends of rubber at the shoulder end (Fig. 14).

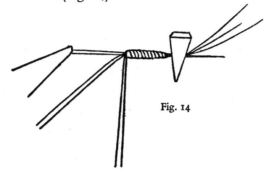

Fig. 14

The needle is now withdrawn from the body, and replaced in the vice by the hook. Place the body on the hook, nearer the tail than the eye, and fix it on top with a couple of turns of tying silk. Wind the tying silk to the eye, and then follow it with turns of one of the remaining ends of the rubber. The other end should form the foundation on which these turns are made (Fig. 15).

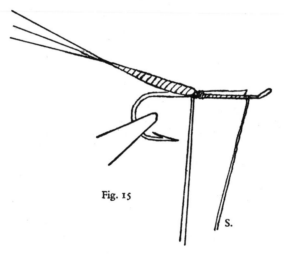

Fig. 15

S.

Other detached bodies can be wound on foundations of bristle or gut, which are placed in the vice as was the needle.

In all cases the bodies should be formed from right to left, instead of from left to right as is the normal procedure on a trout hook.

The detached body of the "Milward-Wanless" fly, illustrated in the coloured plate facing page 96, was formed by winding the body on an eyed piece of wire, as illustrated here. Before the war, these detached body flies were tied on special hooks, one of which is also illustrated here. The idea is that the hackle floats on the surface with the hook in it, and the body cocks up in a more natural way.

Body Wire

THE WHIP FINISH KNOT

The finishing off of a fly is most important, as it is essential that the silk should not become unwound after the fly is tied.

Half hitches may be used, but the most satisfactory method is the "Whip Finish".

Although it is a simple procedure, it is rather difficult to put into words, but the accompanying enlarged drawings should simplify matters.

The loose end of silk is laid against the hook shank, as Fig. 16, forming a small loop. The loose end is retained in this position by lifting up the loop, as Fig. 17. The left-hand side of the loop is then wound round the shank, as Fig. 18. After three or four turns the loop is held taut by the point of a dubbing needle, as Fig. 19. The loose end of the silk is then pulled tightly until the needle rests on the turns of tying silk. The needle is then withdrawn and the silk pulled tight (Fig. 20).

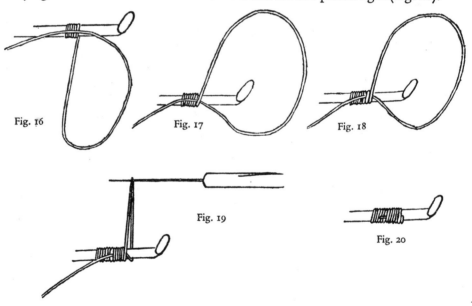

Fig. 16   Fig. 17   Fig. 18

Fig. 19

Fig. 20

The dubbing needle prevents the silk kinking when it is pulled tightly.
See also page 19—Whip Finish Tool.

THE FIGURE OF EIGHT TYING

The reader will find that several types of flies described in the following pages
call for a "figure of eight" tying for positioning the wings.

It is used for those wings that are required to stand out at an angle to the hook
shank and, although it is a very simple procedure, it is more easily explained by
illustrations than the written word.

It is most often used for "hackle-fibre" and "bunch" wings. If the wings
are to stand out at 90 degrees each side of the hook shank, there should be an equal
number of figures of eight on top and underneath the shank. If the wings are to
be more upright, one figure of eight on top of the shank and two or three below
will give the desired effect.

The illustrations below (Figs. 21 go 26) show the figure of eight being used on a
hackle-fibre spent wing pattern. The hackle for the wings is tied in and wound in
the normal way. The fibres are split into two equal sections, moistened and rolled
so that they stand out at right-angles to the hook shank. Assuming that the tying
silk is at the rear of the two sections, the illustrations show the necessary turns that
have to be made to keep them in this position.

Instructions for dressing the types of flies that use the figure of eight for
positioning the wings will be found on pages 81, 83 and 86.

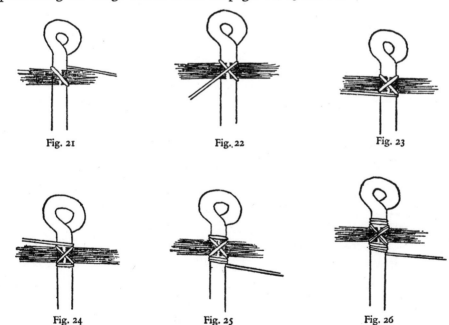

Fig. 21   Fig. 22   Fig. 23

Fig. 24   Fig. 25   Fig. 26

CHAPTER EIGHT

TROUT FLY DRESSING—DRY FLIES
TYING A SIMPLE HACKLED PATTERN

THIS DRESSING IS for the "Quill" series of flies, such as the "Red Quill", "Ginger Quill", "Blue Upright", etc.

Materials required—

    Hook (usually about size 0 or 1)—A larger hook may be used for practice.

    Tail—Fibres from a large old cock's hackle, similar to the hackle being used.

    Body—A stripped quill from the "eye" part of a peacock's tail.

    Hackle—Colour according to the dressing required.

Start winding silk about $\frac{1}{8}$-in. from the eye of the hook. To tie in the silk, hold the end in the left hand, take one turn of the remainder over the hook shank, and then commence winding to the left with the right hand. If the short end is then retained in the left hand for the first three or four turns, these will bind it down sufficiently for the left hand to be released. Cut off tied in end, and wind to a point on the shank where the bend commences. Fig. 27.

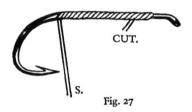

CUT.

S.

Fig. 27

Tail—To make the tail take three or four fibres from a large stiff hackle of the same colour as used for the shoulder hackle. The fibres should be about $\frac{3}{4}$-in. to 1-in. long, and are tied down on top of the shank where the initial tying of silk ended. One turn of the silk is enough, and then put another turn of silk *under* the tail close to the previous one, and another turn round the shank in front of the first one. This will give a smart lift to the tail of the fly. Fig. 28.

Body—For the body we will use a stripped quill from the "eye" feather of a peacock's tail. Tie in the narrow end of the quill close to the tail with two turns of silk, and then wind silk back to starting point. Fig. 29. Now wrap the quill round the shank towards the eye, overlapping each turn very slightly. The bi-coloured

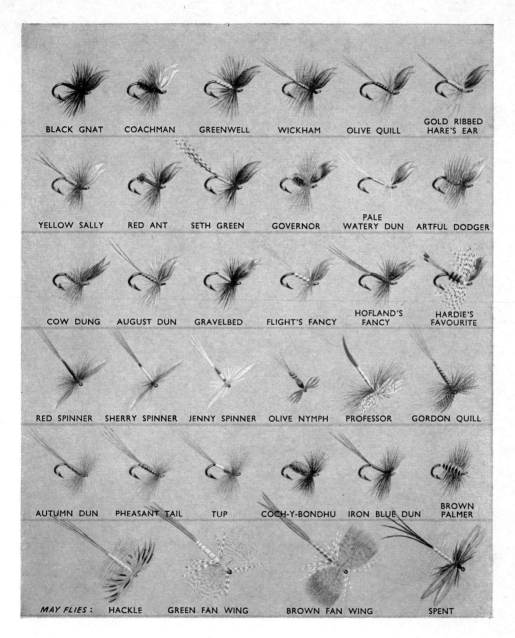

BLACK GNAT   COACHMAN   GREENWELL   WICKHAM   OLIVE QUILL   GOLD RIBBED HARE'S EAR

YELLOW SALLY   RED ANT   SETH GREEN   GOVERNOR   PALE WATERY DUN   ARTFUL DODGER

COW DUNG   AUGUST DUN   GRAVELBED   FLIGHT'S FANCY   HOFLAND'S FANCY   HARDIE'S FAVOURITE

RED SPINNER   SHERRY SPINNER   JENNY SPINNER   OLIVE NYMPH   PROFESSOR   GORDON QUILL

AUTUMN DUN   PHEASANT TAIL   TUP   COCH-Y-BONDHU   IRON BLUE DUN   BROWN PALMER

MAY FLIES: HACKLE   GREEN FAN WING   BROWN FAN WING   SPENT

TROUT FLIES

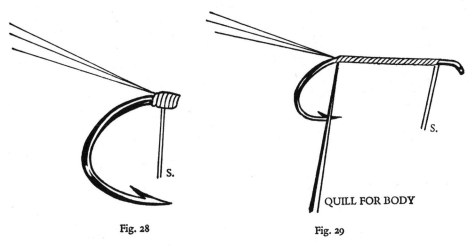

QUILL FOR BODY

Fig. 28   Fig. 29

quill will then give a very good imitation of the rib markings found on many flies. When the silk foundation has been covered, put two turns of silk round quill and cut off surplus. We should now be as Fig. 30. These quills are easier to use, and less brittle, if they are dampened.

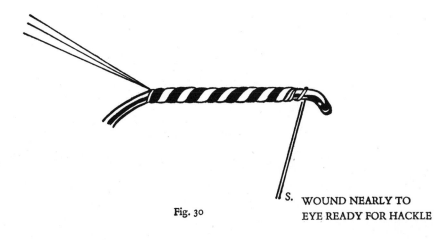

Fig. 30   S. WOUND NEARLY TO
                             EYE READY FOR HACKLE

Hackle—For a dry fly a good stiff-fibred cock's hackle should be used, and for a wet fly a softer one or a hen's hackle. The length of hackle to be used can be judged as follows: Bend hackle in the middle, and the length of the fibres that will stand out should be about the same as the distance between the eye and the point of the hook. Fig. 31.

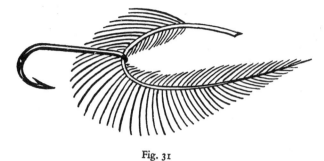

Fig. 31

Hold the hackle by the tip and strip off all the soft fluffy fibres at the base, up to the dotted line as Fig 32. This should leave just the bright, shiny fibres with no soft centre web. Then draw the hackle through the forefinger and thumb so that the fibres stand out at right-angles to the stem, as Fig 33. Tie in the stripped butt on top of the hook shank, close to the eye, leaving just enough room here for the finishing off turns of silk. A tight figure of eight turn should be put round the stem and the silk taken up to where the body ends. If two or three turns are also taken round the stem of the hackle at this stage, this will ensure that the hackle is not pulled out when it is being wound. The stem of the hackle must be laid along the shank to do this, of course. The outside of the hackle must be facing the front, and it is essential that it should be tied on edgeways to the shank, otherwise the fibres will not stand out at right-angles when the hackle is wound. Fig 34. Cut off surplus butt.

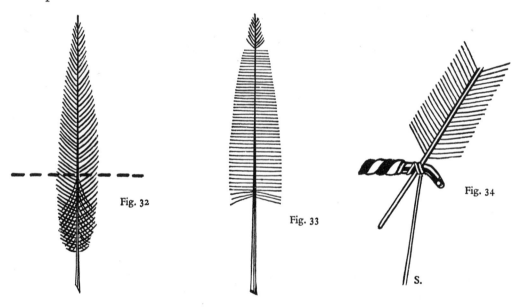

Fig. 32

Fig. 33

Fig. 34

S.

The instructions given for tying in the hackle do not have to be followed blindly. Different people have different methods of doing this, and the one I give is my own. Another very good way is to tie the butt of the hackle along the shank of the hook before the body is formed. When the tail and body are finished, the hackle is bent out at right-angles ready to wind. This method ensures a firm fixture for the hackle.

Some fly tyers prefer to tie their hackles in by the tip instead of the butt, so all I can say is that it is up to the individual to ascertain which method he prefers.

Take the tip of the hackle in the hackle pliers and wind it three or four times clockwise towards the rear of the hook, the turns almost touching. The turns should almost touch but never overlap. If they do the fibres will splay out and give a most unattractive appearance to the fly.

After the turns have been made, allow tip of hackle to hang down in hackle pliers, and wind a couple of turns of silk over it. Then cut off the tip. Now wind silk through hackle fibres towards the eye, binding down the hackle stem but avoiding the fibres. Make a whip finish when the silk is clear of the hackles as Fig. 35.

To wind the silk through the hackle without binding down any of the fibres, keep the silk very taut, working it in between the fibres as you bind down the stem. Use a backwards and forwards motion, going further forward than back, as Fig. 36. Your finished fly should appear as Fig. 37.

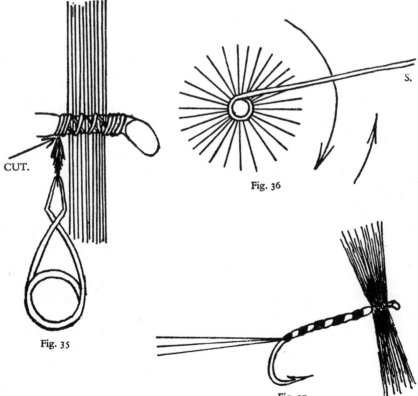

CUT.

Fig. 35

Fig. 36

S.

Fig. 37

TYING A "PALMER" FLY

When the hackle is wound the length of the body, it is referred to as being "tied Palmer".

The "Red Palmer"

Materials required—

    Hook—Size No. 1.
    Rib—Gilt Wire.
    Body—Red or brown seal's fur.
    Hackle—Red cock.

Wind silk to bend of hook and tie in wire rib. No tail is required. Form a dubbing body with the seal's fur and wind to shoulder, as described on page 62.

Take a hackle of the required length and hold it by the tip. Draw the hackle between thumb and forefinger of other hand so that its fibres stand out at right-angles to the stem. Fig. 38. Tie it in by the stem and wind it spirally to the bend of the hook and allow hackle pliers to hang down. Fig. 39.

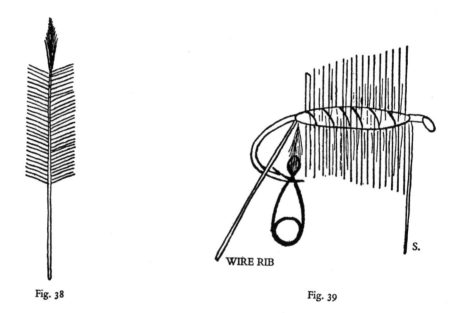

WIRE RIB

S.

Fig. 38   Fig. 39

Now wind the wire rib to the shoulder, working it in and out of the fibres so as not to disturb them, binding down each turn of the hackle stem. Tie in the wire and cut off the surplus. Now cut off tip of hackle. This method makes a very durable fly that will stand a lot of wear and tear.

When a "Palmer" type of May fly is being tied, another hackle at the throat is invariably used (*see* Fig. 40). There are many types of hackle that can be used for this purpose, some of them being French partridge breast feathers, grey partridge breast, Guinea fowl (Gallena), grey duck flank, etc., all natural or dyed various colours.

An illustration of the "French Partridge" hackle May fly will be found in the coloured plate facing page 68.

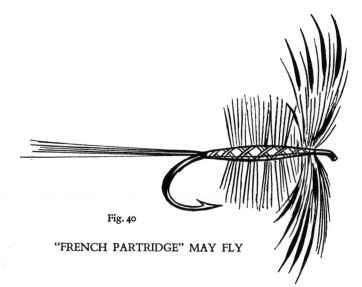

Fig. 40

"FRENCH PARTRIDGE" MAY FLY

TYING A "DOUBLE SPLIT-WING" DRY FLY

The "Iron Blue"

Materials required—

Hook—o or oo.
Tail—Fibres from a large iron blue cock's hackle.
Rib—Orange tying silk.
Body—Mole fur on orange tying silk.
Wings—Cock blackbird.
Hackle—Iron blue cock's.

The hackle should be stiff and bright, and as short in the fibre as possible.
For the wings, a left-hand and a right-hand feather will be needed.
Tie in silk about $\frac{1}{8}$-in. from the eye, wind to bend of hook and tie in tail as described on page 68. Tie in length of silk that is to form the rib.

The mole fur is now "dubbed" on to the tying silk as described on page 62 and wound to the shoulder of the fly to a point that will leave sufficient room between it and the eye for the wings to be tied in. It is better to leave too much room than not enough, and practice will soon give the tyer some idea of the right amount of space to leave.

Now wind the silk rib to the same place, tie it in with the tying silk and cut off the surplus. The fly should now appear as Fig. 41.

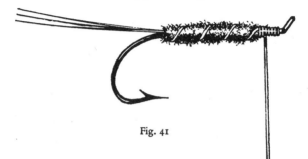

Fig. 41

We are now ready to tie on the wings, which should be prepared as described in chapter VII, page 60.

As previously mentioned, winging is the most difficult operation of all, but if it is carried out properly there is no reason why it should not become as simple as any other. The following points should always be borne in mind—

A. Grip wings tightly.
B. Don't let go until three turns of silk have been firmly drawn down.
C. If wings split, take them off and start again.
D. Make a "bed" of two or three turns of silk. Never tie wings on to bare shank.
E. Don't pull silk after wings are released.

Procedure for tying in wings

Place the wings on top of the hook so that their tips just reach the bend (Fig. 42). Pass silk up between thumb and near side of wings and down between the finger and far side of wings, allowing loop to form above (Fig. 43). Draw silk down gently but firmly so that all fibres come down one on top of the other (Figs. 44 and 45).

Before releasing the "tight grip" on the wings after they are tied in, raise the fingers to a vertical position above the body (Fig. 46) and take two turns of silk round the base of the wings as near to the body as possible, and one more turn round the shank close to the back of the wings. They will then appear as Fig. 47. It

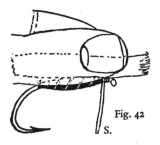

Fig. 42
S.

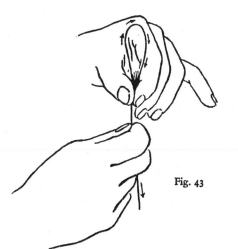

Fig. 43

SILK LOOP

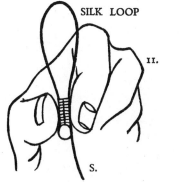

11.

Fig. 44

12.

S.

RIGHT

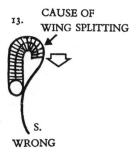

13.

CAUSE OF
WING SPLITTING

S.

WRONG

Fig. 45

may now be necessary to separate the two wings but this can very easily be done by the point of the scissors or dubbing needle. The silk should then be passed between the wings and a turn taken round the shank in front of them. Pass the silk back between the wings, take a turn round the shank, and this will ensure that the two wings stay apart. The wings must be held firmly while the silk is being drawn tight during this part of the operation.

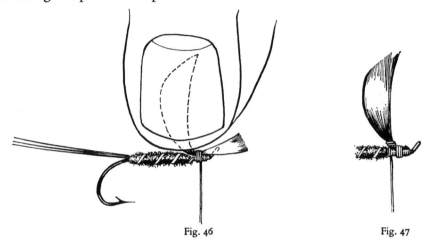

Fig. 46   Fig. 47

When the wings are tied in satisfactorily, the next stage of the proceedings is to tie in and wind the hackle.

Select a good, stiff fibred hackle and tie it in by the butt as close up to the back of the wings as possible. Two hackles may be used to increase the fly's floating capabilities. Wind two or three turns at the back of the wings, then, keeping the hackle taut, make two turns in front of the wings. Tie in the tip of the hackle and finish off with the whip finish. The fly should now be as Fig. 48.

If two hackles were tied in at the rear of the wings, one can be wound at the rear and the other in front.

Fig. 48

TYING ON "ADVANCED" WINGS

Advanced wings make a fly look very attractive and also seem to improve its balance. They were used as single wings in the dressing of the Varients shown on the coloured plate facing page 100, but this method can also be used for "Double Split-Wings".

The main difference in tying in advanced wings is that the wings are tied in *first*, the tail, body and hackle being formed afterwards.

To obtain the forward sweep, the hook is placed in the vice the opposite way round (Fig. 49), the wings are then tied on to the shank in exactly the same way as described in the previous chapter. When the wings are finished, a half hitch should be taken round the hook shank, as, when the hook is turned round for the rest of the fly to be tied, the silk will be the wrong side of the hook for winding clockwise.

A vice which can swing round on its own axis is an advantage here, as the hook need not be removed from the jaws. It is still essential, however, that the half hitch be put in the silk before proceeding with the tying of the body etc.

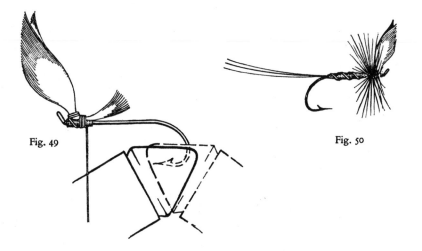

Fig. 49   Fig. 50

The tail should now be tied in and the body formed, but it will only be necessary to wind the hackle at the back of the wings. It need not be carried to front of them; in fact, this will be found to be practically impossible. Your finished fly should now appear as Fig. 50.

I prefer this method of winging to any other, particularly for very small flies. There is no build up of waste material close to the eye, and as the hackle is at the back of the wings only, it simplifies the tying on of the cast.

Any waste material from the wings can be tied down by the body material, and it all helps to make a neater finish to the fly.

TYING SEDGES AND SINGLE-WING DRY FLIES

The "Cinnamon Sedge"

Materials required—

    Hook—Size 1 to 3.
    Rib—Gold wire.
    Body—Two strands of cinnamon turkey tail.
    Body Hackle—Natural red.
    Wing—Cinnamon hen wing quill feather (1 only).
    Front Hackle—Natural red.

This is a fairly simple fly to tie and the procedure is as follows—

First tie a "Palmer" fly as page 72, using the two strands of cinnamon turkey tail for the body. Leave plenty of room between the eye and the body for the wing and front hackle.

For this fly we will use what is known as a "rolled" wing. To obtain this, take one hen wing quill and pull down the fibres until about one inch is projecting to the left (Fig. 51). They should then be torn or cut off, keeping the fibres as much in line as possible. The strip of fibres must then be rolled as one rolls a mat (Fig. 52)

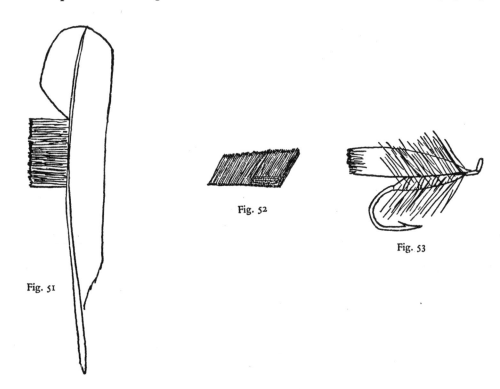

Fig. 52

Fig. 53

Fig. 51

and is now ready for tying in. It does not matter if the fibres split during the rolling, as they can be smoothed together once the wing is tied in. The wing is tied in in the usual way, and left sloping over the back of the fly (Fig. 53).

Now tie in the hackle close to the eye of the hook, and wind the tying silk back to the wing. The hackle is wound in close turns right up to the wing and over the turns of silk which tie it in. Let the tip of the hackle hang down in the pliers and wind the silk back to the eye, binding down the hackle stem but not pushing any of the hackle fibres out of place. The method of doing this is described on page 71. Finish off with the whip finish and the completed fly should be as Fig 54.

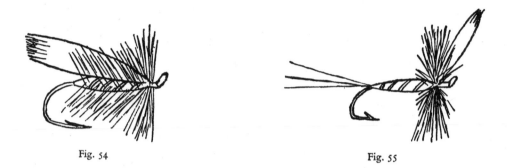

Fig. 54   Fig. 55

This type of wing is sometimes used for single upright winged dry flies, and is usually tied in the "advanced" style. The wing should be tied in before anything else with the hook in the reverse position (Fig. 49, page 77). The body, tail and hackle are put on in that order and the finished fly should appear as Fig. 55.

TYING A DOWN-WINGED FLY

The "Alder"

Materials—

Hook—Size 2 or 3. (A hook with a slightly longer shank is sometimes used for this fly.)
Body—Bronze peacock herl dyed magenta.
Wings—Brown speckled hen wing quill feathers.
Hackle—Black cock.

Place hook in vice and wind silk to bend. No tail is required.

The body is formed of one, or sometimes two, strands of the dyed peacock herl. If two strands are used they can be twisted together, although personally I prefer the following method: Tie in the two herls side by side with the flues towards the rear. The "flue" of these herls runs down the edges of one side of the quill only as shown in Fig. 56. Now wind them towards the eye for about two-thirds of the length of the shank, bringing each turn of the rear quill down on to the turn of the front quill (Fig. 57). Tie in the ends and cut off the surplus. Your fly should now be as Fig. 58.

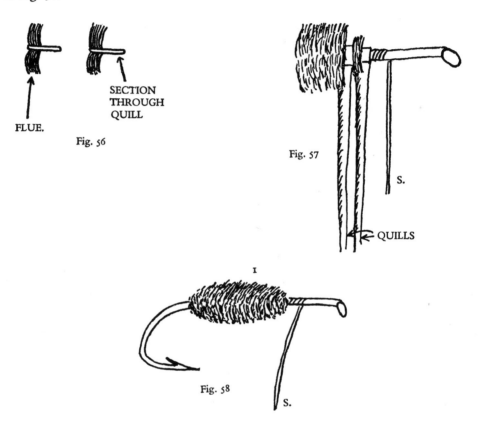

SECTION
THROUGH
QUILL

FLUE.

Fig. 56

Fig. 57

S.

QUILLS

Fig. 58

S.

The next operation is the winging, and the wings should be prepared as follows —Take a strip of the necessary width from the left-hand speckled hen wing feather, and one from the right-hand feather. Place the two strips together with the tips pointing inwards. Repeat this and you then have your pair of wings (Fig. 59). Now tie the wings on to the top of the hook shank. It is important to observe the natural curve of the wings when they are placed together before tying in, otherwise you will have one sweeping upwards and the other downwards.

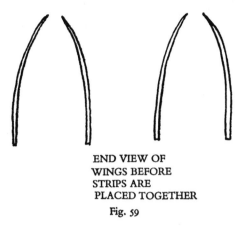

END VIEW OF
WINGS BEFORE
STRIPS ARE
PLACED TOGETHER
Fig. 59

Cut off the surplus roots of the wings, and the fly is now ready for tying in the hackle. This is tied close to the eye of the hook, and the silk is wound back to the point where the wings are tied in. Wind the hackle to the wings covering any waste ends left and also the silk which ties the wings down. Let the tip of the hackle hang down in the pliers and wind the silk back to the eye. Cut off the hackle tip, form the whip finish at the eye of the hook, and seen from above, your fly should be as Fig. 60. The wings may have to be stroked to lay alongside the body, as they should be almost parallel with the hook shank and not stick up into the air.

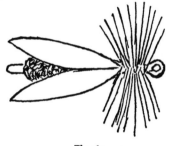

Fig. 60

TYING "BUNCH WING" FLIES
The "Light Cahill"

This method of winging is more popular in America than in the United Kingdom, although our method of tying hackle fibre wings is very similar in effect.

Flank feathers of wildfowl are invariably used, the most common being the mandarin duck and summer duck. For our illustration we will take the "Light Cahill", as shown on the coloured plate facing page 96. This fly was tied by

Mr. Ray Bergman, an expert of this particular method, and one of the most well known fly-tyers in America.

Materials required—

Hook—No. 2 or 3.
Tail—A few fibres as the wings.
Body—Creamy white seal's fur.
Wings—Speckled mandarin duck, light in colour.
Hackle—Ginger.

The body and tail are formed in the usual manner, and we are now ready to tie in the wing.

Mr. Bergman's method is to tie in the tip of the feather pointing over the eye of the hook, as Fig. 61. This means, however, that one feather is required for each fly, and as these feathers are none too plentiful, a dozen flies would work out rather expensive. An alternative method is to tear off a fairly wide strip of fibres from the feather, roll into a bunch, and then tie them in pointing over the eye (Fig. 62). It this method is used care should be taken to see that the tips of the fibres are all in line.

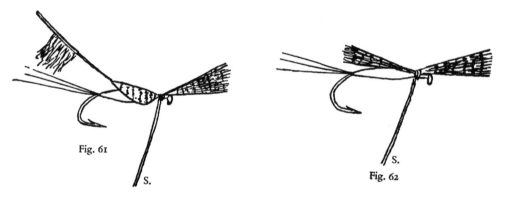

Fig. 61

Fig. 62

Whichever method is used, the procedure from now on is the same.

After the fibres have been *firmly* tied in they should be raised to a vertical position and a couple of turns of silk taken round their extreme base as close to the hook shank as possible. Now take a turn round the hook shank at the rear of the fibres, and this will ensure that they remain upright (Fig. 63). Now cut off surplus roots.

All that remains to be done is to separate the fibres into two equal halves, and the two sections are then kept permanently apart with a figure of eight tying. If the two halves are moistened and rolled, they will stay apart while the figure of eight is being executed. The "figure of eight" is clearly illustrated on page 67.

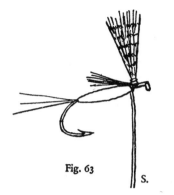

Fig. 63

S.

The hackle is now tied in and wound in the usual way, and the finished fly, as seen from the front, should be as Fig. 64.

Fig. 64

TYING HACKLE POINT WING SPINNERS AND MAYFLIES

The "Iron Blue Spinner" (Male)

Materials required—

Hook—Size oo–o.

Tail—White cock hackle fibres.

Body—White silk, showing a tip of bright red at tail and shoulder, then covered with natural (clear) horsehair.

Wings—The points of two white cock hackles tied "spent".

Hackle—One or two turns only of white cock's hackle.

The thing to remember when tying spinners is the glassy transparency of the natural flies, and the tying should be as light as possible.

The tail is tied in in the usual way and then the length of horsehair for covering the body. Now form the body with, at the tail end, about three turns of bright red tying silk, more turns of white tying silk (make this the colour for tying all the fly), and then another three turns of the red silk at the shoulder. The horsehair should then be wound in even turns to the shoulder and tied in. Cut off the surplus, and the fly should appear as Fig. 65. It will be seen that the two colours of silk will show quite plainly through the horsehair, and that it is the latter that imparts that transparent quality to the fly.

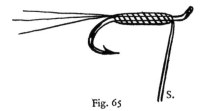

Fig. 65

Now take two small glassy white cock hackles and strip off all the fibres until only two small points are left as Fig. 66. These are tied in one at a time at right-angles to the hook shank, being held in position by a figure of eight winding (Fig. 67). Details of the "figure of eight" tying will be found on page 67. Before the stems of the hackles are cut off, they should be pulled either to the front or to the rear of the fly as Fig. 68. This will ensure that the wings are held securely and will not pull out, and gives a forward or backward sweep to the wings as desired.

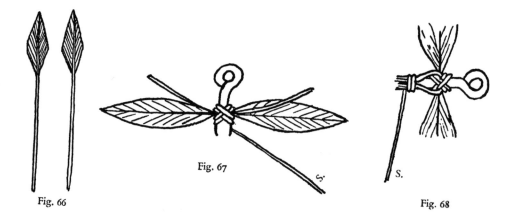

Fig. 66

Fig. 67

Fig. 68

The white hackle is then tied in at the rear of the wings, one turn at the rear and one at the front being quite sufficient. The finished fly should then be as Fig. 69.

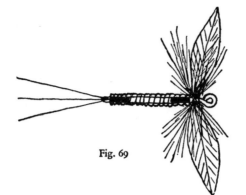

Fig. 69

The "spent" mayfly is tied in exactly the same way, but four hackles are used for the wings instead of two. The points are also kept longer to simulate the flattened wings of the mayfly as it lies on the water (Fig. 70). Stiff saddle or spade hackles are the best for these wings.

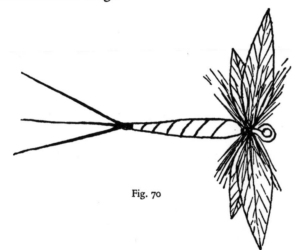

Fig. 70

Single hackle points are sometimes used for the down-winged variety of flies such as the Alder and Sedges. Stiff spade or saddle hackles are the best to use for this purpose, one of the former being illustrated in Fig. 71.

Fig. 71

The soft fibres are stripped from the base of the hackle and it is tied in by the butt on top of the hook shank, so that the tip lies along the back of the fly. The butt is then pulled to the right so that the fibres of the tip are drawn through the turns of tying silk. This draws them into a bunch as Fig. 72.

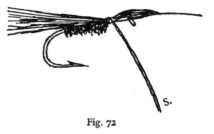

Fig. 72

The hackle is then tied in and wound in front of the wing, covering the turns of tying silk that hold the wing in position. The finished fly should then be as Fig. 73.

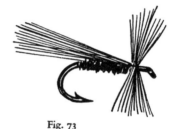

Fig. 73

TYING HACKLE FIBRE WING FLIES

This form of wing is considered to be one of the best types devised. They filter the light to better effect than the more solid types, are very durable and easy to tie. If used as the wings for spinners, they give translucence and improve the buoyancy of the fly.

The actual tying of the wing is simplicity itself. The tip of a bright hackle is tied in at the shoulder and a couple of turns taken round the hook shank. Cut off the tip of the hackle and we now have a simple hackled pattern as Fig. 74. The fibres of the hackle are now divided into two equal sections to stick out at right-angles to the hook shank. An easy way to do this is to moisten the fingers and twist the fibres together, and this will also keep them out of the way whilst they are being set by the turns of tying silk (Fig. 75). To do this we again use the figure of eight tying. One figure of eight on top of the hook will keep the two halves of the fibres separated, and several underneath the hook will push them into the upright position (Fig. 76). Details of the "figure of eight" tying will be found on page 67.

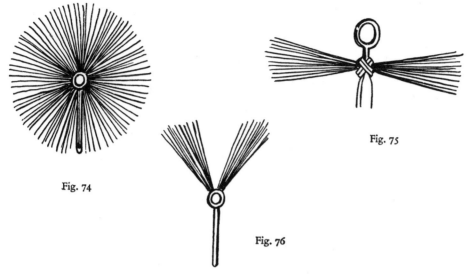

Fig. 74

Fig. 75

Fig. 76

For spent gnats and spinners, the figure of eight should be equal on top and underneath the hook, so that the fibres remain at right-angles to the hook (Fig. 77).

These wings must not be too bushy, although, of course, more turns are needed for mayfly wings.

All that is necessary now is to tie in the hackle and finish off the fly.

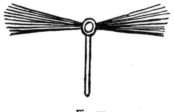

Fig. 77

TYING FAN WING MAY FLIES

Materials required—

Hook—Long shank, up or down eye.
Tail—Three fibres from a cock pheasant tail.
Rib—Oval tinsel.
Body—Raffia.
Wings—A pair of small feathers from the breast of the grey drake.
Hackles—Two medium-large.

Although not universally popular nowadays, this is a very interesting and satisfying type to dress. There are dozens of different dressings, ranging from Halford's exact imitations to concoctions thought up on the spur of the moment.

This method of dressing is also used for the American fan wing flies, illustrated, facing page 58—"Queen of the Waters", "Grizzly King", "Cahill", and "Rube Wood", *see* Dressings, page 103 and 104.

The body, tail and rib are put on in the usual manner, care being taken to make a well-shaped body—thicker at the shoulder than at the tail. Leave plenty of room at the eye of the hook to take the wings and hackles.

Tying in the Wings—Select two of the wing feathers (Fig. 78) as nearly exactly alike as possible. Strip off the soft flue at the bottom and place them back to back (Fig. 79). Place them on top of the hook so that the two stems run along the top and tie them in securely (Fig. 80). Without letting go of them, raise them up and put two or three turns round the stems as close to the hook as possible (Fig. 81).

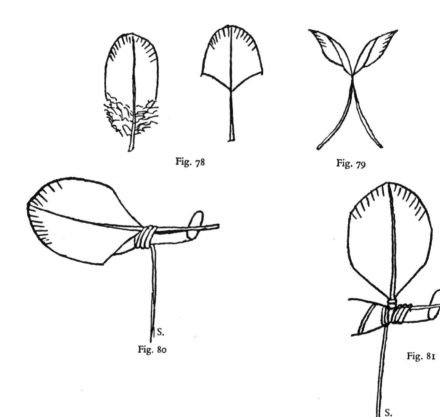

Fig. 78   Fig. 79

Fig. 80   Fig. 81

Now put a couple of turns in front of the wings, pull the stems to the rear and put a couple of turns round them and the hook as Fig. 82. This will keep the wings upright.

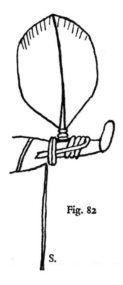

Fig. 82

S.

Now tie in the two hackles at the back of the wings. Wind the whole of one at the back of the wings as a further support for them, and the other one should be wound once or twice round the hook at the back of the wings and then finish up with turns in front of the wings. Wind the silk to the eye through the hackles, finish with the whip finish and the fly should be as Fig. 83.

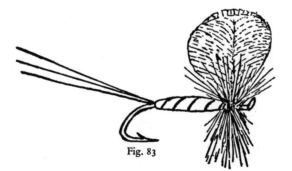

Fig. 83

The wings of a "Fan Wing" fly are obtained from small breast feathers which give the necessary rounded shape required in these flies.

These feathers are tied in exactly the same way as are split dry fly wings, i.e., back to back, upright, and curving outwards.

THE "FORE-AND-AFT" HACKLE FLY

This is a very successful method of dressing, especially for May flies. Not only does it ensure a good floating fly, but it seems to be very attractive to the fish.

It can be added to any dry May fly dressing as all it entails is an extra hackle wound at the tail end of the shank in addition to any at the shoulder. A good steely blue dun hackle is the best, or a good stiff badger hackle.

My favourite dressing, and one that has taken many fish, is as follows—

Tail—Three cock pheasant tail fibres.
Tail Hackle—Blue dun.
Body—Natural raffia ribbed oval gold tinsel.
Wings—Medium blue dun cock hackle fibres tied upright or spent.
Shoulder Hackles—1st, orange; 2nd, dark blue dun.

An illustration of this fly is given here, Fig. 84.

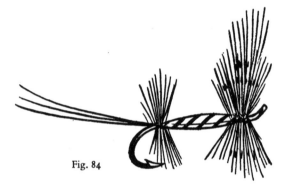

Fig. 84

FLIES TIED IN "REVERSE"

Mr. M. A. Wardle, of Broxbourne, Herts., who sent us the very interesting results of his experiments with "Gantron", also very kindly sent us details of work he has carried out on flies tied in "reverse". This is, flies tied with the hackle at the bend of the hook instead of at the eye.

His theory is that this eliminates the "parachute" effect of flies tied in the normal way, which is caused by the weight of the bend being so far away from the hackle. This causes the fly to land tail first, and to sit unnaturally on the water. This is illustrated in the three drawings below.

He also found that this method of tying improved the "cocking" qualities of the flies. This is because the bend of the hook exerts its righting movement directly through the hackle and wings in a vertical line, whereas, in the orthodox pattern, it has to make its influence felt through the length of the shank.

Also, the weight of the bend being in the hackle, this causes the "reverse" fly to land lightly nose first, and to sit on the water with its tail riding high like the natural. There seems to be no added tendency for the cast to drag down the tail, as might be expected.

Mr. Wardle sent me some patterns of his flies, and when dropped on to water they certainly seemed to bear out his observations. Only a very light tying of hackle is necessary, and he recommends that one side be stripped and the other side cut to a uniform length. Three turns of this hackle will support a fly up to 14, and four turns one up to No. 12.

The only slight disadvantage seems to be a little alteration in the tying technique necessary to finish off the flies, but this can be easily overcome with practice. If wings are used they should be tied sloping backwards to overcome any forward bias caused by the rush of air during casting. The hackle should be wound in front of the wing only, as shown in the illustration.

FLIES TIED "UPSIDE-DOWN"

Mr. Alexander Wanless, the well-known angler and writer, kindly gave me permission to make use of an article of his which appeared in "Angling", March, 1962, issue.

Part of the article was concerned with detached bodies, tied on special hooks, which had the effect of raising the body to the desired angle. Unfortunately the special hooks are not now obtainable, so Mr. Wanless made experiments along quite a new line, in an attempt to produce a fly that would land correctly and look as natural as possible.

The result was flies tied with the bend of the hook uppermost with and without detached bodies. To make them fall correctly the hackles were cut from what would have been the top of the hook had it been tied the right way up. The cut must be square or nearly so, but a very small hackle can be added for legs if necessary. It will be seen that, by using this method, the hook does not enter the water, and Mr. Wanless proved, by experimenting over two seasons, that this type of dressing resulted in many more rises.

The illustrations given below demonstrate three types of fly dressed in the "upside-down" manner. The first shows a fly tied on an ordinary hook, the second one of the detached body type, and the third representing a hatching dun with the thorax floating and the abdomen submerged.

PARACHUTE FLIES

These flies were originated in this country by the well-known fishing tackle firm of Alex. Martin, and two specimens are illustrated in colour on the plate facing page 96.

They differ from orthodox flies in that the hackle is wound on a horizontal plane, and not a vertical one as is usual. To facilitate this Messrs. Alex. Martin use a special hook which they manufacture themselves, which has a small vertical projection on which the hackle is wound.

As these special hooks are not readily obtainable, the amateur who wishes to make his own parachute flies has to resort to makeshifts. Small pieces of gut or bristle can be whipped to the hook shank, but one of the best methods I have seen is as follows—

Tie in the tying silk, make a bed for the wings and tie them in. Now tie in the hackle vertically, as shown in the first of the three illustrations. The projecting stalk is then looped over and tied to the hook shank, as shown in the second illustration.

The body and tail of the fly are now formed, leaving the loop of hackle stalk projecting below, and the tying silk carried to the front of the wings. The hackle is now wound horizontally round the loop of hackle stalk, and to make this operation easier it helps if a dubbing needle is pushed through the loop. The hackle can then be wound quite easily between the needle and the body of the fly.

When sufficient turns have been made, tie down the tip of the hackle in front of the wings. The tying silk is then threaded through the loop of hackle stalk and pulled so that the loop is drawn towards the eye of the hook. The tying silk is then wound in front of the wings again, and the fly finished off with a whip finish. The hackle should be tied in well back of the wings, and one with fairly long fibres should be used.

If only a hackled "Parachute" fly is required, the hackle can be tied in with the butt above the hook shank instead of below, and the procedure carried out on top of the body instead of below it.

CHAPTER NINE

TROUT FLY PATTERNS—DRY FLIES
(Illustrated, facing page 96)

March Brown (E. C. Coombes)
TAIL. Brown partridge fibres.
BODY. Hare's fur spun thinly on yellow silk.
HACKLE. No. 1: Dun Cock hackle.
HACKLE. No. 2: Brown partridge back feather.

Pale Olive Dun (E. C. Coombes)
TAIL. Fibres of light olive dun.
BODY. Very light olive translucent floss, ribbed with white tying silk.
HACKLE. Light olive dun.

Large Dark Olive Spinner (E. C. Coombes)
TAIL. Dark blue dun hackle fibres.
BODY. Three sections:
　　1st. Very light olive seal's fur.
　　2nd Medium olive seal's fur.
　　3rd Very light olive seal's fur.
HACKLE. Light honey dun.

Blue Varient (E. C. Coombes)
TAIL. Light blue dun hackle fibres.
BODY. Blue fur, ribbed light yellow tying silk.
HACKLE. Light blue dun.

Blue Bottle (T. J. Hanna)
BODY (Three-quarters length of shank): Black chenille ribbed with bright blue silk, blue silk tag.
WINGS. Pale blue dun hackle points sloping back over body.
HACKLE. Black, tied in front of wings.
HEAD. (Large.) Black chenille.

Olive Dun (T. J. Hanna)
TAIL. Light olive hackle fibres.
BODY. Light olive translucent plastic.
WINGS. Quill feather from snipe wing cut to shape.
HACKLE. Olive dun.

Lunn's Particular (W. Lunn)
TAIL. Four fibres of natural red from large hackle.
BODY. Undyed hackle stalks from natural Rhode Island Red cock hackle.
WINGS. Two medium blue dun cock hackle points put on flat.
HACKLE. Natural red.
TYING SILK. Pearsall's gossamer, shade 13, crimson.

Houghton Ruby (W. Lunn)
TAIL. Three fibres from white cock hackle.
BODY. Rhode Island hackle stalk dyed red.
WINGS. Two light blue dun hen tips from the breast or back set on flat.
HACKLE. Bright Rhode Island red hackle.
TYING SILK. Pearsall's gossamer, shade 13, crimson.

Winged Yellow Boy (W. Lunn)
TAIL. Pale buff, hackle fibres.
BODY. White hackle stalk dyed medium yellow.
WINGS. Light buff cock hackle points put on flat.
HACKLE. Light buff cock hackle.
TYING SILK. Pearsall's gossamer, pale orange, shade 6A.

Sherry Spinner—Late Evening (W. Lunn)

TAIL. Pale ginger hackle fibres.

BODY. Bright floss silk, deep orange, ribbed with gold wire.

WINGS. Two light blue dun hen tips set on flat.

HACKLE. Bright Rhode Island cock hackle.

TYING SILK. Pearsall's gossamer, pale orange, shade 6A.

Winged Caperer—Welshman's Button (W. Lunn)

BODY. Four or five strands from cinnamon turkey tail feather, two strands from swan feather, dyed yellow to make a ring of yellow in the centre of the body.

WINGS. Coot, bleached and dyed chocolate brown.

HACKLE. One medium Rhode Island cock hackle, one black cock hackle put in front of wings.

TYING SILK. Pearsall's gossamer, shade 13, crimson.

Hill's Red Quill (W. Lunn)

TAIL. Fibres of buff cock hackle.

BODY. Peacock "eye" quill dyed red.

WINGS. Coot, bleached fairly light, tied to slope forward.

HACKLE. Bright Rhode Island large cock hackle.

Tup (H. H. Brayshaw)

TAIL. Fibres of honey dun cock hackle.

BODY. Two sections:
  1st Yellow floss.
  2nd Pink tup wool.

HACKLE. Honey dun cock hackle.

Blue Quill (H. H. Brayshaw)

TAIL. Pale blue dun hackle fibres.

BODY. Quill from peacock "eye" feather, dyed pale blue dun.

WINGS. Pale blue dun hackle points.

HACKLE. Pale blue dun.

Orange Quill (H. H. Brayshaw)

TAIL. Orange hackle fibres.

BODY. Quill dyed orange.

WINGS. Rusty dun hackle points.

HACKLE. Orange.

Sedge (H. H. Brayshaw)

BODY. Light olive quill.

BODY HACKLE. Light olive.

WINGS. Lightly speckled cinnamon brown hen wing feather.

HACKLE. Cinnamon brown tied in front of wings.

Parachute Red Quill (A. Martin)

TAIL. Light blue dun hackle fibres.

BODY. Quill from peacock "eye" feather dyed red.

WINGS. Dark starling tied spent.

HACKLE. Light red.

Parachute Pale Watery (A. Martin)

TAIL. Light blue dun hackle fibres.

BODY. Natural quill from peacock "eye" feather.

WINGS. Light starling tied spent.

HACKLE. Pale watery dun hackle.

Iron Blue (Harry Powell)

TAIL. Iron blue hackle fibres.

BODY. Mole fur dubbing.

HACKLE. Iron blue.

Red Spinner (Harry Powell)

TAIL. Red hackle fibres.

BODY. Red floss ribbed fine flat gold tinsel.

HACKLE. No. 1: Red.

HACKLE. No. 2: Blue dun.

Dark Sedge (Harry Powell)
BODY. Natural quill from peacock "eye" feather.
BODY HACKLE. Red.
WINGS. From dark speckled hen wing quill.
HACKLE. Red, tied in front of wings.

Rough Olive (M. Riesco)
TAIL. Bule dun cock hackle fibres.
BODY. Olive seal's fur, ribbed gold wire.
HACKLE. Olive badger cock hackles.

Half Stone (M. Riesco)
TAIL. Blue dun hackle fibres.
BODY. Two sections:
  1st Natural horse-hair.
  2nd Blue fur (mole).

HACKLE. Blue dun, tied palmer over No. 2 section of body only.

Pheasant Tail Spinner (M. Riesco)
TAIL. Blue dun hackle fibres.
BODY. Fibres from a cock pheasant tail.
WINGS. Light blue dun hackle points.
HACKLE. Golden dun.

Blue Winged Olive—Male (J. W. Dunne)
TAIL. Dark honey.
BODY. Two strands cellulite silk, No. 298 (light brown olive) mixed with two strands, No. 218 (light pink).
RIBBING. Grey gossamer silk.
HACKLE. Six turns of blue dun hen, wound long then clipped.
EYES. Machine silk, terra cotta brown.
TYING SILK. Golden olive.

PATTERNS TIED BY WELL-KNOWN AMATEUR AND PROFESSIONAL FLY TYERS

See Illustrations, facing page 96—Dressings, pages 94 to 99.

COOMBES, E. C. Well-known tackleist and dresser in the Midlands. Flies for the Teme.

HANNA, T. J. Well-known writer and tackleist and fly dresser from Northern Ireland. Wrote *Fishing in Ireland* and many articles in the Fishing Press. Many of his flies are tied with two hackles, one through the other, which are very effective.

LUNN, W. Water Keeper to the Houghton Club, and invented several famous flies. Was a very good Naturalist and kept nymphs in glass containers at home to watch their development. In Hill's *River Keeper* the full dressings of his flies are described.

BRAYSHAW, H. H. Amateur fly-dresser from Devon. He used to breed his own birds for hackles. Tied a very good fly.

MARTIN, A. Well-known tackleist and fly dresser of Glasgow. Famous for his parachute flies, a popular fly. These are tied on special hooks which have a projection standing at right-angles to the hook shank. The hackles when wound on

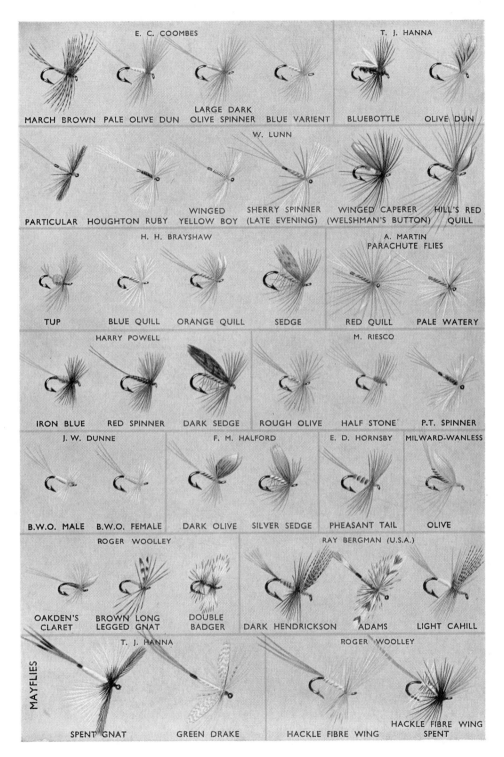

E. C. COOMBES

T. J. HANNA

MARCH BROWN　PALE OLIVE DUN　LARGE DARK OLIVE SPINNER　BLUE VARIENT　　BLUEBOTTLE　OLIVE DUN

W. LUNN

PARTICULAR　HOUGHTON RUBY　WINGED YELLOW BOY　SHERRY SPINNER (LATE EVENING)　WINGED CAPERER (WELSHMAN'S BUTTON)　HILL'S RED QUILL

H. H. BRAYSHAW

A. MARTIN
PARACHUTE FLIES

TUP　BLUE QUILL　ORANGE QUILL　SEDGE　RED QUILL　PALE WATERY

HARRY POWELL

M. RIESCO

IRON BLUE　RED SPINNER　DARK SEDGE　ROUGH OLIVE　HALF STONE　P.T. SPINNER

J. W. DUNNE　　F. M. HALFORD　　E. D. HORNSBY　MILWARD-WANLESS

B.W.O. MALE　B.W.O. FEMALE　DARK OLIVE　SILVER SEDGE　PHEASANT TAIL　OLIVE

ROGER WOOLLEY

RAY BERGMAN (U.S.A.)

OAKDEN'S CLARET　BROWN LONG LEGGED GNAT　DOUBLE BADGER　DARK HENDRICKSON　ADAMS　LIGHT CAHILL

T. J. HANNA

ROGER WOOLLEY

MAYFLIES

SPENT GNAT　GREEN DRAKE　HACKLE FIBRE WING　HACKLE FIBRE WING SPENT

DRY FLIES

this projection lie in the same plane as the hook shank, instead of round it as normally.

POWELL, H. The Wizard of the Usk, as he was known, and an extremely fine fly dresser. Was known all over the world and was as well a very fine fisherman. His two famous flies were "Dog's Body'" and "Powell's Whiskers".

RIESCO, M. Amateur fly-tyer, who for many years has fished the Dove, ties a very new fly. Was for many years Secretary of The British Casting Association and has always shown a keen interest in all forms of angling.

DUNNE, J. W. Famous as the author of *Sunshine and the Dry-fly*. Recommended that the hook be painted white, with special silks, which, when oiled, brought out the colour of the fly and was very translucent.

HALFORD, F. M. One of the most famous fishermen of his day; a keen disciple of the dry fly. Wrote many books, chief of which were *Dry Fly Fishing in Theory and Practice, Floating Flies and How to Dress Them,* and *The Development of the Dry Fly.* Dressed a beautiful fly and, though the moderns are apt to scoff at his exact imitation, he was a great man and did a lot of good work. His *Dry Fly Fishing in Theory and Practice* is still a classic.

HORNSBY, E. D. Known as "Pop" to his many friends. A well-known Devon fly dresser of the 30's. Best known by his pattern of the "Pheasant Tail" which he sent all over the world.

WANLESS, A. Well-known angler and writer. The "Olive" illustrated was tied by the famous Redditch tackle firm of Milwards.

WOOLLEY, ROGER. Well-known tackleist, dresser and writer of the Midlands. Wrote *Modern Trout Fly Dressing*, containing over 400 dressings and very careful instructions, and *The Fly Fishers Flies,* both well worth perusal.

BERGMAN, R. One of U.S.A.'s most famous fly dressers. Wrote the well-known book *Trout* on fishing and fly dressing.

(Illustrated, facing page 96)

**Blue Winged Olive—Female
(J. W. Dunne)**
TAIL. Dark honey cock fibres.
BODY. Three strands cellulite floss silk, No. 298A (pale brown olive) mixed with one strand, 298 (light brown olive) and three quarters strand of No. 287 (insect green). Considerable taper.
RIBBING. White gossamer silk.

HACKLE. Six turns of blue dun hen, wound long then clipped.
TYING SILK. Golden olive.

Dark Olive (F. M. Halford)
TAIL. White gallena (guinea fowl) dyed olive green.
BODY. Herl from condor quill dyed olive green.

WINGS. Coot wing.
HACKLE. Olive green cock.

Silver Sedge (F. M. Halford)
BODY. White floss silk ribbed fine flat silver tinsel.
BODY HACKLE. Ginger cock.
WINGS. Coot.
HACKLE. Ginger tied in front of wings.

Pheasant Tail (E. D. Hornsby)
TAIL. Fibres of golden dun hackle.
BODY. Fibres of cock pheasant tail.
HACKLE. Golden dun cock.

Olive (Milward—Wanless)
TAIL. Fibres of olive hackle.
BODY. (Detached): Well marked quill from peacock "eye" feather dyed light olive.
WINGS. Starling.
HACKLE. Light olive cock.

Oakden's Claret (R. Woolley)
TAIL. Fibres of blue dun cock hackle.
BODY: Claret tying silk.
WINGS. Single starling sloping forward.
HACKLE. Blue dun cock.

Brown Long Legged Gnat (R. Woolley)
BODY. Brown tying silk, with knob of brown wool or fur at thorax.

WINGS. Points of stiff grizzle hackles.
HACKLE. Red grizzle cock, long in fibre and wound sparingly.

Double Badger (R. Woolley)
BODY. Peacock herl.
HACKLE. Badger cock, one tied in at the shoulders and a smaller one at the tail end of the body.

Dark Hendrickson (Ray Bergman, U.S.A.)
TAIL. Whisks of squirrel tail fur.
BODY. Dark blue grey fur.
WINGS. Speckled mandarin duck fibres (flank)
HACKLE. Dark blue dun cock.

Adams (Ray Bergman, U.S.A.)
TAIL. Fibres of grizzle hackles.
BODY. Blue grey wool or fur.
WINGS. Two grizzle hackles tied spent.
HACKLE. Red grizzle cock.

Light Cahill (Ray Bergman, U.S.A.)
TAIL. Mandarin duck speckled flank, light shade.
BODY. Creamy white fur.
WINGS. Mandarin duck speckled fibres (flank), light shade.
HACKLE. Ginger cock.

MAY FLIES

Spent Gnat (T. J. Hanna)
TAIL. Three cock pheasant tail fibres.
BODY. White translucent plastic.
WINGS. Dark blue dun hackle. Points tied spent.
HACKLE. Badger cock.

Green Drake (T. J. Hanna)
TAIL. Three cock pheasant tail fibres.
BODY. Light olive plastic.
WINGS. Mallard drake breast feathers dyed green drake and cut to shape.
HACKLE. Yellowish green cock.

Hackle Fibre Wing (R. Woolley)

TAIL. Three fibres from a cock pheasant tail.

BODY. Natural raffia, ribbed silver oval tinsel.

BODY HACKLE. Medium olive cock.

WINGS. Fibres of large honey dun cock hackle dyed light olive (tied upright).

SHOULDER HACKLE. Badger cock dyed yellow.

Hackle Fibre Wing Spent (R. Woolley)

TAIL. Three fibres from a cock pheasant tail.

BODY. Natural raffia, ribbed oval silver tinsel.

BODY HACKLE. Badger cock.

WINGS. Dark blue dun cock hackle (large) fibres tied spent.

SHOULDER HACKLE. Black cock.

(Illustrated, facing page 100)

Gravel Bed

BODY. Lead coloured tying silk.

WINGS. Woodcock wing feather, not too heavily marked.

HACKLE. Black cock's long in fibre.

Yellow Sally

BODY. Yellowish buff dyed seal's fur, ribbed primrose tying silk.

WINGS. Any fine fibred wing feather dyed a deep primrose.

HACKLE. Natural light ginger cock's.

Black Gnat

BODY. Black tying silk.

WINGS. Starling wing feather tied small.

HACKLE. Black cock's.

Black Ant

BODY. Black tying silk, well waxed and tied to shape of ant's body then varnished over with celluloid varnish.

WINGS. Two small pale blue cock's hackles.

HACKLE. Black cock's.

Olive Quill

TAIL. Three whisks as hackle.

BODY. Peacock quill dyed olive.

WINGS. Medium starling wing feathers.

HACKLE. Dyed medium olive cock's.

Gold Ribbed Hare's Ear

TAIL. Three strands as hackle.

BODY. Hare's fur spun on yellow silk, ribbed flat gold tinsel.

WINGS. Pale wing feather of a starling.

HACKLE. Some longer strands of the body picked out with the dubbing needle.

B.W.O. Spinner (Male)

TAIL. Pale gold hackle fibres.

BODY. Brown red silk covered by natural horse hair.

WINGS. Pale blue dun cock hackle points tied spent.

HACKLE. Pale gold.

B.W.O. Spinner (Female)

TAIL. Pale ginger.

BODY. Natural horse-hair over gold silk.

WINGS. Pale blue dun cock hackle points tied spent.

HACKLE. Pale ginger.

Pale Watery Spinner (Male)

TAIL. Pale cream cock hackle fibres.

BODY. Pale yellow tying silk with orange at tail and shoulder, covered with natural horse-hair.

WINGS. Pale blue dun cock hackle points tied spent.

HACKLE. Pale cream cock.

Pale Watery Spinner (Female)

TAIL. Pale golden yellow cock hackle fibres.

BODY. Pale yellow silk covered with natural horse-hair.

WINGS. Pale blue dun cock hackle points tied spent.

HACKLE. Pale golden yellow.

Iron Blue Spinner (Male)

TAIL. White cock hackle fibres.

BODY. White silk with a tip of bright red at tail and shoulder, covered with natural horse-hair.

WINGS. Glassy white cock hackle points tied spent.

HACKLE. One turn only of white cock hackle.

Iron Blue Spinner (Female)

TAIL. Fibres of medium blue dun grizzled hackles.

BODY. Claret silk covered by natural horse-hair.

WINGS. Points of medium blue dun grizzled cock hackle tied spent.

HACKLE. Medium blue dun grizzled cock hackle.

Driffield Dun

TAIL. Pale ginger cock fibres

BODY. Pale blue fur, ribbed yellow tying silk.

WINGS. Tied forward, pale starling.

HACKLE. Pale ginger cock.

Adjutant Dun

TAIL. Three strands as hackle.

BODY. Striped quill of the adjutant or dyed blue peacock quill.

WINGS. Wing feathers of a starling.

HACKLE. Natural or dyed blue dun cock's.

August Dun

TAIL. Brown ginger cock.

BODY. Brown floss silk, or brown quill ribbed yellow horse-hair.

WINGS. Pale mottled hen pheasant wing.

HACKLE. Brown ginger cock.

Coachman

BODY. Bronze peacock herl.

WINGS. Duck or goose or any white wing feather.

HACKLE. Natural light red, ginger or light brown cock's.

Governor

BODY. Bronze peacock's herl, with golden yellow floss silk tip, followed by one turn of flat gold tinsel at tail-end of body.

WINGS. Feather from a hen pheasant's wing.

HACKLE. Natural reddy brown cock's.

Artful Dodger

BODY. Purple wool, ribbed fine gold wire.

WINGS. Cock pheasant's wing feather.

HACKLE. Blood red cock, ribbed down body.

Cinnamon Quill

TAIL. Fibres of ginger cock hackle.

BODY. Pale cinnamon quill, found at root-ends of some peacock quills.

HACKLE. Ginger cock.

Autumn Dun

TAIL. Palest blue dun cock fibres.

BODY. Undyed pale heron herl.

HACKLE. Pale blue dun cock.

Brown Palmer

BODY. Brown wool or dyed seal's fur ribbed flat gold tinsel (ribbing optional, as in all Palmers).

HACKLE. Brown cock's ribbed down body.

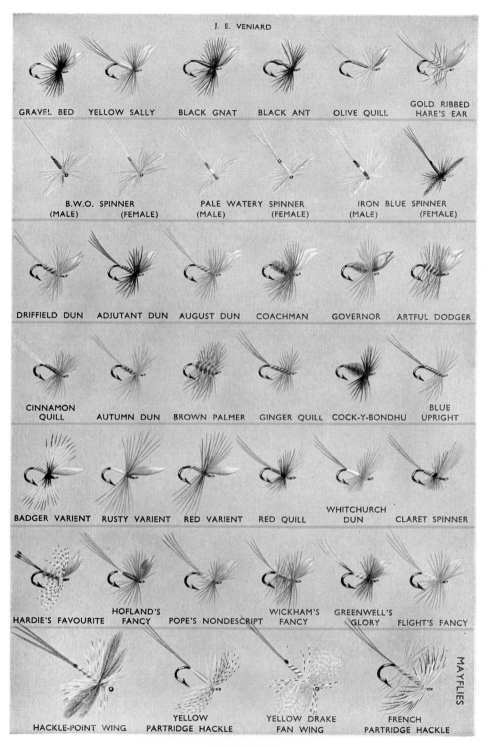

J. E. VENIARD

| GRAVEL BED | YELLOW SALLY | BLACK GNAT | BLACK ANT | OLIVE QUILL | GOLD RIBBED HARE'S EAR |

B.W.O. SPINNER (MALE)   (FEMALE)   PALE WATERY SPINNER (MALE)   (FEMALE)   IRON BLUE SPINNER (MALE)   (FEMALE)

DRIFFIELD DUN   ADJUTANT DUN   AUGUST DUN   COACHMAN   GOVERNOR   ARTFUL DODGER

CINNAMON QUILL   AUTUMN DUN   BROWN PALMER   GINGER QUILL   COCK-Y-BONDHU   BLUE UPRIGHT

BADGER VARIENT   RUSTY VARIENT   RED VARIENT   RED QUILL   WHITCHURCH DUN   CLARET SPINNER

HARDIE'S FAVOURITE   HOFLAND'S FANCY   POPE'S NONDESCRIPT   WICKHAM'S FANCY   GREENWELL'S GLORY   FLIGHT'S FANCY

HACKLE-POINT WING   YELLOW PARTRIDGE HACKLE   YELLOW DRAKE FAN WING   FRENCH PARTRIDGE HACKLE

MAYFLIES

DRY FLIES

Ginger Quill
TAIL. Ginger cock hackle fibres.
BODY. Undyed peacock quill from the eye.
HACKLE. Ginger cock.

Coch-y-Bondhu
BODY. Bronze peacock herl, with a flat gold tinsel tip.
HACKLE. Furnace cock with black tips.

Blue Upright
TAIL. Medium blue dun cock's hackle fibres.
BODY. Well marked peacock quill from the eye part of peacock tail feather.
HACKLE. Medium blue dun cock's.

Red Quill
TAIL. Red cock hackle fibres.
BODY. Peacock quill from eye, dyed red.
WINGS. Pale blue cock hackle fibres, tied upright.
HACKLE. Red cock.

Whitchurch Dun
TAIL. Pale ginger cock hackle fibres.
BODY. Primrose floss silk.
WINGS. Pale blue cock hackle fibres, tied upright.
HACKLE. Pale ginger cock.

Claret Spinner
TAIL. Cream cock hackle fibres.
BODY. Claret floss silk, ribbed gold wire.
WINGS. Pale blue cock hackle fibres, tied upright.
HACKLE. Red cock's.

Hardie's Favourite
TAIL. Three or four fibres of golden pheasant tippet.

Badger Varient
BODY. Undyed peacock quill from eye.
WINGS. Starling wing, tied to slope forward over eye of hook.
HACKLE, Badger cock, large.

Rusty Varient
BODY. Yellow floss.
WINGS. From partridge wing feather, tied to slope forward over eye of hook.
HACKLE. Bright rusty dun cock, large.

Red Varient
BODY. Undyed peacock quill from the eye.
WINGS. Starling, tied to slope forward over eye of hook.
HACKLE. Red cock hackle, large.

BODY. Claret floss silk, ribbed bronze peacock herl.
WINGS. From the wing feather of a woodcock.
HACKLE. Light partridge breast (grey).

Hofland's Fancy
TAIL. Three whisks as hackle.
BODY. Darkish reddy brown tying silk.
WINGS. Woodcock's or hen pheasant's wing.
HACKLE. Natural red cock's.

Pope's Nondescript
TAIL. Red cock hackle fibres.
BODY. Apple green floss tied with crimson silk, which may be shown at tail and thorax, ribbed flat gold tinsel.
WINGS. Starling wing.
HACKLE. Red cock.

Wickham's Fancy
TAIL. Three strands as hackle.

BODY. Alternate ribbing of flat gold tinsel and natural red cock's hackle.

WINGS. From the wing feather of a starling.

HACKLE. Natural red cock.

Greenwell's Glory

BODY. Waxed yellow tying silk, ribbed fine gold wire.

WINGS. Darkest starling or hen blackbird wing feather.

HACKLE. Light furnace cock's.

Flight's Fancy

TAIL. Three whisks as hackle.

BODY. Palest yellow floss silk, ribbed flat gold tinsel.

WINGS. Palest starling's wing feather.

HACKLE. Light ginger or honeydun cock's.

Hackle Point Wing May Fly

TAIL. Three fibres cock pheasant tail.

BODY. Yellow raffia, ribbed oval silver tinsel.

WINGS. Points of blue dun cock's hackles.

HACKLE. Light grizzled.

Yellow Partridge Hackle May Fly

TAIL. Three fibres of cock pheasant tail.

BODY. White floss silk.

1ST HACKLE. Light yellow cock.

2ND HACKLE. Grey partridge dyed yellow.

Yellow Drake Fan Wing May Fly

TAIL. Three fibres of cock pheasant tail.

BODY. Yellow raffia, ribbed oval gold tinsel.

WINGS. Duck breast feather dyed yellow.

1ST HACKLE. Yellow cock.

2ND HACKLE. Grey partridge.

French Partridge Hackle May Fly

TAIL. Three fibres of cock pheasant tail.

BODY. Natural raffia, ribbed oval gold tinsel.

BODY HACKLE. Olive cock.

HACKLE. French partridge.

(Illustrated, facing page 68)

Red Ant

BODY. Crimson tying silk, bronze peacock herl tag.

WINGS. Medium starling wing.

HACKLE. Natural blood red cock.

Seth Green

TAIL. A few strands of the breast feather of a teal.

BODY. Bright green floss silk, ribbed yellow tying silk.

WINGS. Either from the wing-feather of a landrail or from a wild duck's wing.

HACKLE. Natural red cock.

Pale Watery Dun

TAIL. Fibres of pale olive yellow cock.

BODY. Pale watery yellow quill.

WINGS. Palest starling wing.

HACKLE. Pale olive yellow cock.

Cowdung

BODY. Snuff colour wool or seal's fur.

WINGS. From the landrail wing.

HACKLE. Dark ginger cock.

Red Spinner

TAIL. Fibres of red cock hackle.

BODY. Red horse-hair on bare hook.

WINGS. Tied spent of bright medium blue cock hackle fibres, or two small medium blue cock hackle tips.

HACKLE. Red cock.

Sherry Spinner

TAIL. Fibres of palest ginger cock hackle.

BODY. Pale gold coloured quill, or plastic over gold coloured floss.

WINGS. Tied spent of glassy pale blue dun cock hackle fibres or two small pale blue cock hackles.

HACKLE. Palest ginger cock.

Jenny Spinner

TAIL. Fibres of white cock hackle.

BODY. White horse-hair or quill, showing a tip of bright red at tail and shoulder.

WINGS. Spent, of glassy white cock hackle fibres, or two white cock hackle tips.

HACKLE. White cock.

Pheasant Tail

BODY. Cock pheasant tail fibres, ribbed gold wire.

HACKLE. Golden dun cock.

TAIL. Golden dun cock hackle fibres.

Professor (Bunch Wing)

TAIL. A few long fibres of red ibis feather.

BODY. Yellow tying or floss silk, ribbed either gold, silver, or black tying silk.

WINGS. From the flank feather of a grey mallard.

HACKLE, Natural ginger cock.

Gordon Quill (Bunch Wing)

TAIL. Bronze blue-grey hackle fibres.

BODY. Peacock quill.

WING. Mandarin duck flank.

HACKLE. Bronze blue-grey cock.

May Fly, French Partridge Hackle

TAIL. Cock pheasant tail fibres.

BODY. Natural raffia, ribbed gold oval tinsel.

BODY HACKLE. Blue dun cock.

HACKLE. French partridge.

May Fly, Brown Fan Wing

TAIL. Cock, pheasant tail fibres.

BODY. Brown floss, ribbed gold oval tinsel.

WING. Brown mallard breast.

HACKLE NO. 1. Brown cock.

HACKLE NO. 2. Grey partridge breast.

May Fly, Green Fan Wing

TAIL. Cock pheasant tail fibres.

BODY. Greenish yellow floss.

RIB. Oval gold tinsel.

HACKLE. Grey partridge breast.

WINGS. Greenish-yellow mallard breast.

May Fly, Hackle Point Wing (Spent)

TAIL. Black cock hackle fibres.

BODY. Natural raffia, ribbed silver oval.

WINGS. Four dark blue dun hackle points tied "spent".

BODY HACKLE. Yellow cock.

HACKLE, Blue dun cock.

(Illustrated, facing page 58)

Fan-Wing Queen of the Waters

TAIL. Golden pheasant tippet fibres.

BODY. Orange floss silk.

WING. Grey mallard breast.

HACKLE. Brown cock tied palmer.

Fan-Wing Grizzly King

TAIL. Scarlet ibis.

BODY. Green floss, ribbed gold flat tinsel.

WING. Teal breast.

HACKLE. Grizzle cock.

Fan-Wing Cahill
TAIL. Brown mandarin duck fibres.
BODY. Blue-grey fur.
WINGS. Brown mandarin duck flank.
HACKLE. Brown cock.

Fan-Wing Rube Wood
TAG. Scarlet floss.
TAIL. Teal flank fibres.
BODY. White chenille.
WING. Grey mallard breast.
HACKLE. Brown cock.

(Not Illustrated)

Blue Dun
TAIL. Dark olive hackle fibres.
BODY. Olive tying silk ribbed gold wire.
WINGS. Dark starling or snipe wing.
HACKLE. Dark olive cock.

Iron Blue Dun (Female)
TAIL. Pale blue dun cock hackle fibres.
BODY. Dark peacock quill dyed claret.
WINGS. Cock blackbird wing.
HACKLE. Dark blue dun cock.

Iron Blue Dun (Male)
TAIL. Dark brown olive cock hackle fibres.
BODY. Dark peacock quill dyed olive.
WINGS. Cock blackbird.
HACKLE. Dark brown olive cock.

Olive Dun (1)
TAIL. Olive cock hackle fibres.
BODY. Olive quill.
WINGS. Snipe or starling wing.
HACKLE. Olive cock.

Olive Dun (2)
TAIL. Olive cock hackle fibres.
BODY. Waxed yellow tying silk ribbed gold wire.
WINGS. Snipe or starling wing.
HACKLE. Olive cock.

Grey Hen and Rusty
HOOK. 12–14.
BODY. Fibres from a cock pheasant's tail. Must be a good red colour.
HACKLE. Medium Blue Dun cock hackle, stiff and bright.

Blue Winged Olive (1)
TAIL. Green olive cock hackle fibres.
BODY. Heron herl dyed greenish yellow, ribbed gold wire.
WINGS. Dark starling or coot wing.
HACKLE. Green olive cock.

Blue Winged Olive (2)
TAIL. Green olive cock hackle fibres.
BODY. Greenish-yellow seal's fur, ribbed gold wire.
WINGS. Smoky blue hackle points.
HACKLE. Green olive cock.

Dogsbody
TAIL. Three fibres from a cock pheasant's tail.
BODY. Camel coloured (fawn) wool or seal's fur, well picked out.
RIB. Oval gold tinsel.
HACKLE. Grizzle cock hackle, with a red/brown one tied in front.

July Dun
TAIL. Medium olive cock hackle fibres.
BODY. Heron herl dyed yellow, ribbed gold wire.
WINGS. Dark starling wing.
HACKLE. Medium olive cock.

Ash Dun
TAIL. Light grey dun hackle fibres.
BODY. Silver grey silk.
WINGS. Light starling wing.
HACKLE. Light grey dun cock.

Whirling Blue Dun
TAIL. Ginger cock hackle fibres.

BODY. Smoke grey seal's fur on yellow tying silk.

WINGS. Dark starling wing.

HACKLE. Ginger cock.

Pale Evening Dun

TAIL. Pale honeydun cock hackle fibres.

BODY. Pale yellow seal's fur.

WINGS. Starling wing.

HACKLE. Pale honeydun cock.

Blue Dun Spinner

TAIL. Red cock hackle fibres.

BODY. Red-brown seal's fur ribbed gold wire.

WINGS. Tips of two small medium blue dun cock hackles, or hackle fibres, tied spent.

HACKLE. Red cock.

March Brown Spinner

TAIL. Red cock hackle fibres.

BODY. Red silk covered by horse-hair.

WINGS. Tips or fibres of medium blue dun cock hackles.

HACKLES. Red cock.

Iron Blue Spinner

TAIL. Medium blue dun cock hackle fibres.

BODY. Claret quill or horse-hair.

WINGS. Tips or fibres of medium blue dun cock hackles.

HACKLE. Medium blue dun cock.

Olive Spinner

TAIL. Medium olive cock hackle fibres.

BODY. Horse-hair over yellow tying silk.

WINGS. Tips or fibres of medium blue dun cock hackles.

HACKLE. Medium olive cock.

Light Sedge

BODY. Pale ginger fur or pale brown turkey tail fibres dyed yellow.

BODY HACKLE. Pale ginger cock.

WINGS. Hen pheasant wing.

SHOULDER HACKLE. Pale ginger cock tied in front of wings.

Dark Sedge

BODY. White wool ribbed gold wire.

BODY HACKLE. Furnace cock.

WINGS. Woodcock wing.

SHOULDER HACKLE. Furnace cock.

Orange Sedge

BODY. Orange floss silk or fur ribbed gold wire.

BODY HACKLE. Ginger cock.

WINGS. Plain brown hen wing.

SHOULDER HACKLE. Ginger cock.

Red Sedge

BODY. Dark red fur ribbed gold wire.

BODY HACKLE. Red cock.

WINGS. Plain brown hen wing.

SHOULDER HACKLE. Red cock.

Welshman's Button (Male)

BODY. Dark chocolate brown quill.

BODY HACKLE. Furnace cock.

WINGS. Plain brown hen wing.

SHOULDER HACKLE. Furnace cock.

Welshman's Button (Female)

As for male, but with two or three turns of cinnamon turkey tail at tail end of fly, and a paler wing.

Silver Horns

BODY. Dark green olive tying silk.

BODY HACKLE. Black cock.

WINGS. Waterhen or blackbird wing.

SHOULDER HACKLE. Black cock.

HORNS. Fibres of barred teal breast feather tied in at the head. (These should be nearly twice the length of the fly.)

Grannom

BODY. Dark heron herl with a small knob of green fur at tail end.

BODY HACKLE. Pale ginger cock.

WINGS. Hen pheasant or partridge wing.

SHOULDER HACKLE. Pale ginger cock.

The Hoolet

HOOK. No. 6 Long shank (light wire).
BODY. Bronze peacock herl.
WINGS. Piece cut from the wing feather of a brown owl, rolled and tied on flat.
HACKLE. Light Red game wound over front of wings sedge style.

Stone Fly

BODY. Hare's fur and yellow seal's fur mixed, ribbed yellow silk.
WINGS. Hen pheasant wing, or four dark blue dun cock hackles tied low over back.
HACKLE. Dark grizzle cock.

February Red

BODY. Claret quill.
WINGS. Speckled hen wing, or two dark brown grizzled hackles tied low over back.
HACKLE. Dark grizzled blue dun cock.

Winter Brown

BODY. Dark brown quill.
WINGS. Speckled hen wing, or two dark brown grizzled hackles tied low over back.
HACKLE. Dark dun cock.

Willow Fly

BODY. Peacock quill from eye dyed pale orange.
WINGS. Two small medium grizzled dun cock hackles tied low over back.
HACKLE. Brownish dun cock.

Needle Fly

BODY. Dark or medium olive tying silk, with dirty yellow fur dubbed at tail.
WINGS. Two small blue dun cock hackles tied low over back.
HACKLE. Medium grizzled blue dun cock.

Gravel Bed

BODY. Dark quill from stem of a peacock tail.

WINGS. Fibres of hen pheasant tail feather or two small dark grizzled cock hackles tied flat over back.
HACKLE. Black cock.

McLeod's Olive

TYING SILK. Lt. Olive or yellow.
TAIL. Fibres from an olive hackle.
BODY. Two turns of flat gold tinsel followed by medium olive wool or seal fur.
HACKLE. Medium olive hen hackle.
WINGS. From starling wing feather.

Grey Gnat (to be dressed as the Brown Gnat in coloured plate facing page 96).

BODY. Undyed peacock quill from "eye" part of feather.
THORAX. Heron herl.
WINGS. Two small pale blue dun cock hackle tips.
HACKLE. Blue dun cock.

Olive Gnat

BODY. Olive tying silk or quill from peacock "eye" dyed olive.
THORAX. Olive herl.
HACKLE. Olive cock.
WINGS. Two small dark grizzled cock hackles.

Claret Spinner

TAIL. Cream cock hackle fibres.
BODY. Claret floss silk.
WINGS. Starling wing.
HACKLE. Red cock.

Claret Quill

TAIL. Claret cock hackle fibres.
BODY. Peacock quill from "eye" dyed claret.
WINGS. Starling wing.
HACKLE. Claret cock.

Mole Fly

BODY. Dark olive tying silk ribbed with gold wire.

WINGS. Mottled hen pheasant wing, tied in forward position.

HACKLE. Red cock with black butt tied from shoulder to tail.

Red Quill

TAIL. Red cock hackle fibres.

BODY. Quill from peacock "eye" either undyed or dyed red.

WINGS. Starling wing.

HACKLE. Red cock.

Blue Quill

TAIL. Medium blue dun cock hackle fibres.

BODY. Peacock quill from "eye" undyed.

WINGS. Starling wing.

HACKLE. Medium blue dun cock.

If hackled patterns of the above are required, a pale blue dun shoulder hackle should be incorporated, and the wings omitted. Hackle fibre wings can be used in place of the starling wing feathers.

Black Beetle

WING CASES. Black cock tail feather or magpie tail feather.

BODY. Bronze peacock herl.

LEGS. Black cock hackle.

Brown Beetle

WING CASES. Brown hen wing.

BODY. Bronze peacock herl.

LEGS. Brown cock hackle.

Red Beetle

WING CASES. Blue feather from outside of mallard wing. (Blue-white tip.)

BODY. Red wool or seal's fur.

HACKLE. Grizzled cock.

Dark Princess

BODY. Yellow silk.

HACKLES. Red and furnace cock wound palmer fashion, but two or three turns of the yellow silk to be left showing as a tag.

Gilchrist Spinner

TAIL. Fibres of red cock hackle.

BODY. One-quarter orange peacock quill from "eye" and three-quarters of brown ditto.

WINGS. Four blue dun cock hackle points.

HACKLE. Natural red cock.

MAY FLIES (Not Illustrated)

Fan Wing

1. TAIL. Three strands of black fur.
   BODY. Raffia ribbed black tying silk.
   WINGS. Undyed grey mallard breast.
   HACKLE. Ginger cock.

2. TAIL. Three strands of cock pheasant tail.
   BODY. Raffia ribbed yellow tying silk.
   WINGS. Dyed yellow mallard breast.
   HACKLE. Dyed yellow.

3. TAIL. Three strands of cock pheasant tail.
   BODY. Raffia ribbed gold oval tinsel.
   WINGS. Dyed pale olive mallard breast.
   HACKLE. 1st. Feather from outside woodcock wing.
   2nd. Dyed pale olive cock.

4. TAIL. Three strands of brown mallard shoulder.
   BODY. Raffia ribbed crimson silk.
   WINGS. Mallard breast dyed as substitute for summer duck.
   HACKLE. Body hackle of pale ginger, shoulder hackle dyed olive cock.

Hackle Wing

5. TAIL. Three strands of cock pheasant tail.
   BODY. Raffia ribbed gold wire.

WINGS. Dark blue dun hackle fibres tied upright.

HACKLE. 1st. Orange.
           2nd. Dark blue dun cock.

6. TAIL. Three strands of cock pheasant tail.

BODY. Raffia ribbed gold oval tinsel.

WINGS. Fibres of grizzle cock hackle dyed green drake.

HACKLE. Body hackle ginger cock, shoulder hackle grizzled cock dyed yellow.

7. TAIL. Three strands of cock pheasant tail.

BODY. Raffia dyed yellow, ribbed gold wire.

WINGS. Grizzled cock hackle fibres dyed "green drake".

HACKLE. Grizzled cock dyed yellow down body, brown olive cock at shoulder.

8. TAIL. Three strands of cock pheasant tail.

BODY. White floss silk ribbed crimson tying silk.

WINGS. Fibres of dark dun cock hackle.

HACKLE. Natural red.

Hackled

9. TAIL. Three strands of cock pheasant tail.

BODY. Raffia ribbed oval gold tinsel.

HACKLES. Grizzled cock dyed yellow down body, greenish yellow cock at shoulder.

10. TAIL. Three strands of cock pheasant tail feather.

BODY. Raffia dyed yellow, ribbed with gold wire.

HACKLES. Ginger cock down body,

grizzle cock dyed yellow at shoulder.

11. TAIL. Three strands of cock pheasant tail.

BODY. Cream seal's fur, ribbed gold wire.

HACKLES (at shoulder only):
    1st. Grizzled cock dyed yellow.
    2nd. Hen pheasant breast feather.

12. TAIL. Three strands of cock pheasant tail.

BODY. Yellow seal's fur, ribbed gold oval tinsel.

HACKLES (at shoulder only):
    1st. Hen pheasant breast feather.
    2nd. Summer duck or substitute.

13. TAIL. Three strands of cock pheasant tail.

BODY. Natural raffia, ribbed with gold oval tinsel and a badger hackle.

HACKLES. Grey partridge dyed yellow with French partridge dyed green at head.

14. TAIL. Three strands of cock pheasant tail.

BODY. Natural raffia, ribbed with silver oval tinsel and a badger hackle.

HACKLES. Grey partridge with French partridge at head.

Spent

15. TAIL. Three fibres of cock pheasant tail.

BODY. Yellow raffia, ribbed brown silk.

WINGS. Medium blue dun hackle points (4), or hackle fibres of the same shade, tied spent.

HACKLE. As wings, but of a slightly paler shade.

16. TAIL. Three fibres of cock pheasant tail.

BODY. Raffia or floss silk, ribbed red tying silk.

WINGS. The points of four dun hackles, or hackle fibres of the same shade, tied spent.

HACKLE. Inner of natural red cock, outer of dark blue dun cock.

17. TAIL. Three long stiff black cock hackle fibres.

BODY. Raffia ribbed silver oval tinsel.

WINGS. Four dark blue dun cock hackle points, or hackle fibres of the same shade, tied spent.

HACKLE. Dark dun cock down body and at shoulder.

18. TAIL. Three long stiff black cock hackle fibres.

BODY. Raffia ribbed silver wire.

WINGS. The points of four medium blue dun cock hackles, or hackle fibres of the same shade, tied spent.

HACKLE. Badger cock down body, dark blue dun cock at shoulder.

The bodies of May flies that have been tied with raffia grass may be improved with the addition of a coat of celluloid varnish.

VARIENTS (or VARIANTS)

Dark Varient

BODY. Dark quill from the base of a peacock "eye" tail.

WINGS. Starling wing.

HACKLE. Large grizzle cock hackle dyed blue dun.

Light Varient

BODY. Quill from peacock "eye" undyed.

WINGS. Light starling wing.

HACKLE. Light blue dun cock, large.

Brown Varient

BODY. Cock pheasant tail fibres ribbed with gold wire.

WINGS. Woodcock wing.

HACKLE. Large red cock.

Black Varient

BODY. Very dark peacock quill from base of "eye" tail.

WINGS. Starling wing.

HACKLE. Black cock, large.

Gold Varient

BODY. Flat gold tinsel.

WINGS. Starling wing.

HACKLE. Large medium blue dun cock.

Silver Varient

As above but with flat silver tinsel body.

The wings of these flies should be small and thin, and tied to slope forward over the eye of the hook. (*See* illustrations facing page 100 and instructions page 50.)

Midges

BODIES. Thin black heron herl, a strand of brown speckled turkey tail, black tying silk tipped with silver tinsel, or undyed quill from peacock "eye" feather with two turns of black herl at shoulder.

HACKLES. Black cock, starling neck badger cock, or dark grizzle cock.

CANADIAN AND AMERICAN DRY FLIES

The first American dry flies were tied by the late Theodore Gordon around 1890, the only dry flies available before this being patterns tied in Britain.

His first ones were tied from samples and instructions sent to him by the late F. M. Halford; consequently, many of the patterns used today have British origins. Nevertheless, Gordon did not believe in using foreign patterns, and he copied many natural American insects.

His name is perpetuated in the fly that bears his name—the "Gordon"—the dressing of which is given below. He referred to this himself as the "Golden Spinner" and the dressing which is given immediately below the "Gordon" he called the "Blue Quill Gordon".

The result of his efforts and the efforts of those who followed him, has been the building up of a range of dry fly patterns for use in every part of the United States.

It was not only in the sphere of dry flies that Gordon was famous, as the streamer fly, which is now so universally popular, is reckoned to have originated from his "Bumblepuppy" which he used successfully for salmon, bass and pike. There are several variations of this dressing, one of which is given in the streamer fly dressings on page 149, and illustrated in the coloured plate, facing page 150.

The following dry fly patterns are shown in the colour plate, facing page 96—"Hendrickson", "Adams", and "Light Cahill". Others illustrated, facing pages 58 and 68, are the "Queen of the Waters", "Grizzly King", "Cahill", "Rube Wood", "Seth Green", "Governor", and "Gordon Quill".

Gordon
TAIL. Fibres of speckled mandarin.
BODY. Gold floss silk, ribbed gold tinsel.
WINGS. Speckled mandarin flank bunched.
HACKLE. Badger cock.

Quill Gordon
TAIL. Fibres of brassy blue dun cock hackle.
BODY. Undyed peacock quill from "eye" tail.
WINGS. Speckled mandarin flank bunched.
HACKLE. Brassy blue dun cock.

Fox (Ray Bergman)
TAIL. Fibres of honey hackle.
BODY. Grey fur.
WINGS. Grey mallard flank, bunched.
HACKLE. Mixed honey and ginger cock.

Blue Fox (Ray Bergman)
TAIL. Fibres of grizzle hackle.
BODY. Blue-grey fur.
WINGS. Tips of two grizzle hackles.
HACKLE. Mixed grizzle and blue dun cock.
BODY. Blue-grey fur.
WINGS. Tips of two grizzle hackles.
HACKLE. Mixed grizzle and blue dun cock.

March Brown
TAIL. Brown hackle fibres.
BODY. Brown cellophane, ribbed with gold wire.
WINGS. Brown mallard shoulder, bunched.
HACKLE. Brown cock.

Pink Lady (Translucent)

TAIL. Brown hackle fibres.
BODY. Cellophane over pink silk.
WINGS. Dark blue dun hackle tips.
HACKLE. Brown cock.

Royal Coachman (Fan Wing)

TAIL. Fibres of golden pheasant tippet.
BODY. Bronze peacock herl with a centre of scarlet silk.
WINGS. White mandarin breast feathers.
HACKLE. Brown cock.

Badger Bi-visible

TAIL. Badger hackle tips.
HACKLE. Badger cock tied "Palmer" very close, with a white hackle at the front.

Black Bi-visible

TAIL. Black hackle tips.
HACKLE. Black cock tied "Palmer"very close, with a white hackle at the front.

Brown Bi-visible

TAIL. Brown hackle tips.
HACKLE. Brown cock tied "Palmer" very close, with a white hackle at the front.

Blue Bi-visible

TAIL. Blue dun hackle tips.
HACKLE. Blue dun cock tied "Palmer" very close, with a white hackle at the front.

Orange Fish Hawk

BODY. Orange floss ribbed with gold tinsel, and a gold tinsel tip.
HACKLE. Badger cock.

Bradley

TAIL. Fibres of brown hackle.
BODY. Mole fur.
WINGS. Grey mallard flank, bunched.
HACKLE. Brown cock.

Black Spider

TAIL. Black hackle fibres.
BODY. Flat gold tinsel.
HACKLE. Black cock.

Blue Spider

TAIL. Blue dun hackle fibres.
BODY. Flat gold tinsel.
HACKLE. Medium blue dun cock.

Campbell's Fancy

TAIL. Golden pheasant crest feather.
BODY. Flat gold tinsel.
WINGS. Grey mallard flank tied as a bunch-wing.
HACKLE. Furnace cock.

Coty

TAIL. Fibres of blue dun cock's hackle.
BODY. Blue dun fur mixed with a little red fur.
WINGS. Tips of two blue dun cock's hackles.
HACKLE. Blue dun cock.

Ginger Quill

TAIL. Fibres of ginger cock's hackle.
BODY. Stripped peacock quill, dyed ginger.
WINGS. Speckled mandarin flank tied as a bunch-wing.
HACKLE. Ginger cock.

Mosquito

TAIL. Fibres of dark grizzle cock's hackle.
BODY. Dark quill from peacock tail—stripped.
WINGS. Tips of two dark grizzle cock hackles.
HACKLE. Dark grizzle cock.

Cahill Quill

TAIL. Fibres of brown cock hackle.
BODY. Undyed quill from peacock "eye" tail.
WINGS. Speckled mandarin flank bunched.
HACKLE. Brown cock.

AUSTRALIAN AND NEW ZEALAND DRY FLIES

Most of the dry flies used in Australasia are of British origin, mainly because nearly all the flies obtainable are tied in Britain. They are gradually being superseded as fly-tying develops, and a range of patterns of natural insects is being built up.

Many of the British patterns are still ideal for certain waters, some of these being the "Coch-y-bondhu", "Alder", "Hare's Ear", "Black Gnat", and "Red Spinner".

The patterns given below are of purely Australian or New Zealand origin.

Brown Ant
BODY. Brown silk tied to shape of ant, abdomen, waist, chest.
WINGS. Two white hackle points, tied flat.
HACKLE. Brown cock.

Black Ant
BODY. Black silk tied to shape of ant, abdomen, waist, chest.
WINGS. Two white hackle points tied flat.
HACKLE. Black cock.

Termite
BODY. Yellow silk.
WINGS. Two white hackle points, tied flat.
HACKLE. Very small grey cock.

Grasshopper
BODY. Lemon silk.
WINGS. Oak turkey wing feather, tied flat. On each side of the wing cases tie in six golden pheasant tippet fibres to extend along the side of the body and protrude a quarter-of-an-inch beyond the hook.
HACKLE. Grey cock.

Bogong Moth
BODY. Grey chenille.
WINGS. Oak turkey wing feather, tied in flat.
HACKLE. Grizzle cock.

Black Beetle
BODY. Black chenille.
LEGS. Four fibres crow wing cut short.
HACKLE. Black cock.

Chafer Beetle
TAIL. Three short golden pheasant tippet fibres.
BODY. Tail end four turns black ostrich herl, remainder golden brown ostrich herl.
HACKLE. Red-black cock.

Damsel Fly
TAIL. Half-inch dyed red cock hackle.
BODY. Bottle green silk, ribbed silver tinsel.
HACKLE. Grizzle cock.

Summer's Day
TAIL. Three red hackle fibres.
BODY. Red and orange dyed seal's fur.
HACKLE. One cock hackle dyed red, one dyed orange.

Hare's Ear
TAIL. Red cock hackle fibres.
BODY. Brown squirrel, ribbed gold wire.
WINGS. Starling wing.
HACKLE. Fibres picked out from body.

A "FORE AND AFT" HACKLED MAYFLY

"PARTRIDGE AND ORANGE" HACKLED WET FLY

March Brown
HOOK. Painted white.
TAIL. Three blue dun cock hackle fibres.
BODY. Pale honey colour floss silk.
WINGS. Dark grizzle cock hackle points.
HACKLE. Blue dun cock.

Black Spinner
TAIL. Three black cock hackle fibres.
BODY. Centre quill of black cock feather.
HACKLE. Two black cock hackles.

Golden Spinner
HOOK. Painted white.
TAIL. Three blue dun cock hackle fibres.
BODY. Deep honey colour floss silk.
HACKLE. Blue dun cock.

Orange Spinner
HOOK. Painted white.
TAIL. Three black-red cock hackle fibres.
BODY. Pale orange floss silk.
HACKLE. Black-red cock.

Brown Sedge
BODY. Pale cinnamon floss silk.
HACKLE. Ginger cock, tied palmer.
WINGS. Speckled brown partridge tail feather.
THROAT HACKLE. Ginger cock.

Grey Sedge
BODY. White floss silk.
HACKLE. Grey cock, tied palmer.
WINGS. Grey duck wing.
THROAT HACKLE. Grey cock.

Stone Fly
BODY. White floss silk.
WINGS. Grey duck wing.
HACKLE. Grey cock.

CHAPTER TEN

TROUT FLY DRESSING—WET FLIES
TYING A HACKLED WET FLY

THESE ARE ABOUT the easiest flies to tie, and it is a good idea for the beginner to start on these so that he may get used to handling tools and materials.

The "Partridge and Orange"

Materials required—

> **Hook**—0-1.
> **Body**—Orange floss silk.
> **Hackle**—Brown partridge back feather.

This is one of the "Partridge" series of North Country and Yorkshire wet flies. On some patterns a grey partridge breast feather is used, as in the "Partridge and Yellow".

Tie in tying silk a short distance from the eye, and wind to the bend of the hook. Tie in a short length of the floss silk and wind tying silk back to starting point. Wind the floss silk to starting point, making several turns thicker as the shoulder of the fly is reached so as to make a shaped body (Fig. 85).

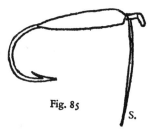

Fig. 85
S.

Now tie in partridge hackle by the butt, after stripping off the soft fluffy fibres from the base. The outer side of the feather should be towards the eye of the hook. Wind two or three turns of the hackle, making the turns from the eye towards the bend of the hook. Very close together, of course. Tie in and cut off tip of hackle. Wind silk through hackle as described on page 71, and finish off with whip finish. The finished fly should be as Fig. 86.

For a fly such as the "Blue Dun" a tail of hackle fibres, a rib of tying silk and a dubbing body are required, but the procedure is the same. A blue dun hen's hackle or similar soft cock's hackle would be used, of course.

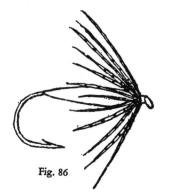

Fig. 86

The hackles of wet flies should be well stroked back after the winding, as this makes for easy entry into the water. Stiffer hackles should be used if the fly is to be used in fast water, as some anglers like plenty of "kick" to their flies under these conditions.

TYING A WINGED WET FLY

This method of tying covers a large range of patterns, and can be used for imitations of naturals such as the "March Brown", "Blue Dun", etc., or for fancies such as the "Butcher", "Woodcock and Green", "Grouse and Claret", etc.

The "March Brown"

Materials required—

Hook—Hook 2–4.
Tail—Fibres from speckled partridge tail or brown partridge back.
Rib—Gold wire.
Body—Darkish hare's fur, from the ear.
Hackle—Brown partridge back feather.
Wings—Mottled hen pheasant secondary wing feathers.

Tie in silk about $\frac{1}{8}$-in. from the eye of the hook, and wind to bend of hook. Tie in tail fibres. Tie in wire for rib. Now dub hare's fur on to silk as shown on page 62, and wind to shoulder. Wind rib and cut off surplus. Tie in hackle by the butt after stripping off the soft fibres from the base. Make two turns of the hackle, tie in the tip and cut off the surplus. Now, with thumb and forefinger, reach up from underneath hook and draw all the fibres downwards. It helps if the fingers are moistened. Take two or three turns of silk over the top of the hackle only (diagonally towards the rear of the hook and this will hold them in place and point them to the rear of the hook as Fig. 87).

The wings are prepared as described on page 60, but, instead of the tips pointing outwards as for a dry fly, they must point inwards so that they will appear as a single wing when tied in.

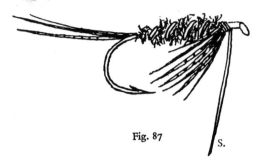

Fig. 87

S.

The procedure for tying on the wing is also the same as for the dry fly, *see* page 74, except that the wing does not have to be lifted into the upright position once it has been tied on to the hook shank. Cut off the surplus roots of the wings, and make one or two turns of silk to form a tapered head. Finish off with a whip finish and varnish head. The sweep of the wings is controlled by whichever edge of the wings is placed on to the hook shank as Figs. 88 and 89.

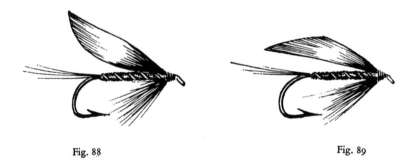

Fig. 88   Fig. 89

There is very little difference in tying this sort of fly and a fly like the butcher, the only difference being that a tinsel body has to be used, and this is tied in at the tail end of the fly and wound in even turns to the shoulder. The tinsel should be cut into a point to make its tying in smoother, and it is important that the tying silk, when it is wound back to the shoulder of the fly, forms a smooth even bed on which the tinsel will lie in neat, even turns.

For practice on this type of fly a "Silver March Brown" can be tied, the materials being exactly the same as for the "March Brown", except that the fur body and wire rib are replaced by a flat silver tinsel body. A silver wire rib is optional.

TYING THE "MALLARD" AND "TEAL" SERIES OF WET FLIES

The mallard and teal ducks supply many of the fly-tyers' wing materials, but for the above flies it is the soft speckled shoulder feathers of the mallard and the black and white barred flank feathers of the teal that are required. This should be borne in mind when ordering materials, as I have known many tyers to order "Mallard Wings" or "Teal Wings" when in actual fact it was the body feathers they wanted.

Fig. 90 shows an illustration of a teal flank feather and as it appears when used as the wing of the "Peter Ross".

The mallard brown shoulder feathers are used for such well-known flies as the "Mallard and Claret", "Connemara Black", "Fiery Brown", "Golden Olive", etc.

The "Peter Ross"

Materials required—

Hook—Size according to the type of water, and usually larger for sea trout than loch fishing.

Tail—Fibres of golden pheasant tippet feather.

Body—Tail half flat silver tinsel. remainder red seal's fur, ribbed with oval silver tinsel.

Hackle—Black.

Wings—Barred teal flank feathers.

The body and tail and hackle are formed as described for the "March Brown" in the foregoing chapter. The forming of the wing is rather more difficult when

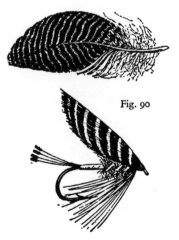

Fig. 90

using the soft breast and flank feathers, but the actual procedure is exactly the same. The soft fibres are stripped from the base of the pair of feathers being used, and the sections pulled down in the same manner, as described on page 60. The tips of the sections to point inwards, of course. If only single sections are used, the wing sometimes has a flimsy appearance, and if a stouter wing is required, double sections should be used.

TYING A WET MAY FLY

Materials required—

    Hook—Long shank, 3–5.
    Tail—Three strands from a cock pheasant's tail.
    Rib—Gold wire.
    Body—Yellow lamb's wool.
    Hackle—Speckled grey mallard flank dyed greenish-yellow.

The procedure for tying these flies is very similar to that for tying an ordinary hackled wet fly.

The body and tail are formed in the usual way but, when tying in the mallard feather, it is better to tie it in by the tip instead of the butt, owing to the rather thick stem on these feathers. Two turns of the feather should suffice, and the fibres should be stroked towards the rear when the surplus is cut off, and a few turns of silk over the roots will keep them in this position. The finished fly should appear as Fig. 91.

Fig. 91

TYING NYMPHS AND BEETLES

If a nymph is required without wing cases, all that is necessary is a hackled wet fly with a dubbing body much thicker at the shoulder so that a distinct hump is formed. Only one or two turns of the hackle for the legs should be used (Fig. 92).

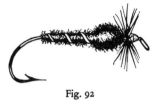

Fig. 92

To tie a nymph with wing cases—

The "March Brown Nymph"

Materials required—

Hook—2–4.

Winged Cases—Woodcock wing feather.

Tail—Three strands of brown mallard shoulder or brown partridge back feather.

Rib—Gold wire.

Body—Darkish hare's fur from root of ears.

Thorax—As for body.

Hackle—One turn of a small brown speckled grouse hackle.

Tie in a very small hackle for the legs, and then wind tying silk to about one-third of the distance between the eye and the bend of the hook. Now tear off a strip of fibres from the Woodcock wing feather and tie in as Fig. 93. The fibres should be stroked towards the eye of the hook so as to be out of the way while the

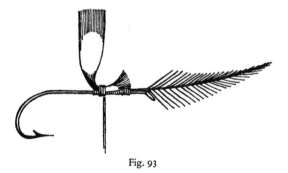

Fig. 93

rest of the body is formed. Continue winding silk to the bend of the hook and tie in the tail and wire rib. Dub the fur on to the silk and wind it up to the wing cases. Now wind rib as far as the wing cases, tie it in and cut off the surplus. Dub more fur on to the silk and wind it in front of the wing cases to form thorax. Now bring the wing cases down over the thorax, tie in and cut off the surplus. Wind one turn of the hackle, cut off the tip, and finish off with a whip finish. The finished nymph should now be as Fig. 94.

A very good method of making effective looking Mayfly nymphs, is to tie in the wing cases right at the bend of the hook, after the tail fibres have been fixed. The fur body is then wound on, and thickened at the front as described on page 119. The wing cases are then brought down and tied in at the front of the hook. The wire rib is now wound evenly, but fairly widely from the tail end, a large gap being left where the wing cases proper should hump up. The result is a very realistic looking segmented body.

For a beetle, the wing cases should be tied in at the bend of the hook so that they reach from the bend to the eye as Fig. 95.

Fig. 94   Fig. 95

If nymphs or any other kind of wet flies are required to sink rapidly, a base of electrical fuse wire can be wound on first. This material is easier to use than lead wire that is usually advocated.

CHAPTER ELEVEN

TROUT FLY PATTERNS—WET FLIES

(Illustrated, facing page 122)

Winged Pheasant Tail
BODY. Fibres of cock pheasant tail, ribbed gold wire.
HACKLE. Red cock.
WINGS. Woodcock wing.

McGinty
TAIL. Three strands as hackle.
BODY. Alternate quarters of browny orange and black chenille, or yellow and black chenille.
HACKLE. Ginger cock.
WINGS. From the white tipped feathers from a wild duck wing.

Yellow Dun
TAIL. A few fibres as hackle.
BODY. Yellow mohair, yellow floss or yellow tying silk.
HACKLE. Light yellow dun cock or the breast feather of a dotterel.
WINGS. Lightest starling wing.

Rube Wood
TAG. Red floss silk.
TAIL. A few whisks as hackle, or a few strands of a woodcock feather.
BODY. White chenille.
HACKLE. Natural ginger cock.
WINGS. From the grey flank feather of a mallard.

Cinnamon
TAIL. Three whisks as hackle.
BODY. Rich cinnamon-brown floss or tying silk.
HACKLE. Natural light brown cock.
WINGS. Brown owl or brown hen wing.

Cockwing Dun
TAIL. A few fibres as hackle.
BODY. Blue fur on yellow tying silk.
HACKLE. Olive dun cock.
WINGS. Starling wing.

Salmon Pink
TAIL. A few strands as hackle.
BODY. Pink wool or seal's fur, ribbed fine gold wire.
HACKLE. The grey breast hackle of a partridge.
WINGS. Hen pheasant wing.

Hoskins
TAIL. Three long fibres of the golden pheasant crest feather.
BODY. Lemon yellow floss silk with flat gold tinsel tip.
HACKLE. Dyed or natural blue dun cock.
WINGS. American wood-duck flank.

Laramie
TAIL. A short piece of the floss silk used on the body.
BODY. Scarlet floss silk, ribbed flat silver tinsel.
HACKLE. Dyed or natural blue dun cock.
WINGS. Grey mallard flank feathers.

Wickham's Fancy
TAIL. Red cock hackle fibres.
BODY. Flat gold tinsel, ribbed gold wire.
HACKLE. Red cock, from shoulder to tail.
WINGS. Starling wing.

March Brown Silver
TAIL. Two strands as hackle.
BODY. Flat silver tinsel, ribbed oval silver tinsel.
HACKLE. Darkish brown partridge back feather.
WINGS. Hen pheasant wing.

Woodcock Greenwell
BODY. Waxed yellow tying silk, ribbed gold wire.
HACKLE. Light furnace hen.
WINGS. Woodcock wing.

Royal Governor
BODY. Divided into thirds, the two outer thirds of bronze peacock herl, and the inner of scarlet floss silk.
HACKLE. Ginger cock.
WINGS. Hen pheasant wing.

Broughton's Point
BODY. Claret tying silk.
HACKLE. Mixed black and dyed scarlet cock.
WINGS. Starling wing.

Grizzly King
TAIL. Red ibis.
BODY, Green floss silk, ribbed flat gold tinsel.
HACKLE. Grizzle cock.
WINGS. Grey mallard flank feather.

Brown Owl
BODY. Mixed cream and gold coloured mohair.
HACKLE. Light furnace cock.
WINGS. Brown owl wing.

Queen of the Waters
TAG. Flat gold tinsel.
BODY. Orange floss silk, ribbed fine gold oval.
HACKLE. Natural browny-red or ginger cock, ribbed up body.
WINGS. From the faintly marked flank feather of a mallard.

Cairn's Fancy
BODY. Blue floss silk, ribbed fine flat silver tinsel.
HACKLE. Black hen.
WINGS. Starling wing.

Olive Cow Dung
BODY. Dark olive seal's fur.
HACKLE. Dark ginger cock.
WINGS. Landrail wing.

Gordon
TAG. Flat gold tinsel.
TAIL. Brown mallard or mandarin duck.
BODY. Yellow floss silk, ribbed gold tinsel.
HACKLE. Brassy blue dun cock.
WINGS. Brown mallard shoulder or mandarin duck flank.

Malloch's Favourite
TAIL. Red cock hackle fibres.
BODY. Peacock quill from eye, tipped with silver.
HACKLE. Blue dun hen.
WINGS. Woodcock wing.

Purple Dun
TAIL. Three or four whisks as hackle.
BODY. Purple wool or mohair.
HACKLE. Dark brown hen.
WINGS. Starling wing.

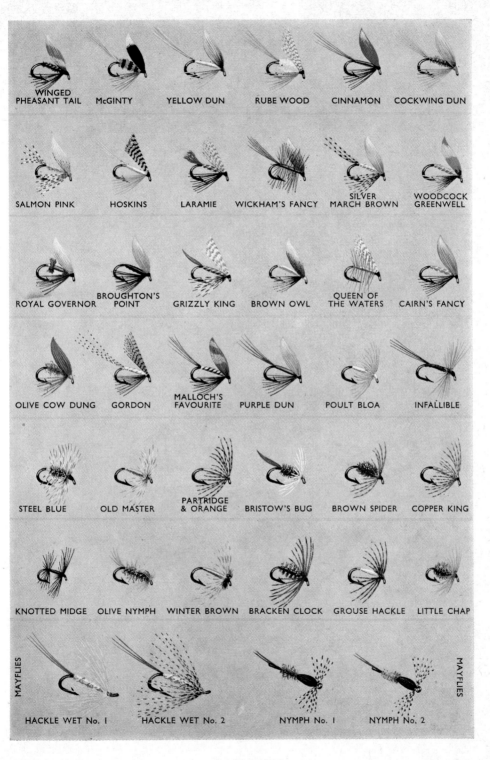

WINGED PHEASANT TAIL | McGINTY | YELLOW DUN | RUBE WOOD | CINNAMON | COCKWING DUN

SALMON PINK | HOSKINS | LARAMIE | WICKHAM'S FANCY | SILVER MARCH BROWN | WOODCOCK GREENWELL

ROYAL GOVERNOR | BROUGHTON'S POINT | GRIZZLY KING | BROWN OWL | QUEEN OF THE WATERS | CAIRN'S FANCY

OLIVE COW DUNG | GORDON | MALLOCH'S FAVOURITE | PURPLE DUN | POULT BLOA | INFALLIBLE

STEEL BLUE | OLD MASTER | PARTRIDGE & ORANGE | BRISTOW'S BUG | BROWN SPIDER | COPPER KING

KNOTTED MIDGE | OLIVE NYMPH | WINTER BROWN | BRACKEN CLOCK | GROUSE HACKLE | LITTLE CHAP

MAYFLIES

HACKLE WET No. 1 | HACKLE WET No. 2 | NYMPH No. 1 | NYMPH No. 2

MAYFLIES

WET FLIES

Poult Bloa
BODY. Pale yellow tying silk.
HACKLE. Underside wing feather of a grouse.

Infallible
BODY. Mole fur dubbed on crimson or claret tying silk, which may be shown at tail end of body.
HACKLE AND WHISKS. Dark blue dun cock.

Steel Blue
BODY. Thin peacock herl, ribbed gold wire with three turns of orange silk at tail end.
HACKLE. Well grizzled bright blue cock, from shoulder to tail.

Old Master
BODY. Ash-coloured floss silk.
HACKLE. From the inside wing feather of a woodcock.

Patridge and Orange
BODY. Bright orange floss or tying silk.
HACKLE. Brown partridge back feather.

Bristow's Bug
TAIL. Red wool or ibis feather.
BODY. Green peacock herl, ribbed fine silver wire.
HACKLE. From inside (or list) of a creamy white hen's hackle.

Brown Spider
BODY. Bronze peacock herl.
HACKLE. Brown partridge back feather.

Copper King
BODY. Copper coloured tinsel.
HACKLE. Brown partridge back feather.

Knotted Midge
BODY. Black tying silk.
HACKLE. Black cock, one at tail end of hook, one at shoulder end.

Olive Nymph
BODY AND THORAX. Olive seal's fur, ribbed fine gold wire.

HACKLE. Olive hen.
WING CASES. Strip from starling wing.

Winter Brown
BODY. Dull orange floss or tying silk.
HACKLE. From the inside feather of a woodcock wing.
HEAD. Peacock herl.

Bracken Clock
BODY. Bronze peacock herl and red silk.
HACKLE. From cock pheasant neck, brown with black edge.

Grouse Hackle
BODY. Yellow floss or tying silk with one turn of flat gold tinsel at tail.
HACKLE. Grouse neck.

Little Chap
BODY. Brown peacock herl.
HACKLE. Medium dun cock.

MAY FLIES

Hackled Wet

1. TAIL. Three strands from cock pheasant tail feather.

   BODY. Yellow lamb's wool ribbed gold wire.

   HACKLE. Slightly speckled buff feather from the hen pheasant breast, tied half-way down the body.

2. TAIL. Three strands of cock pheasant tail feather.

   BODY. Yellow lamb's wool, ribbed gold wire.

   HACKLE. Speckled grey mallard flank feather, dyed greenish yellow.

Nymphs

1. WING CASES. The dark part of hen pheasant tail feather.

   TAIL. Three short strands of cock pheasant tail feather.

   BODY AND THORAX. Brownish olive seal's fur, ribbed gold wire.

   LEGS. Grey partridge breast feather.

2. WING CASES. Dark part of hen pheasant tail feather.

   TAIL. Three short strands of cock pheasant tail feather.

   BODY. Three turns at tail end of dirty yellow seal's fur, remainder of body and thorax brownish olive.

   LEGS. Dark brown partridge back feather.

(Illustrated, facing page 124)

Woodcock and Green

TAIL. A few strands of golden pheasant tippet.

BODY. Green wool or seal's fur, ribbed fine silver wire.

HACKLE. Dyed green cock.

WINGS. Woodcock wing.

Cardinal

TAIL. Red ibis.

BODY. Red floss silk, ribbed fine gold wire.

HACKLE. White cock dyed same colour as wings.

WINGS. Dyed red swan, ibis or duck.

Connemara Black

TAIL. Small golden pheasant crest feather.

BODY. Black wool or seal's fur, ribbed fine oval silver tinsel.

HACKLE. Inner of natural black cock, outer from the blue feather of the wings of a blue jay.

WINGS. From the bronze shoulder feather of a mallard.

Peter Ross

TAIL. Golden pheasant tippet fibres.

BODY. Tail half flat silver tinsel, shoulder half red seal's fur, ribbed silver oval tinsel.

HACKLE. Black cock.

WINGS. Teal flank feathers.

Professor

TAIL. A few long fibres of red ibis feather.

BODY. Yellow tying or floss silk, ribbed either gold tinsel or black tying silk.

HACKLE. Natural ginger cock.

WINGS. From the flank feather of a grey mallard.

Mallard and Blue

TAIL. Two or three fibres of a golden pheasant tippet.

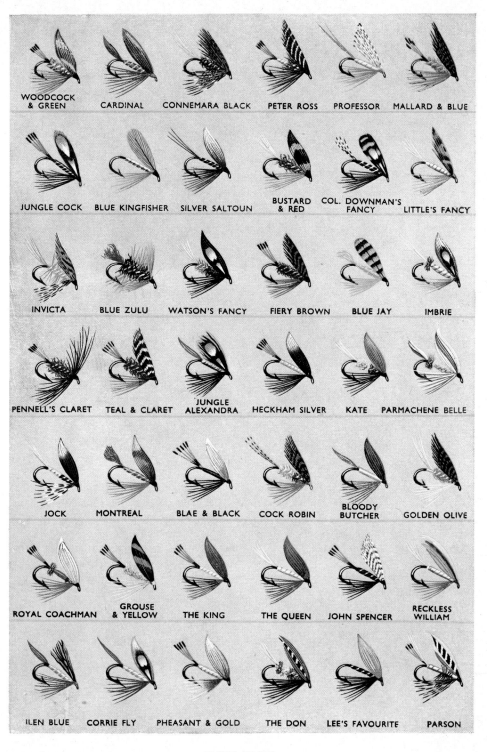

WET FLIES

BODY. Light blue seal's fur, ribbed fine silver wire.

HACKLE. Blue cock.

WINGS. The bronze shoulder feather of a mallard.

Jungle Cock

TAIL. Three or four fibres of a golden pheasant tippet feather.

BODY. Black floss silk, ribbed gold wire.

HACKLE. Black cock.

WINGS. Two jungle cock neck feathers.

Blue Kingfisher

BODY. Flat silver tinsel, ribbed fine silver oval.

HACKLE. Dyed light blue cock.

WINGS. Two black feathers of the kingfisher, left untrimmed.

Silver Saltoun

TAIL. Three whisks as hackle.

BODY. Black tying silk, ribbed fine silver wire.

HACKLE. Black cock.

WINGS. Lightest starling wing.

Bustard and Red

TAIL. A small golden pheasant crest feather.

BODY. Bright red seal's fur, ribbed fine gold wire.

Watson's Fancy

TAIL. Small golden pheasant crest feather.

BODY. Half red and half black floss or dubbing, ribbed silver tinsel.

HACKLE. Black cock.

WINGS. From crow wing, with small jungle cock feather each side.

HACKLE. Natural blood-red hen, sparsely dressed.

WINGS. From the Florican bustard barred wing feather.

Col. Downman's Fancy

TAIL. Teal fibres.

BODY. Black floss silk, ribbed silver tinsel.

HACKLE. Black cock.

WINGS. Jay wing with small jungle cock each side.

Little's Fancy

TAIL. Golden pheasant crest feather.

BODY. Flat silver tinsel.

HACKLE. Ginger cock.

WINGS. Hen pheasant centre tail.

Invicta

TAIL. Golden pheasant crest feather.

BODY. Yellow seal's fur or wood, ribbed oval gold tinsel.

HACKLE. Ginger cock.

HEAD HACKLE. Blue jay.

WINGS. Hen pheasant centre tail.

Blue Zulu

TAIL. Red wool.

BODY. Black dubbing ribbed fine silver tinsel.

HACKLE. Dyed blue cock.

Fiery Brown

TAG. Orange floss.

TAIL. Tippet fibres.

BODY. Fiery brown seal's fur, ribbed gold oval.

HACKLE. Fiery brown cock.

WINGS. Brown mallard shoulder.

Blue Jay

TAIL. Leave a short length of the floss used for the body and tease it out with a dubbing needle.
BODY. Light blue floss, ribbed fine gold wire.
HACKLE. Light blue cock, same colour as body.
WINGS. The blue feathers from a jay wing.

Imbrie

TAIL. Three long fibres from the crest feather of a golden pheasant.
BODY. White floss silk, ribbed flat gold tinsel, with two tags at the tail end—the first of green peacock herl and the second of flat gold tinsel.
HACKLE. Natural light red or ginger cock.
WINGS. Dark starling wing feather with an inset of jungle cock feather on each side.

Pennell's Claret

TAIL. Golden pheasant tippet fibres and crest fibres.
BODY. Claret seal's fur, ribbed fine gold wire or oval tinsel.
HACKLE. A long fibred furnace cock.

Teal and Claret

TAIL. Tippet fibres.
BODY. Claret dubbing, ribbed gold tinsel.
HACKLE. Claret cock.
WINGS. Teal flank.

Jungle Cock Alexandra

TAIL. Scarlet ibis.
BODY. Silver tinsel, ribbed silver wire.
HACKLE. Black cock.
WINGS. Green peacock herl with jungle cock each side.

Heckham Silver

TAIL. Three or four fibres of the golden pheasant tippet feather.
BODY. Flat silver tinsel, ribbed fine silver oval.
HACKLE. Black cock.
WINGS. The white tipped feather from a wild duck wing.

Kate

TAIL. Whole feather of a golden pheasant crest.
BODY. Halved, the tail end being canary yellow and the remainder scarlet seal's fur. The whole body is ribbed with oval gold tinsel.
HACKLE. Natural black cock.
WINGS. From the fawny brown feathers on the jay's wing.

Parmachene Belle

TAIL. Red and white duck.
BUTT. Black ostrich herl.
BODY. Yellow floss silk or wool, ribbed flat gold tinsel.
HACKLE. Dyed scarlet cock mixed with white cock.
WINGS. White duck or swan with a stripe of red ibis feather on each side. The ibis should be about half the width of the duck or swan.

Jock

TAIL. Smallest whole feather of a golden pheasant crest.
BODY. Halved, the tail end being of yellow and the remainder black floss silk. The whole body is ribbed with fine gold oval tinsel.
HACKLE. The small spotted guinea fowl neck hackle (Gallena).
WINGS. The white tipped feather from a wild duck wing.

(Illustrated, facing page 124)

Montreal

TAIL. A piece of the floss silk used for the body.
BODY. Red floss silk, ribbed gold wire.
HACKLE. Light red cock.
WINGS. Woodcock wing.

Blae and Black

TAIL. A few fibres of golden pheasant tippet.
BODY. Black floss, wool or seal's fur.
HACKLE. Black hen.
WINGS. Wild duck wing.

Cock Robin

TAIL. Three strands of brown mallard.
BODY. 1st half golden olive, 2nd half scarlet seal's fur, ribbed oval gold tinsel.
HACKLE. Natural dark red cock.
WINGS. Brown mallard shoulder.

Bloody Butcher

TAIL. Scarlet ibis.
BODY. Silver tinsel ribbed silver wire.
HACKLE. Blood red cock.
WINGS. Purple feather from outside mallard wing.

Golden Olive

TAG. Orange floss.
TAIL. Golden pheasant crest feather.
BODY. Golden olive seal's fur, ribbed gold oval.
HACKLE. Golden olive cock.
WINGS. Brown mallard shoulder.

Royal Coachman

TAIL. A few strands of golden pheasant tippet.
BODY. Divided roughly into thirds, the two outer thirds of bronze peacock herl, and the inner of scarlet floss silk.

HACKLE. Natural light red cock.
WINGS. Any white wing feather.

Grouse and Yellow

TAIL. Fibres of a golden pheasant tippet.
BODY. Canary yellow seal's fur, ribbed gold wire.
HACKLE. Dyed canary yellow cock.
WINGS. Wing or tail feather of a grouse.

The King

TAIL. Golden pheasant tippet.
BODY. Gold tinsel.
HACKLE. Royal blue cock.
WINGS. Swan or duck wing dyed crimson.

The Queen

TAIL. Golden pheasant crest.
BODY. Silver tinsel.
HACKLE. Crimson cock.
WINGS. Swan or duck wing dyed royal blue.

John Spencer

TAIL. Golden pheasant tippet.
BODY. Black floss, ribbed silver oval tinsel.
HACKLE. Black cock.
WINGS. Grey mallard flank feather.

Reckless William

TAIL. Golden pheasant crest feather.
BODY. Half flat silver tinsel, half pink floss silk.
HACKLE. Orange cock.
WINGS. Emerald green swan wing, hen pheasant centre tail dyed emerald green outside, topping over all.

Ilen Blue

TAIL. Scarlet ibis.

BODY. Flat gold tinsel, ribbed gold oval tinsel.

HACKLE. Scarlet cock.

WINGS. Fibres of blue peacock neck feather.

Corrie Fly

TAIL. Scarlet ibis.

BODY. Silver tinsel, ribbed silver wire.

HACKLE. Bright claret cock.

WINGS. Grey mallard wing quill, with jungle cock each side.

Pheasant and Gold

TAIL. Whisks of golden pheasant tippet.

BODY. Flat gold tinsel, ribbed fine gold oval.

HACKLE. Soft feather from front of hen pheasant wing.

WINGS. Hen pheasant wing.

The Don

TAG. Round silver tinsel and yellow floss.

TAIL. Topping.

BUTT. Green peacock herl.

BODY. One-third at tail yellow, two-thirds claret seal's fur, ribbed gold oval tinsel.

HACKLE. Black cock.

WINGS. Lightly dressed, dun turkey tail, with a strip of teal flank each side.

Lee's Favourite

BODY. Black floss, ribbed flat silver.

HACKLE. Black cock.

WINGS. Jay wing primary feather.

Parson

TAIL. Mixed golden pheasant crest and tippet feather.

BODY. Flat silver tinsel, ribbed fine silver oval.

HACKLE. Black cock with a throat hackle of blue jay wing feather.

WINGS. Heavily marked teal flank, over a foundation of dyed yellow and scarlet swan feather. A golden pheasant crest over the back of the wing.

(Illustrated, facing page 58)

Alexandra

TAIL. Red ibis feather and peacock herl.

BODY. Flat silver tinsel.

HACKLE. Black hen.

WINGS. About six to eight strands of bright green peacock sword herl, with an inset on each side of red ibis feather.

Butcher

TAIL. Red ibis.

BODY. Flat silver tinsel.

HACKLE. Black cock.

WINGS. The blue back feathers from the wild duck wing.

Mallard and Claret

TAIL. Fibres of a golden pheasant tippet.

BODY. Deep claret seal's fur, ribbed fine gold wire.

HACKLE. Natural light red cock, or hen.

WINGS. Bronze mallard shoulder.

March Brown

TAIL. Two strands as hackle.

BODY. Hare fur, spun on brown silk, ribbed olive tying silk.

HACKLE. Darkish brown partridge back feather.

WINGS. Hen pheasant wing.

Grouse and Orange

TAIL. Three or four fibres of gold pheasant tippet.

BODY. Orange seal's fur, ribbed gold wire.

"BUTCHER" LAKE AND SEA TROUT FLY

"MALLARD AND CLARET" LAKE AND SEA TROUT FLY

A MAYFLY NYMPH

"ZULU" HACKLED WET FLY

HACKLE. Dyed orange cock.
WINGS. Tail feather of a grouse.

Teal Blue and Silver
TAIL. A few strands of golden pheasant tippet.
BODY. Flat silver tinsel, ribbed fine silver oval.
HACKLE. Bright blue cock.
WINGS. From the flank feathers of a teal.

Alder
BODY. Bronze peacock herl, ribbed well waxed claret sewing silk.
HACKLE. Black cock or hen.
WINGS. Brown speckled feather from hens' wing.

Cinnamon Sedge
BODY. A strand from a cinnamon turkey tail feather, ribbed with gold wire.
HACKLE. Ginger cock tied down body. (For dry flies another hackle is wound in front of wings.)
WINGS. Landrail.

Blue Dun
TAIL. Fibres of medium blue dun hen's hackle.
BODY. Blue fur from rabbit, mole or water rat, ribbed yellow tying silk or silver wire, or left unribbed.
HACKLE. Medium blue dun hen.
WINGS. Starling.

February Red
BODY. Reddish claret mohair at tail, remainder lightish brown.
HACKLE. Dark grizzle dun cock.
WINGS. Speckled hen wing.

Kingfisher
TAIL. A few strands of the golden pheasant tippet feather.

BODY. Red floss silk, ribbed white tying silk.
HACKLE. Grey dun cock.
WINGS. Grey mallard flank feathers.

Fiery Brown
TAIL. Golden pheasant tippet or (when the brown owl wing is used) red ibis.
BODY. Reddish brown seal's fur, ribbed gold wire.
HACKLE. Natural red cock hackle.
WINGS. Bronze mallard shoulder feather or (occasionally) the wing-feather of a brown owl.

Demon
TAIL. Golden pheasant crest feather.
BODY. Embossed gold tinsel.
HACKLE. Light claret cock.
WINGS. Feathers from jungle-cock neck, strip of brown mallard over.

Grannom
BODY. Hare fur spun on brown silk. Work in a little green floss silk at tail end of body to represent the eggs of the insect.
HACKLE. Pale ginger cock.
WINGS. From the wing-feather of a partridge.

Olive Dun
TAIL. Fibres from olive cock hackle.
BODY. Waxed yellow tying silk, ribbed or not, with gold wire, or olive dubbing, ribbed gold wire, or olive quill.
HACKLE. Blue dun hen.
WINGS. Hen blackbird wing.

Zulu
TAIL. Red ibis feather or red wool.
BODY. Black wool or seal's fur, ribbed fine flat silver tinsel.
HACKLE. Black cock.

Partridge and Yellow
BODY. Yellow tying silk, ribbed or not with flat gold.
HACKLE. Grey partridge, breast feather.

Red Tag
TAG. Red floss.
BODY. Bronze peacock herl, with tip of gold or silver under tag.
HACKLE. Red cock.

Snipe and Purple
BODY. Purple floss or tying silk.

HACKLE. From the small wing-feather of a snipe.

Priest
TAIL. Fibres of red ibis feather.
BODY, Flat silver tinsel, ribbed fine silver oval.
HACKLE. Natural badger cock.

Waterhen Bloa
BODY. Water rat fur spun on yellow tying silk.
HACKLE. Underside wing-feather of a water hen.

NYMPHS (Not Illustrated)

Blue Dun (Early Olive Dun)
WING CASES. Dark starling wing.
TAIL. Three short fibres of a dark olive hen's hackle.
BODY. Dark olive seal's fur, ribbed gold wire.
THORAX. Dark olive seal's fur.
LEGS: One turn of a short dark olive hen's hackle.

Iron Blue
WING CASES. Waterhen wing.
TAIL. Three short fibres from a soft white cock's hackle.
BODY. Mole fur on claret tying silk.
THORAX. Mole fur.
LEGS. One turn of a short iron blue dun hen's hackle.

Olive Dun
BODY. Olive seal's fur, ribbed with gold wire.
THORAX. Olive seal's fur.
LEGS. One turn of a short olive hen's hackle.

Green Peter (Sedge Pupae—Irish).
BODY. Green seal fur, and a slip of dark green olive goose feather, tied in at tail and brought down over body and tied in

at head—the whole ribbed with gold tinsel to give it a segmented effect.
WING. Dark mottled hen pheasant wing, tied to lie along the side of the body—not on top.
HACKLE. A few fibres of mallard scapular fibres tied underneath, and a couple of turns of ginger hen hackle.
HOOK. No. 9 or 10.

May Fly
WING CASES. Dark part of a hen pheasant centre tail.
TAIL. Three short fibres from a cock pheasant tail.
BODY. Natural seal's fur, ribbed gold wire.
THORAX. Natural seal's fur.
HACKLE. Grouse neck feather.

Gnat Larvae
WING CASES. Starling wing.
TAIL. Fibres of medium olive cock hackle.
BODY. Peacock quill dyed dark olive.
THORAX. Mole fur (a fairly large pad).
HACKLE. Large blue dun hen hackle clipped to leave $\frac{1}{4}$ in. of fibres, and two turns only.

Blue Winged Olive Dun
WING CASES. Goose breast feather dyed pale olive.

TAIL. Three short fibres of a grizzled hen's hackle, dyed yellow.

BODY. Heron's herl dyed olive, ribbed gold wire.

THORAX. Dark olive seal's fur.

LEGS. One turn of a grizzled hen's hackle, dyed yellow.

Pale Watery Dun

WING CASES. Pale starling wing.

TAIL. Three short fibres of a pale ginger hen's hackle.

BODY. Pale ginger fur on light yellow tying silk.

THORAX. Pale yellow or ginger fur.

LEGS. One turn of a pale ginger hen's hackle.

March Brown

WING CASES. Woodcock wing.

TAIL. Three short fibres of a brown partridge back feather.

BODY. Brown seal's fur, ribbed gold wire.

THORAX. Brown seal's fur.

LEGS. One turn of a grouse neck feather.

Lake Olive Dun

WING CASES. Cock pheasant tail fibres.

TAIL. Partridge breast dyed yellow.

BODY. Yellow-olive seal's fur, ribbed with gold wire.

THORAX. Yellow-olive seal's fur.

HACKLE. Yellow-olive hen—short in fibre.

LAKE FLIES

These, as a rule, are fancy flies, made to attract by form and colour rather than to imitate any particular natural fly. They do not, of course, rule out the use of imitations of naturals, especially if there happens to be a hatch on.

The range of fancy flies produced by fly dressers and anglers is very extensive, but the best known are the "Teal", "Mallard", "Grouse", and "Woodcock" series, which derive their names from the wing material that is used. Several of these are illustrated in the plates of flies, facing pages 58 and 124.

The combinations that can be made up from these materials are too numerous for listing here, but I have given a list of the "Mallard" series, and the fly-tyer can substitute his wing material as he fancies. It is generally assumed that the hackle should be the same colour as the body, but this is not a hard and fast rule. The tails also may be varied, golden pheasant tippet fibres or crests, strips of red ibis, or tufts of silk and wool being the most popular.

The wing materials are—

Teal—Black and white barred flank feathers.

Mallard—Small brown speckled shoulder feathers.

Grouse—Speckled tail feathers.

Woodcock—Wing quills.

Mallard and Green (Hook sizes 2–3)

TAIL. Tippet fibres.

BODY. Green seal's fur, ribbed silver oval tinsel.

HACKLE. Green hen.

WINGS. Brown mallard shoulder.

Mallard and Black

TAIL. Tippet fibres.

BODY. Black seal's fur, ribbed silver oval tinsel.

HACKLE. Black hen.

WINGS. Brown mallard shoulder.

Mallard and Red
TAIL. Tippet fibres.
BODY. Red seal's fur, ribbed gold oval tinsel.
HACKLE. Red hen.
WINGS. Brown mallard shoulder.

Mallard and Orange
TAIL. Tippet fibres.
BODY. Orange seal's fur, ribbed gold oval tinsel.
HACKLE. Orange hen.
WINGS. Brown mallard shoulder.

Mallard and Silver
TAIL. Tippet fibres.
BODY. Flat silver tinsel, ribbed oval silver tinsel.
HACKLE. Blue (or black) hen.
WINGS. Brown mallard shoulder.

Mallard and Gold
TAIL. Tippet fibres.
BODY. Flat gold tinsel, ribbed oval gold tinsel.
HACKLE. Black (or ginger) hen.
WINGS. Brown mallard shoulder.

LAKE FLIES (Not Illustrated)

Mallard and Yellow
TAIL. Tippet fibres.
BODY. Yellow seal's fur, ribbed oval gold tinsel.
HACKLE. Yellow hen.
WINGS. Brown mallard shoulder.

Mallard, Red and Yellow
TAIL. Tippet fibres.
BODY. Tail half red seal's fur, shoulder half yellow, whole ribbed gold oval tinsel.
HACKLE. Black (or orange) hen.
WINGS. Brown mallard shoulder.

In addition to the above series and the lake flies illustrated, facing page 124 are—

March Brown Gold
TAIL. Fibres of brown partridge.
BODY. Gold flat tinsel, ribbed gold oval tinsel.
HACKLE. Brown partridge back feather.
WINGS. Hen pheasant wing.

Red Palmer
BODY. Peacock herl or red seal's fur, ribbed gold wire.
HACKLE. Red cock from shoulder to tail.

Jungle Cock and Silver
TAIL. Golden pheasant tippet fibres or a small crest.
BODY. Flat silver tinsel, ribbed oval silver tinsel.
HACKLE. Blue or black.
WINGS. Two jungle cock feathers back to back.

Worm Fly
This is usually tied as two "Red Tag" flies in tandem, the hooks joined by a piece of nylon monofilament or wire. Hook sizes 12–14.
TAIL. Rear Fly only. Red wool, red silk or any red feather.
BODIES. Bronze Peacock Herl.
HACKLES. Tied at front of each fly-dark red/brown hen. Coch-y-hondhu or black are sometimes used as alternatives.

Silver Zulu
TAIL. Red wool.
BODY. Flat silver tinsel, ribbed silver wire.
HACKLE. Black cock.

Johnson's Favourite
TAIL. Golden pheasant tippet fibres.
BODY. Flat gold tinsel.
HACKLE. Grizzle cock dyed flame, wound palmer.
WINGS. Brown mallard shoulder.

Sam Slick
TAIL. Tippet fibres.
BODY. One-third at tail yellow floss silk, remainder brown seal's fur, whole ribbed oval gold tinsel.
HACKLE. Brown partridge back feather.
WINGS. Speckled partridge tail.

Ke-He
TAIL. Golden pheasant tippet fibres.
BODY. Bronze peacock herl—fairly thick.
HACKLE. Medium red/brown.

Dunkeld
TAIL. Small golden pheasant crest.
BODY. Flat gold tinsel ribbed oval gold tinsel.
HACKLE. Orange cock from shoulder to tail.
WINGS. Brown mallard shoulder with jungle cock either side.

Pennell's Black and Silver
TAG. Oval silver tinsel.
TAIL. Golden pheasant crest and tippet fibres.
BODY. Black floss silk, ribbed oval silver tinsel.
HACKLE. Black cock tied long.

Blue and Orange
TAIL. Small golden pheasant crest feather.
BODY. Tail half blue floss silk, remainder orange floss silk, ribbed with silver oval tinsel.
HACKLE. Bright blue cock.
WINGS. Widgeon or wild duck grey quill feather.

The Poacher
TAIL. Fibres from a golden pheasant red body feather.
BODY. 1st. third gold coloured floss, mohair or seal fur, remainder Peacock herl.
RIBS. Fine oval gold tinsel over entire body.
HACKLE. Red/Black cock or hen.
The body should be tapered and the hackle bushy.

Loch Ordie Tandem. This is a rather unique type of trout fly, and is used for dapping on lakes, especially in the extreme north of Scotland. A length of floss silk is added to the line, and this, with the aid of the wind, carries the fly over the surface. It is while the fly is just "scuffing" the water that its taking qualities have been found most effective.

It is dressed as follows—

Two hooks tied in close tandem, and thickly hackled "palmer" fashion with brown hackles. A white hackle is wound at the head.

Fig. 96

In most instances, a small treble hook whipped to gut is also tied in at the head to trail at one side. This "appendage" should not reach more than three-quarters the length of the fly (*see* Fig. 96).

Variations of this pattern can be made by lengthening the distance between the two tandem hooks, and by adding floss silk bodies of different colours.

Other patterns of dapping flies can be tied on single hooks, and the "Wilson" dry salmon fly hook shown on page 27 is ideal for this purpose, the flying treble being omitted.

To obtain really thick hackling of these patterns, two hackles should be tied in and wound round the hook shank together.

SEA TROUT FLIES

Most of the patterns used for lake flies will be found suitable for sea trout, but they are usually tied on hooks two or three sizes larger. Those patterns with plenty of tinsel in the body are to be preferred, my favourite being the teal blue and silver.

Smaller patterns of salmon flies can also be used to good effect, and multi-hook lures similar to those illustrated in the coloured plates, facing pages 212 and 236.

These are quite simple to make up. The additional hooks are of the eyeless type, being whipped on to short lengths of gut or wire in line with the main hook, Fig. 97.

Each hook is then dressed as for the body of the particular pattern being tied. By that I mean that if it was a "Teal, Blue and Silver", each hook would have a silver tinsel body and a tail of tippet fibres. The hackle is wound on the main hook in the usual way, and the wings tied in to extend the whole length of the lure.

For extra strength the turns of silk which bind the gut or wire to the hook shanks, should be well varnished before the bodies are put on.

Fig. 97

The following patterns of sea trout flies are in addition to those illustrated facing page 124.

Mason
TAG. Round silver tinsel or silver wire.
TAIL. Dyed blue duck or goose fibres.
BODY. White silk ribbed flat silver tinsel.
HACKLE. Dark blue cock.
WINGS. "Married" strands of dark blue, light blue, and white duck or goose feathers.

Ramsbottom's Favourite
TAIL. Red ibis.
BODY. Yellow seal's fur ribbed oval gold tinsel.
HACKLE. Coch-y-bondhu cock or hen.
WINGS. "Married" strands of red, yellow, and blue duck or goose feathers.

Dugmore's Fancy
BODY. Black silk ribbed flat silver tinsel.
HACKLE. Black cock.
WINGS. Brown mallard shoulder feather.

Tippet and Black
TAIL. A few fibres of small golden pheasant tippet.

BODY. Black seal's fur ribbed oval silver tinsel.
HACKLE. Black cock.
WINGS. A few fibres of golden pheasant tippet.
(The body hackles of this fly can be varied as for the "Mallard" series of patterns.)

SEA TROUT FLIES (Not Illustrated)

Black and Orange
TAIL. Golden pheasant tippet fibres.
BODY. Tail half hot orange seal's fur, remainder black ditto, ribbed with oval gold tinsel.
WINGS. Brown mallard shoulder.

General Eagle's Fairy
TAG. Silver oval tinsel and yellow floss silk.
TAIL. Golden pheasant crest feather.
BUTT. Scarlet wool.
BODY. Silver tinsel, ribbed silver wire.
HACKLE. Black cock.
WINGS. Grey mallard flank feather.

General Eagle's Jungle Cock
Same as the "Fairy" with jungle cock either side.

General Eagle's Fancy
TAG. Silver tinsel and yellow floss silk.
TAIL. Golden pheasant crest feather.
BODY. Black floss silk, ribbed oval silver tinsel.
HACKLE. Claret cock.
WINGS. Fibres of golden pheasant tippet, with brown mallard over.

Golden Ranger
TAIL. Brown mallard fibres.
BODY. Oval gold tinsel.
HACKLE. Badger cock dyed scarlet.
WINGS. Lightly dressed of a few fibres of golden pheasant tippet, brown mallard and green peacock herl.

The Winsum
TAG. Silver tinsel and yellow floss silk.
TAIL. Golden pheasant crest feather.
BUTT. Red wool.
BODY. Flat silver tinsel ribbed silver wire.
HACKLE. Badger cock, dyed scarlet.
WINGS. Lightly dressed mixed fibres of tippet, green and red goose, teal flank, and brown mallard shoulder.

Carter's Pale Blue
BODY. Pale slaty blue floss, ribbed flat silver tinsel.
HACKLE. Pale slaty blue cock.
WINGS. Yellow goose, brown mallard should over.

Oakley's Fly
TAIL. Three fibres of cock pheasant tail.
BUTT. Peacock herl.
BODY. Lamb's wool.
HACKLE. Badger cock.
WINGS. Grey mallard flank, dyed pale yellow.

Welsh Blue Palmer
TAG. Flat silver tinsel.
TAIL. Golden pheasant crest feather.
BODY. Peacock herl, ribbed flat silver tinsel.
HACKLE. Medium blue dun cock from shoulder to tail.

Grouse and Orange
TAG. Silver tinsel.

TAIL. Golden pheasant crest feather.

BODY. Orange floss silk, ribbed oval gold tinsel.

HACKLE. Brown speckled grouse back feather tied half-way down body, clipped underneath for legs and left long over back to form part of the wings.

WINGS. Added to grouse, fibres of tippet, red, yellow, green goose, brown mallard shoulder over and a topping over all.

John Storey

TAIL. Red hackle fibres.

BODY. Peacock herl ribbed with scarlet silk.

WINGS. Grey mallard flank.

HACKLE. Red.

AMERICAN WET FLIES

Until the 1890's fly fishing in America was primarily of the wet fly variety; consequently a large number of patterns was built up to suit the vast territory available to the angler.

Although some of them had British origins, most of them had names, and were as distinctive, as the territory where they were used. Such flies as the "Adirondack", "Cupsuptic", "Hudson", "Potomac", "Rio Grande King", and the "Utah", the dressings of which are given below.

There must be at least six or seven hundred catalogued American wet fly patterns. Some of these, illustrated in the coloured plates facing pages 122 and 124 are the "McGinty", "Rube Wood", "Hoskins", "Laramie", "Royal Governor", "Grizzly King", "Queen of the Waters", "Gordon", "Cardinal", "Professor", "Parmachene Belle", "Montreal", and the "Royal Coachman".

Adirondack

TAG. Yellow floss silk.

TAIL. Black hackle tips.

BODY. Grey seal's fur.

HACKLE. Orange cock.

WINGS. White duck wing.

Cupsuptic

BODY. Silver tinsel.

HACKLE. Crimson cock tied palmer.

WINGS. Guinea fowl wing over brown turkey tail.

Potomac

BODY. Bright green floss silk, ribbed yellow floss silk.

HACKLE. Brown cock.

WINGS. Cinnamon hen wing.

Hudson

TAG. Orange floss silk.

TAIL. Strip of green duck or goose wing.

BODY. Dark brown almost black seal's fur, ribbed gold tinsel.

HACKLE. Orange cock.

WINGS. Light brown turkey tail.

Rio Grande King

TAG. Gold tinsel.

TAIL. Strip of yellow duck or goose quill feather.

BODY. Black chenille.

HACKLE. Brown cock.

WINGS. White duck wing.

Utah

BODY. Cinnamon seal's fur, ribbed gold tinsel.

HACKLE. Ginger cock.

WINGS. Cinnamon hen wing.

CANADIAN AND AMERICAN WET FLIES (Not Illustrated)

Abbey
TAIL. Golden pheasant tippet fibres.
BODY. Red floss silk, ribbed oval gold tinsel.
HACKLE. Natural red cock.
WINGS. Grey mallard flank.

Academy
TAIL. Red cock hackle fibres.
BODY. Bronze peacock herl, red floss tip.
HACKLE. Natural red cock.
WINGS. Claret duck or goose wing.

Beaverkill
TAIL. Fibres of grey mallard breast feather.
BODY. White silk floss.
HACKLE. Red cock, tied palmer.
WINGS. Starling wing.

Black Prince
TAIL. Crimson hackle fibres.
BODY. Black silk floss, ribbed silver oval tinsel.
HACKLE. Black cock.
WINGS. Crow wing.

Catskill
TAIL. Fibres of brown mallard shoulder feather.
BODY. Orange floss silk.
HACKLE. Red cock, tied palmer.
WINGS. Brown mallard shoulder.

Coachman Leadwing
BODY. Bronze peacock herl.
HACKLE. Dark red cock.
WINGS. Coot or waterhen wing.

Cooper
BODY. Orange floss silk.
HACKLE. Black cock.
WINGS. Cinnamon turkey tail.

Kingdom
BODY. White floss silk, ribbed blue tying silk.
HACKLE. Natural red cock.
WINGS. Brown mottled turkey tail.

Light Fox
TAIL. Yellow wool.
BODY. White seal's fur, ribbed oval gold tinsel and tip of round gold tinsel.
HACKLE. Yellow cock.
WINGS. Grey duck wing.

Mershon
TAIL. Black hackle fibres.
BODY. Black silk floss.
HACKLE. Black cock.
WINGS. White tipped duck wing quill feather—to show white tip.

Montreal Silver
TAIL. Scarlet wool.
BODY. Flat silver tinsel.
HACKLE. Claret cock.
WINGS. Woodcock wing.

Neversink
TAIL. Fibres of grey mallard breast feather.
BODY. Light yellow floss silk.
HACKLE. Yellow cock.
WINGS. Grey mallard flank feather.

Orange Miller
TAIL. Scarlet ibis.
BODY. Orange chenille, ribbed gold oval tinsel and tip of round gold tinsel.
HACKLE. White cock.
WINGS. White duck wing.

Parmachene Beau
TAG. Black ostrich herl.

TAIL. Red and white hackle or duck quill fibres.

BODY. Light yellow floss silk, ribbed silver oval tinsel.

HACKLE. Mixed, red and white cock.

WINGS. Married red and white duck wing (red in centre) and jungle cock feather each side.

Dr. Burke

TAIL. Fibres of peacock sword tail feather.

BODY. Flat silver tinsel ribbed silver wire.

HACKLE. Yellow cock.

WINGS. White duck wing, with jungle cock each side.

Furguson

TAIL. Yellow and crimson hackle fibres.

BODY. Yellow floss ribbed gold tinsel and gold tinsel tip.

HACKLE. Green cock.

WINGS. Cinnamon turkey tail with a yellow stripe of duck wing each side.

Gosling

TAIL. Grey hackle fibres.

BODY. Green floss silk.

HACKLE. Grey cock.

WINGS. Grey duck wing.

Hoskins

BODY. Yellow floss silk.

HACKLE. Medium blue dun cock.

WINGS. Grey duck wing.

Ingersol

TAIL. Fibres of cock pheasant tail.

BODY. Orange chenille, ribbed oval gold tinsel.

HACKLE. Brown cock.

WINGS. Mottled turkey tail.

King of the Waters

TAIL. Fibres of grey mallard breast feather.

BODY. Dark red floss, ribbed flat gold tinsel.

HACKLE. Dark red cock.

WINGS. Grey mallard flank feather.

Peter Ross (American)

TAIL. Fibres of golden pheasant tippet.

BODY. Yellow floss silk, ribbed gold oval tinsel.

HACKLE. Light ginger cock.

No Wings.

Pink Wickham

TAIL. Light red hackle fibres.

BODY. Pink floss silk.

HACKLE. Natural light red cock tied palmer.

WINGS. Starling wing.

Ray Bergman

TAIL. Brown mallard fibres.

BODY. Dark orange seal's fur or wool.

HACKLE. Brown cock.

WINGS. Grey dick wing.

Saranac

TAIL. A golden pheasant crest feather.

BODY. Claret floss silk, ribbed oval gold tinsel and tip of round gold tinsel.

HACKLE. Claret cock.

WINGS. Golden pheasant tippet.

Swiftwater

TAIL. Fibres of grey mallard breast.

BODY. Bronze peacock herl with orange silk centre.

HACKLE. Natural red cock.

WINGS. White duck wing.

AUSTRALIAN AND NEW ZEALAND WET FLIES

Owing to the fact that fly-tying in Australia and New Zealand has not reached anything like full development, most of the flies used in Australasia are of British origin. They are usually tied on larger sizes of hooks than those used in Britain, for, as a rule, the fish are much bigger.

A range of distinctive patterns is being built up, however, the most well known probably being the "Matuka" series. This is a "streamer" type of fly which has a hackle tied along the top of the hook only, with its tip projecting well beyond the bend. This is illustrated in the coloured plate facing page 150, in the chapter devoted to streamer flies.

Popular British patterns are the "Alexandra", "Butcher", "Hardie's Favourite", "March Brown", "Peter Ross", "Coachman", "Greenwell's Glory", "Wickham's Fancy", and "Red Tag".

The patterns given below are of Australian or New Zealand origin—

Up Stream Nymph
HOOK. Painted white.
TAIL. Three blue dun hackle fibres.
BODY. Palest honey silk, ribbed fine flat silver tinsel.
THORAX. Oak turkey wing.

Mid-Water Nymph
TAIL. Black cock hackle fibres (or to suit colour of body).
BODY. Black silk, ribbed fine silver tinsel. (Alternative colours: green, red, yellow.)

Caddis Nymph
BODY. Straw coloured dry grass stems, protruding quarter-of-an-inch beyond bend of hook, and bound in with pale yellow floss up to eye, finishing off with black tying silk to represent head.
HACKLE. One turn grizzle cock.

Beetle
BODY. Black wool.
RIBBING. Fine flat silver tinsel.
WING CASES. Strips of green peacock herl.

Bumble Bee
BODY. Alternate turns of black and yellow chenille.

HACKLE. Natural red cock.
WINGS. Grey duck wing.

Bredbo
BODY. Golden yellow floss silk, ribbed oval gold tinsel.
HACKLE. Brown partridge back feather.
WINGS. Golden pheasant tippet fibres under speckled hen wing quill feather.

Cooma
BODY. Yellow floss silk ribbed black tying silk.
HACKLE. Light red cock.
WINGS. Blue mallard wing quill feather, with narrow strip of dyed red duck quill feather at base.

Jindabyne
TAIL. Fibres of natural red cock hackle.
BODY. Orange floss silk ribbed with black tying silk.
HACKLE. Red cock.
WINGS. Dark teal flank feather.

Tumut
BODY. Bronze peacock herl.
HACKLE. Light red cock.
WINGS. Grey duck wing.

CHAPTER TWELVE

HAIR WING FLIES

THE USE OF HAIR instead of feathers for wings has become increasingly popular for use in fast streams, especially on the west coast of America, mainly because it has more "life" when wet. It is used mainly for wet flies, especially those of the "Streamer" variety, but there are one or two instances where it can be used for dry flies. These are of the down-winged variety such as stone flies and sedges. Hair is of no use for the upright winged type of fly, as hair being heavier than feathers, flies made in this fashion are top-heavy and fall on their sides.

Although hair is used on patterns that represent natural flies, it is used mostly on those flies that are supposed to represent the small food fish on which the larger fish feed. This type of fly and the dressing thereof is dealt with in the chapters "Streamer Flies" and "Flies for Sea Fishing", so we will confine ourselves here to dry flies, one or two of the smaller patterns of wet flies, and hair-winged salmon flies. Illustrations of these types will be found in the coloured plate facing page 146.

The furs selected for the wings of these flies, should be as near as possible in colour to the feathers that would be used if feathered wing patterns were being tied. By that I mean a blue-grey fur should be used for a "Blue Dun", a brown one for "Sedges", a mottled one for such flies as the "March Brown" and "Alder". The following list will no doubt provide a useful guide—

Blue-grey fur for the "Dun's", etc.	Dyed bucktail.	Brown mottled fur for "March Brown", etc.	Barred brown squirrel tail.
Grizzled fur for "Grizzly King", etc.	Grey squirrel tail.	White fur for "Coachman", etc.	Undyed bucktail, Dyed bucktail or
Brown fur for "Sedges", etc.	Brown squirrel tail.	Blue, red, yellow, green, etc., for sea trout flies, salmon flies, etc.	goat hair.

HOW TO DRESS A HAIR-WINGED FLY

The dressing of hair-winged flies is very simple, and, as far as the dry fly is concerned, the same principles are followed as if one was tying a feathered pattern. The tail and body are formed, the wing tied in, and the hackle put on last. The last sequence is most important as it gives the tyer extra turns of silk to hold the slippery hair, since the hackle is wound over these turns and conceals them.

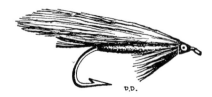

A common fault when tying hair wings is to use far too much hair, which results in a fly that is poorly balanced and which has an ugly lump where the wing joins the hook. About 1/16th of an inch is ample for a fly as large as a No. 5. Give the hair a twist before cutting it from the skin, and the resulting thickness will provide the necessary measurement. Do not cut the hair from the skin until ready to tie in the wing.

After cutting, remove any long, uneven hairs so that the wing has a neat and regular appearance. If any fine body fur is present in the hair, comb *some* of it out with a needle as this will help to keep the head small. Do not remove all of it otherwise the wing will look lean and scraggy.

The best way to attach a hair wing is as follows—

Form tail and body, and be sure to leave plenty of room at the eye to take the wing and hackle. Now take a few turns of silk round the bare hook that is left, at about the centre of where the wing is to be fastened. Apply a little thin cellire varnish to these turns, and also a little on the butt end of the wing. Hold the wing on the near side of the hook in an almost vertical position and secure with one turn of silk (Fig. 98). Pull the silk taut and the hair will roll on to the top of the hook shank. A little assistance may have to be given to the hair to make it do this, but if one attempts to put the hair on top of the hook before pulling the silk tight, it will be pulled to the far side. Hold the hair very tightly during this part of the procedure.

Now take about three turns of silk to the left and make a half hitch. Grasp the silk with the left hand, raise the wing with the right hand, and take one turn of silk round the wing only, as close as possible to the previous turn. Lower the wing and take two or three more turns around wing and hook towards the left. This should bring you to a point just over the beginning of the body. Now take several

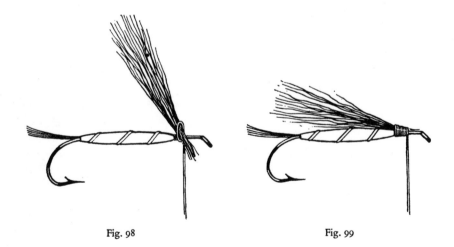

Fig. 98   Fig. 99

turns to the right and make a half hitch. Cut off the surplus hair which lies over the eye by raising it and laying the scissors flat. This will cut them on the slant and also very close to the turns of silk. The fly should now be as Fig. 99. The silk should now be wound to the right to cover the hair left exposed after the cutting and then back to the left to the point where the wing was first tied in. This will ensure that the wing is safely kept in position and not pulled out easily.

When using this type of wing for dry flies, the hair may be separated into two equal parts by figure of eight turns. It will be found that this causes the wing to be raised slightly, which seem to improve the taking qualities of the fly.

Another method of tying in hair wings, to ensure that they will not come adrift, is as follows—

Use only half the required thickness of hair and tie it in at the required position by its middle (see Fig. 100).

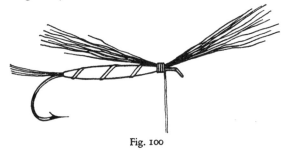

Fig. 100

Fold the front section to the rear (as Fig. 101) and then bind this down with two or three turns of silk. This will lock the fibres far more securely than any other method, but can only be used when plain coloured hairs are being used. It will not do for the "badger" type of hair that shows a distinct bar.

I am grateful to Mr. A. S. Rooke, of Claremorris, County Mayo, for this idea.

Fig. 101

For a dry fly the procedure for tying the hackle is as follows—

Strip the soft flue from the base of the hackle and tie it in by the butt as close up to the wing as possible. Wind the hackle to the right in close turns, covering all the silk that holds the wing. Leave the hackle pliers hanging down and carefully wind the silk through the hackle until the eye is reached. Tie in the tip of the hackle and cut off the surplus. Finish with a whip finish, and the completed fly should be as Fig. 102.

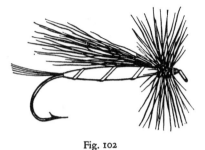

Fig. 102

For a wet fly the hackle may be put on first in the usual manner, but care must be taken to ensure that sufficient room is left for the wing to be secured properly.

When winging hair-winged salmon flies with mixed colours the procedure is exactly the same, but it is even more important that not too much hair is used. Start with the bottom colour and work to the right, each colour to be as close to the last as possible. When all the colours are on the hook, secure the wing as explained previously as though just a single wing had been secured to the top of the hook shank.

WET FLIES (Illustrated, facing page 146)

Cahill
TAIL. Brown hackle fibres.
BODY. Grey fur.
HACKLE. Brown cock.
WINGS. Barred brown squirrel tail.

Montreal
TAIL. Scarlet hackle fibres.
BODY. Claret floss silk.
RIB. Flat gold tinsel.
HACKLE. Claret cock.
WINGS. Plain brown squirrel tail.

Princess
TAIL. Golden pheasant tippets paired, or
   orange polar bear fur.
BODY. Oval gold tinsel.
WINGS. Lower—yellow bucktail; middle
   —orange bucktail; upper—grey squirrel
   tail.

McGregor
TAIL. Golden pheasant crest.
BODY. Orange chenille.
RIB. Silver tinsel.
HACKLE. Grizzle cock.
WINGS. Grey squirrel tail and jungle cock.

ADDITIONAL PATTERNS

Black Prince
TAIL. Scarlet hackle fibres.
BODY. Black floss silk, ribbed silver oval tinsel.
HACKLE. Black cock.
WINGS. Bucktail dyed black.

Governor
TAG. Scarlet floss silk.
BODY. Bronze peacock herl.
HACKLE. Natural red cock.
WINGS. Brown barred squirrel tail.

Professor
TAIL. Scarlet hackle fibres.
BODY. Yellow floss silk, ribbed flat gold tinsel.
HACKLE. Natural red.
WINGS. Grey squirrel tail.

Queen of the Waters
BODY. Orange wool or seal's fur, ribbed gold tinsel.
HACKLE. Brown cock (tied palmer).
WINGS. Grey squirrel tail.

Sawtooth (Ray Bergman)
TAIL. Fibres of spotted guinea fowl.
BODY. Orange chenille ribbed oval gold tinsel.
HACKLE. Guinea fowl speckled neck feather.
WINGS. Brown barred squirrel tail fibres.
SIDES. Jungle cock.

Cummings
BODY. Shoulder half claret seal's fur, tail half yellow floss silk, ribbed oval gold tinsel.
HACKLE. Claret cock.
WINGS. Brown bucktail.
SIDES. Jungle cock.

Gibson Girl
TAIL. Fibres of golden pheasant tippet.
BODY. Orange wool, ribbed gold tinsel and gold tinsel tip.
HACKLE. Dark brown cock.
WINGS. Brown bucktail.
SIDES. Jungle cock.

WET FLIES (Not Illustrated)

Golden Demon
TAIL. Yellow hackle fibres.
BODY. Flat gold tinsel, ribbed oval gold tinsel.
HACKLE. Orange cock.
WINGS. Brown bucktail.
SIDES. Jungle cock.

Surveyor
TAIL. White and brown bucktail.
BODY. Shoulder half yellow chenille, tail half gold tinsel. Gold tinsel rib through chenille.
HACKLE. Grizzle and brown cock mixed.
WINGS. White and brown bucktail.

Umpqua
TAIL. White bucktail.
BODY. Two-thirds scarlet chenille, one-third yellow wool, ribbed silver oval tinsel.
HACKLE. Brown cock.
WINGS. White and scarlet bucktail.

Red Trude
TAIL. Fibres of scarlet cock's hackle.
BODY. Scarlet floss silk ribbed with oval silver tinsel.
HACKLE. Natural red cock.
WINGS. Plain brown squirrel tail.

Bobbie Dunn

TAIL. Crimson bucktail.

BODY. Copper wire or heavy oval gold tinsel.

WING. Lower section white, bucktail, middle red bucktail, top brown bucktail.

Silver Ant

TAIL. Yellow bucktail.

BODY. Flat silver tinsel.

HACKLE. Crimson cock.

WINGS. Black bucktail.

Thor

TAIL. Orange hackle fibres.

BODY. Scarlet chenille.

HACKLE. Brown cock.

WINGS. White bucktail.

Van Luven

TAIL. Dyed red bucktail.

BODY. Red floss silk or seal's fur, ribbed oval silver tinsel.

HACKLE. Brown cock.

WINGS. White bucktail.

Silver King

TAIL. Fibres of scarlet cock's hackle.

BODY. Flat silver tinsel.

HACKLE. Natural red cock.

WINGS. White bucktail.

DRY FLIES (Illustrated, facing page 146)

Blue Dun

TAIL. Grey bucktail.

BODY. Blue-grey fur, or the stripped quill from the "eye" of a peacock tail.

WINGS. Grey bucktail.

HACKLE. Blue dun cock.

Grizzly King

TAIL. Red hackle fibres.

BODY. Green floss silk.

RIB. Flat gold tinsel.

WINGS. Grey squirrel tail.

HACKLE. Grizzle cock.

Brown Sedge

BODY. Strands of cinnamon turkey tail.

RIB. Gold wire.

BODY HACKLE. Brown cock.

WINGS. Brown squirrel tail.

FRONT HACKLE. Brown cock.

March Brown

TAIL. Brown hackle fibres.

BODY. Hare's fur ribbed with gold wire.

WINGS. Barred brown squirrel tail.

HACKLE. Brown and grizzle cock mixed (or "cree" hackle, which has brown, black and white bars).

ADDITIONAL PATTERNS

Black Gnat

BODY. Black ostrich herl.

WINGS. Dyed grey bucktail or goat hair.

HACKLE. Black cock.

Cowdung

BODY. Dark olive seal's fur.

WINGS. Dyed grey bucktail or goat hair.

HACKLE. Brown cock.

Gold Ribbed Hare's Ear
TAIL. Grizzle cock hackle fibres.
BODY. Hare's fur ribbed gold wire.
WINGS. Dyed grey bucktail or goat hair.
HACKLE. Long fibres of hare's fur, or "cree" (black/brown barred) cock.

Grey Sedge
BODY. Grey seal's fur, ribbed silver wire.
WINGS. Grey squirrel fur from tail.
HACKLE. Grizzle cock.

McGinty
TAIL. Scarlet hackle fibres.
BODY. Alternate bars of black and yellow chenille.

WINGS. From grey squirrel tail.
HACKLE. Natural red cock.

Royal Wulff
TAIL. Brown bucktail.
BODY. Bronze peacock herl with scarlet floss silk centre section.
WINGS. White bucktail.
HACKLE. Natural red cock.

White Wulff
TAIL. White bucktail.
BODY. Cream seal's fur.
WINGS. White bucktail.
HACKLE. Badger cock.

HAIR WING SALMON FLIES

Silver Doctor (Illustrated opposite)
TAG. Round silver tinsel.
TAIL. Golden pheasant crest, green peacock herl.
BUTT. Red wool.
BODY. Flat silver tinsel.
HACKLE. Light blue cock.
THROAT. Spotted guinea fowl.
WINGS. Plain brown squirrel tail with red, yellow and blue bucktail each side.

Grey Wulff (Dry) (Illustrated opposite)
TAIL. Brown bucktail.
BODY. Blue-grey fur.
WINGS. Brown bucktail.
HACKLE. Blue-grey cock.

Studley
TAG. Round silver tinsel and yellow floss.
TAIL. Golden pheasant crest, with pale blue chatterer above and below.
BUTT. Black ostrich herl.
BODY. In four, three, two or one sections (according to size of hook) of yellow

floss, each section butted with black herl and veiled above and below with pale blue chatterer.
THROAT HACKLE AND WINGS. Yellow mohair, bucktail or polar bear fur.
HEAD. Black varnish.

Jock Scott (Illustrated opposite)
TAG. Round silver tinsel.
TAIL. Golden pheasant crest and Indian crow.
BUTT. Black ostrich herl.
BODY. In two equal parts:
    I. (Rear) yellow floss ribbed flat silver tinsel, with black ostrich herl at joint and "veiled" with Toucan.
    2. Black floss ribbed with silver tinsel and a black hackle.
SHOULDER HACKLE. Spotted guinea fowl.
WINGS. Teal breast with crown polar bear or bucktail either side; over this two or three green peacock sword fibres and whisps of dyed scarlet, yellow and blue polar bear fur or bucktail.

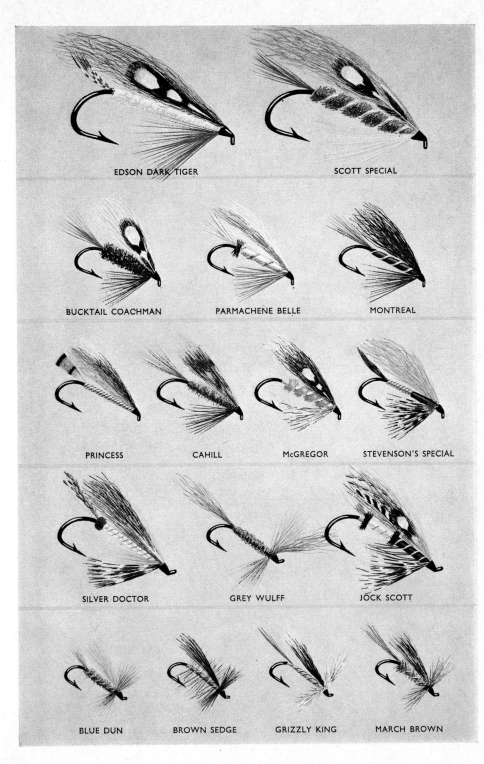

EDSON DARK TIGER   SCOTT SPECIAL

BUCKTAIL COACHMAN   PARMACHENE BELLE   MONTREAL

PRINCESS   CAHILL   McGREGOR   STEVENSON'S SPECIAL

SILVER DOCTOR   GREY WULFF   JOCK SCOTT

BLUE DUN   BROWN SEDGE   GRIZZLY KING   MARCH BROWN

HAIR WING FLIES

SHOULDERS. Jungle cock.
CHEEKS. Blue chatterer or kingfisher.
HEAD. Black varnish.

Coke's Infallible
TAG. Flat or oval gold tinsel.
TAIL. Golden pheasant crest and Indian crow.
BUTT. Black ostrich herl.

BODY. In equal sections, varying in number with size of hook, of black floss ribbed with fine oval gold tinsel, each section butted with black herl, and veiled above and below with Indian crow.
THROAT HACKLE AND WINGS. Black mohair, bucktail or polar bear fur.
HEAD. Black varnish.

There are no established hair-wing dry fly patterns for salmon fishing, the "Grey Wulff", which is given here, being a larger dressing of the trout fly of that name. *See also* Dressings on page 145 and 146.

For further hair-wing salmon flies *see* pages 238 and 239 and Illustrations facing page 212.

BUCKTAIL FLIES (Illustrated, facing page 146)

Coachman
TAIL. Crimson hackle fibres.
BODY. Peacock herl.
HACKLE. Brown cock.
WINGS. White bucktail and jungle cock.
HEAD. Black varnish.

Stevenson's Special
TAIL. Spotted guinea fowl dyed red.
BODY. Rear half oval gold tinsel, front half black chenille.

HACKLE. Spotted guinea fowl dyed yellow.
WINGS. Yellow bucktail.
HEAD. Black varnish.

Parmachene Belle
TAG. Peacock herl.
TAIL. Scarlet and white hackle fibres.
BODY. Yellow wool.
RIB. Flat gold tinsel.
HACKLE. Scarlet and white cock.
WINGS. Scarlet and white bucktail.
HEAD. Black varnish.

HAIR WING STREAMER FLIES (Illustrated, facing page 146)

Edson Dark Tiger
TAIL. Guinea fowl or barred mandarin duck.
BODY. Yellow chenille.
HACKLE. Scarlet cock.
WINGS. Brown bucktail and jungle cock.
HEAD. Black varnish.

Scott Special
TAG. Round silver tinsel.
TAIL. Scarlet.
BODY. Light brown wool.
RIB. Flat silver tinsel.
HACKLE. Yellow cock.
WINGS. Yellow bucktail and jungle cock.
HEAD. Black varnish.

Further dressings of hair-winged flies will be found among the patterns of streamer flies, pages 149 to 153. As these streamers are flies with a particular function, I think this is less confusing than if they were lumped together with hair wing flies in general.

CHAPTER THIRTEEN

STREAMER FLIES

THIS TYPE OF FLY is immensely popular in America, but its possibilities in the United Kingdom have never been seriously considered. The nearest approach we have to it is the "lure", which consists usually of two or three hooks in tandem with a long wing. The idea is very much the same, of course, the main difference being that many of the "streamers" are tied to represent the small fish on which game fish feed, whereas most of the lures are just brightly coloured "attractors".

In the United States they are used to catch every type of game fish, including brown and rainbow trout, sea trout (steelheads), salmon, bass, pike and perch.

They are usually tied on long-shanked hooks, but they can also be tied on the usual shorter shanked hooks, the "streamer" effect being obtained by the wing projecting well beyond the bend of the hook.

As will be readily understood, the wing is the most important part of the fly as it is this that gives the streamer its "form" and "life" when it is submerged. In their order of importance, the qualities required of a "streamer" are action, form, flash and colour. They should be trim, streamlined and not too heavily dressed.

The materials most used for wings are hair and long hackles, others being peacock herl and marabou plumes. The best hackles are long, thin saddle hackles.

Jungle cock is used profusely to simulate the eye of the quarry.

The procedure for dressing hair-winged patterns is given in the chapter on hair-winged flies, the hackles for these patterns being put on before or after the wing, according to the pattern being dressed. Some patterns have no hackle at all.

When hackle wings are used they are either put on in bunches, or back to back in pairs to form a neat, single wing. Sometimes two pairs of different colours are used, one colour inside, sheathed by the other colour. A good illustration of this type is the "Spencer Bay Special" in the coloured plate facing page 150. This has an outer pair of black/red hackles and inner pair of blue. The "Professor" and "Black Ghost" illustrated facing page 150 have wings formed of one pair of hackles only.

Quite effective heads can be put on these flies by building up with several coats of black "cellire" varnish, and then painting on an eye. In America special beads

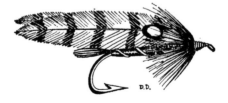

are obtainable with "eyes" already painted on, as illustrated in Fig. (*b*), page 156.

Among the dressings of the streamer flies, given on the following pages, will be found many with hair wings. The method of dressing of this particular wing will be found under the heading "Hair Wing Flies" on page 140, and two patterns are illustrated facing page 146: "Edson Dark Tiger" and "Scott Special", the dressings of which will be found on page 147.

(All these Patterns are Illustrated, facing page 150)

Matuka
BODY. Yellow seal's fur ribbed with flat silver tinsel.
HACKLE. Hen pheasant side feathers along top of hook only, and tip of feather protecting at rear.
HEAD. Black varnish.

Spencer Bay Special
TAIL. Fibres of golden pheasant tippets.
BODY. Flat silver tinsel.
HACKLE. Mixed, yellow and light blue cock.
WINGS. Two blue hackles back to back inside, and two furnace (red/black) hackles outside.
SHOULDERS. Jungle cock.
HEAD. Black varnish.

Chief Needabeh
TAG. Silver tinsel.
BODY. Scarlet floss.
RIB. Oval silver tinsel.
HACKLE. Mixed, yellow and scarlet cock.
WINGS. Two yellow hackles back to back inside, and two orange hackles outside.
SHOULDERS. Jungle cock.
HEAD. Black varnish.

Nancy
TAG. Round silver tinsel.
BODY. Flat gold tinsel.
RIB. Oval silver tinsel.
HACKLE. Yellow cock.
WINGS. Two long green hackles back to back, with two shorter orange hackles outside.

CHEEKS. Any light brown mottled feather.
HEAD. Black varnish.

Blue Devil
TAIL. Golden pheasant crest.
BODY. Flat gold tinsel.
HACKLE. Grizzle cock, with golden pheasant crest feather under.
WINGS. Grizzle hackles, back to back.
CHEEKS. Blue peacock feathers, and blue kingfisher feathers.
HEAD. Black varnish.

Barnes Special
TAIL. Jungle cock.
BODY. Flat silver tinsel.
HACKLE. White cock, tied full.
WINGS. Mixed red and white bucktail below, then two yellow hackles back to back with two grizzle hackles outside of these.
HEAD. Black varnish.

Professor
TAIL. Scarlet.
BODY. Yellow floss silk.
RIB. Flat gold tinsel.
HACKLE. Brown cock, wound as collar.
WINGS. Grizzle hackles.
HEAD. Black varnish.

Bumble Puppy
TAIL. Scarlet ibis.
BODY. White chenille.
RIB. Flat silver tinsel.
HACKLE. Grey mallard flank.

WINGS. White bucktail below, white goose or swan above.
SHOULDERS. Jungle cock.
HEAD. Black varnish.

White Marabou
BODY. Flat silver tinsel.
RIB. Round silver tinsel.
HACKLE. Scarlet cock.
WINGS. White marabou plumes topped by several strands of green peacock herl.

SHOULDERS. Jungle cock.
HEAD. Black varnish.

Black Ghost
TAIL. Golden pheasant crest.
BODY. Black wool or floss.
RIB. Flat silver tinsel.
HACKLE. Golden pheasant crest.
WINGS. White hackles.
SHOULDERS. Jungle cock.
HEAD. Black varnish.

(Not Illustrated)

Alaska Mary Ann Bucktail
TAIL. Red hackle fibres.
BODY. Ivory or light tan silk.
RIB. Flat silver tinsel.
WING. White bucktail.
CHEEKS. Jungle cock.
HEAD. Black varnish.

Alexandra Streamer
TAIL. Narrow section of red goose.
BODY. Embossed silver tinsel.
RIB. Oval silver tinsel narrow.
THROAT. Black saddle hackle wound on as a collar.
WING. Green peacock herl.
HEAD. Black varnish.

Ames Rogue Bucktail
TAIL. Red hackle fibres.
BODY. Varnished thread, greenish-black on top and red below.
THROAT. Ginger hackle wound on as a collar.
WING. White bucktail.
HEAD. Red varnish.

Ballou Special Streamer
TAIL. One or two golden pheasant crest feathers curving downward.
BODY. Flat silver tinsel.

WING. Red bucktail, with two white marabou feathers over.
TOPPING. Green peacock herl.
CHEEKS. Jungle cock.
HEAD. Black varnish.

Bauman Bucktail
TAIL. Section of barred woodduck or mandarin duck.
BODY. Orange silk.
RIB. Flat gold tinsel.
THROAT. Red hackle.
WING. White bucktail over which yellow bucktail.
TOPPING. Green peacock sword fibres.
CHEEKS. Jungle cock.
HEAD. Black varnish with red eye.

Brown Falcon Bucktail
TAG. Embossed silver tinsel.
BUTT. Red silk.
BODY. Embossed silver tinsel, butted just behind the head with red silk.
WING. White bucktail over which yellow bucktail.
SHOULDER. Brown saddle hackle on each side.
CHEEKS. Jungle cock.
HEAD. Black varnish.

MATUKA

SPENCER BAY SPECIAL

CHIEF NEEDABEH

NANCY

BLUE DEVIL

BARNES SPECIAL

PROFESSOR

BUMBLEPUPPY

WHITE MARABOU

BLACK GHOST

STREAMER FLIES

Highlander Streamer

TAIL. Barred wooduck feather.

BODY. Flat silver tinsel.

WING. Two dyed green highlander saddle hackles, with plymouth rock saddle hackle each side.

THROAT. Green highlander saddle hackle with plymouth rock saddle hackle ahead of this, tied as a collar.

CHEEKS. Jungle cock.

HEAD. Black varnish.

Silver Grey Streamer

TAIL. Barred wooduck feather.

BODY. Flat silver tinsel.

WING. Two orange saddle hackles, with grey plymouth rock saddle hackle each side.

CHEEKS. Jungle cock.

THROAT. Grey plymouth rock saddle hackle tied as a collar.

HEAD. Black varnish.

Catskill Bucktail

TAIL. Red wool.

BODY. Flat silver tinsel.

RIB. Oval silver tinsel.

WINGS. White bucktail, with red bucktail over.

TOPPING. Two or three strands of green sword peacock herl.

CHEEKS. Jungle cock.

HEAD. Black varnish.

Colonel Bates Streamer

TAIL. Red duck shoulder feather.

BODY. Flat silver tinsel.

THROAT. Dark brown saddle hackle.

WING. Two yellow saddle hackles, with slightly shorter white saddle hackle each side.

SHOULDERS. Grey teal breast feathers.

CHEEKS. Jungle cock.

HEAD. Red varnish.

Dick's Killer Bucktail

TAG. Flat gold tinsel.

TAIL. Golden pheasant tippet rather long.

BODY. Peacock herl.

WING. Yellow bucktail.

TOPPING. A few strands from a wooduck or mandarin duck breast feather.

SHOULDERS. Red turkey feathers.

CHEEKS. Jungle cock.

HEAD. Black varnish.

Dr. Burke Streamer

TAIL. Sword peacock fibres.

BODY. Medium flat silver tinsel.

RIB. Oval silver tinsel.

THROAT. Yellow cock hackle.

WING. Four white saddle hackles.

CHEEKS. Jungle cock.

HEAD. Black varnish.

Edson Light Tiger Bucktail

TAG. Narrow flat gold tinsel.

TAIL. Barred wooduck or mandarin duck feather.

BODY. Bronze peacock herl, wound fairly thick.

WING. Yellow bucktail.

TOPPING. Tips of two small red neck hackles, two thirds as long as wing.

CHEEKS. Jungle cock, short.

HEAD. Black varnish.

Fraser Streamer

BUTT. Two turns of dull orange chenille.

BODY. Bright green wool, thick.

RIB. Fine oval tinsel, silver.

WING. Four white neck hackles.

SHOULDERS. Short yellow neck hackle, extending two-thirds the length of wing.

CHEEKS. Jungle cock.

HEAD. Black varnish.

Mansfield Bucktail

TAIL. Golden pheasant tippet.
BODY. Black silk, dressed full.
RIB. Flat silver tinsel.
WINGS. White bucktail over which orange bucktail, same size.
CHEEKS. Jungle cock.
HEAD. Black varnish.

Muddler Minnow

TAIL. Fibres from an "oak" turkey wing quill.
BODY. Flat gold tinsel.
WINGS. Black, or white and black mixed impala hair. (Bucktail as a substitute.) With two strips from an "oak" turkey wing quill each side, both hair and wing fibres to reach to end of tail.
HACKLE. Bunch of deer body hair spun round hook, and sloping backwards.
HEAD. Butts of deer body hair cut to shape.

Montreal Streamer

TAIL. Narrow strip red duck wing feather.
BODY. Flat silver tinsel.
RIB. Oval silver tinsel.
THROAT. Magenta cock hackle.
WING. Four magenta saddle hackles.
SHOULDERS. Brown turkey tail feathers, medium width, one third as long as the wing.
HEAD. Black varnish.

Moose River Streamer

BODY. Flat silver tinsel.
WING. White bucktail, over which four golden badger neck hackles.
TOPPING. Peacock herl.
SHOULDERS. Golden pheasant tippet, one third as long as the wing.
HEAD. Black varnish.

Red Phantom Streamer

TAIL. Red hackle fibres.
BODY. Bright red wool.

RIB. Flat silver tinsel.
WINGS. White marabou feathers.
HEAD. Black head with white eye.

Sanborn Streamer

TAG. Flat gold tinsel.
BODY. Black silk, wound thick.
RIB. Flat gold tinsel.
THROAT. Bright yellow cock hackle.
WING. Bright yellow neck hackles.
CHEEKS. Jungle cock.
HEAD. Black varnish.

Sanders Streamer

BODY. Flat silver tinsel.
WINGS. White bucktail, over which four grizzly saddle hackles.
CHEEKS. Jungle cock.
HEAD. Black varnish.

Greyhound Streamer

TAG. Narrow flat silver tinsel.
TAIL. Red hackle fibres.
BODY. Red silk, thinly dressed.
RIB. Flat silver tinsel.
THROAT. Peacock herl, under which white bucktail, and under this red dock hackle.
WING. Four grey saddle hackles.
SHOULDERS. Jungle cock extending one-third the length of wing.
CHEEKS. Jungle cock short.
HEAD. Black varnish.

Green Drake Streamer

TAG. Flat gold tinsel.
TAIL. Black hackle fibres.
BUTT. Peacock herl.
BODY. Yellowish brown silk.
RIB. Black silk.
THROAT. Light brown cock hackle.
WING. Two olive green saddle hackles, outside of which are two medium brown saddle hackles, one on each side.
CHEEKS. Jungle cock, long.
HEAD. Black varnish.

Jane Craig Streamer

BODY. Flat silver tinsel.

THROAT. White cock hackle.

WING. Six white saddle hackles.

TOPPING. Bright green peacock herl.

CHEEKS. Jungle cock.

HEAD. Black varnish.

Brown Ghost Streamer

TAG. Flat silver tinsel.

BODY. Dark brown silk.

RIB. Narrow flat silver tinsel.

THROAT. Four or five strands peacock herl under which small bunch white bucktail, slightly longer than hook, beneath which golden pheasant crest feather curving upwards.

WING. Golden pheasant crest feather with four medium brown saddle hackles over.

SHOULDER. Teal body feather, dyed brown.

CHEEKS. Jungle cock.

HEAD. Black varnish.

Silver Minnow Bucktail

BODY. Medium flat silver tinsel, over fine wire.

RIB. Oval silver tinsel.

THROAT. Red cock hackle.

WING. White bucktail over grey squirrel tail hair.

TOPPING. Peacock herl.

HEAD. Red varnish.

Wesley Special Bucktail

TAIL. Golden pheasant tippet.

BODY. Flat silver tinsel.

RIB. Oval silver tinsel.

THROAT. Black cock hackle.

WING. White bucktail, over which blue-grey bucktail.

CHEEKS. Jungle cock.

HEAD. Black varnish.

Yellow Peril Streamer

BODY. Flat gold tinsel.

RIB. Oval gold tinsel.

THROAT. Yellow cock hackle.

WINGS. One red saddle hackle, between two grizzle saddle hackles.

CHEEKS. Jungle cock.

HEAD. Black varnish.

Brown Bomber Streamer

TAIL. Yellow hackle fibres.

BODY. Dark orange wool.

RIB. Narrow gold oval tinsel.

THROAT. Yellow bucktail.

HACKLE. Yellow cock.

WINGS. Four medium brown saddle hackles.

SHOULDERS. Yellow goose shoulder.

HEAD. Black varnish.

Binns Streamer

TAIL. A section of red and white goose shoulder feathers.

BODY. Medium flat silver tinsel.

RIB. Oval silver tinsel.

THROAT. Red and white saddle hackles, tied as a collar.

WINGS. Two matched pairs, section of white goose married between two sections of yellow goose, all equal widths.

SHOULDERS. Gallena hen breast.

HEAD. Black varnish.

Black Lure. (British). Sometimes referred to as "Black Leech".

HOOK. Long shank, or two or three short shanked in tandem.

BODY. Black seal fur, wool or floss.

RIB. Flat or oval silver tinsel.

WINGS. Two black cock or hen hackles. The hen hackles will give a broad wing, the cock hackles a slim one.

CHAPTER FOURTEEN

FLIES FOR SEA FISHING

FLY FISHING FOR SALT-WATER FISH is becoming increasingly popular amongst sportsmen, but it has been a well-known method to professional fishermen for many years.

In America flies have been used for more than 80 years, and in Ireland, on the coast of Donegal, they have been in use even longer.

The mere fact that flies are used by those more interested in the food or monetary value of the fish than in its sporting qualities, proves the efficiency of this method of fishing.

When tying flies for sea fishing, it must be borne in mind that the whole object is to imitate some form of marine life that will be acceptable to the fish. The flies used by the Donegal fishermen are tied to represent herring fry and consist solely of long white hairs whipped to a hook. White goat hair is the most popular, but fibres from a white goose feather can also be used. Pollack and coal fish are taken on this particular fly, and, of course, mackerel, which will take any lure.

In one instance an angler off Yarmouth, Isle of Wight, using a feathered trace with nine hooks, hauled it in to find a mackerel on each hook.

Another fisherman, using feathered mackerel lures offshore, landed a 22 lb. tope. One lure was in the fish's nose and another was fixed in the back of its head.

With such instances as these on record, it is difficult to understand why this method of fishing for mackerel is not more popular.

The streamer fly, which is discussed on page 148, is only a more elaborate variation of this fly, but its elaborations are necessary for the wide range of fish and waters for which it is used.

The salt water flies are usually very simple in construction, and those fly-tyers who are within reach of good sea fishing can turn to good account the experience they have gained tying their own trout or salmon flies.

The bodies are made of silver or gilt tinsel, or of bright silk or silk chenilles ribbed with tinsel. Owing to the length of wing, tails are mostly unnecessary.

The wing materials that can be used are numerous and, in addition to the hair already mentioned, the following items can be utilised. Long neck and saddle hackles of domestic fowl in natural shades or dyed bright colours, yellow, red and white being the most popular. Bear fur, bucktail, both natural and dyed, and goose feathers used as when tying salmon flies, or with just the tip making a large wing.

In most cases hackles on the body or throat are not necessary, but can be useful if contrasts of colouring are required, i.e., white wing/red hackle, red wing/white hackle, etc.

Many patterns are made attractive by building up the heads with several coats of "Cellire" varnish and painting on an eye.

I have given illustrations of five different types of fly and also five additional dressings. Three are illustrated on the frontispiece.

PATTERNS ILLUSTRATED, PAGE 156

(a) **Hook.** Long shank.
    Wing. White bucktail.
    Head. Red varnish.

(b) **Hook.** Long shank.
    Wings. Five or six long grizzle neck or saddle hackles.
    Hackle. Scarlet cock.
    Head. Black varnish with white "eye".

(c) **Hook.** Long shank.
    Tail. Red and white goose feathers.
    Body. Embossed silver tinsel.
    Wing. Marabou plumes, white.
    Cheeks. Red hackle tips and jungle cock.
    Head. Black varnish.

(d) **Hook.** Long shank.
    Body. Red chenille ribbed broad silver tinsel.
    Wing. Strips of a white goose quill feather, back to back.
    Head. Black varnish.

(e) **Hook.** Long shank.
    Body. Flat silver tinsel or red or white chenille.
    Wing. Tips of two red or white goose stiff shoulder feathers, back to back.
    Head. Black varnish, with yellow "eye".

ADDITIONAL PATTERNS

The following dressings may be useful, although with the considerable materials available the combinations at the disposal of the fly dresser are legion:

    Hook. Long shank.
    Wings. Five or six long white and long crimson hackles.
    Hackle. Mixed—red and white cock.
    Head. White chenille.

    Hook. Long shank.
    Body. White chenille.
    Hackle. Red cock.

Wings. Five or six white saddle hackles.
Head.   White varnish with black "eye".

Hook.   Long shank.
Hackle. White cock.
Wings. Five or six long white and long blue neck hackles.
Head.   Black varnish.

Hook.   Long shank.
Hackle. A few strands of red bucktail tied underneath hook.
Wings. White bucktail with a strip of blue goose either side.
Head.   Black varnish with red "eye".

Hook.   Long shank.
Hackle. Large Black cock.
Wings. Red cock hackle projecting well beyond bend.
Head.   Black varnish with white "eye".

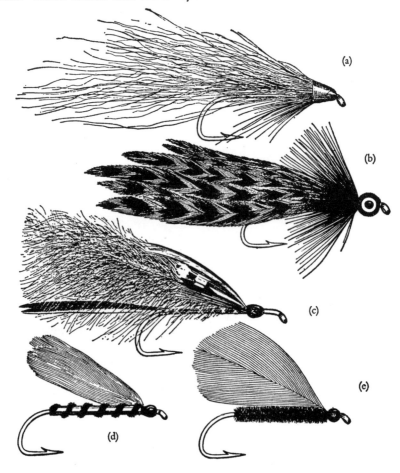

WHISKERBUGS

Mr. A. Dalberg, of Stockholm, who very kindly sent me samples of these flies, adapted them from American patterns. The American originals were dressed with hair, but Mr. Dalberg has used very long-fibred hackles for his patterns.

They are used for fishing from rocks, and fished on or just below the surface of the water. A spinner similar to that shown on page 159 can be used with advantage.

The bodies of the flies all have thick chenille (*see* page 30) bodies, the chenille being left exposed at the tail and also sometimes at the head.

The hackles are all wound very closely "Palmer" fashion, and then all the top fibres are trimmed off close to the body. Some of the side fibres are also removed so that all the remaining ones point downwards. The result is a "shrimpy" type of fly, with a long "beard" running the length of the body. This rather unique method of dressing the flies, causes them to swim in the upside-down position as shown in the illustration. This characteristic is even further developed by the "balancer" shown, and by building up the head. The "balancer" is loose fitting on its wire attachment so that it imparts flash when moving through the water. They can be dressed on either single or double salmon hooks and can vary in size from 7/0 to No. 8.

Mr. Dalberg is a very well-known fisherman in Sweden, as well as being a progressive fly-dresser, and has often appeared successfully at the International Bait Casting tournaments held in this country. Three of his "Whiskerbug" dressings are given below—

No. 1.

Body: Yellow chenille, shown at head, and red chenille at tail end.

Hackles: Alternate natural red and dyed yellow hackles—very long in fibre, cut along top and sides.

No. 2.

Body: Yellow chenille, shown at tail end only.

Hackles: One blue one at head, remainder black—very long in fibre and cut along top and sides.

No. 3.

Body: Orange chenille, shown at tail and head.

Hackle: Natural red, very long in fibre and cut along top and sides.

CHAPTER FIFTEEN

FLIES FOR PIKE AND PERCH FISHING

IT IS INTERESTING to note that the largest British rod caught pike was taken on a fly. It was the fabulous pike of Loch Ken, taken in the latter part of the eighteenth century by John Murray, gamekeeper to Lord Kenmure. Although its exact weight is not known, measurements of its skull by the late Dr. C. Tate Regan, a famous authority on fish, resulted in an estimated weight of 70 lb. or more.

The fly used was, of course, an outsize specimen, using the whole of a peacock's "eye" feather for the wing.

For some unknown reason, little experimental work has been carried out in this sphere of fly fishing, although one very modern method, passed on to me by an American friend, utilizes flies tied on straight-eyed hooks in conjunction with a small spinner as per the illustration below. By using a light threadline outfit I have had some fine sport with large perch and good sized pike in the 3–4 lb. range, and have found variations of the streamer and hair-winged flies described on pages 140 and 148 to be the best killers.

These experiences took place in the late fifties and early sixties, but just before going to press for this edition of the "Guide" two results of what can be achieved by fly fishing were brought to my notice, one accidental and the other deliberate.

The first was the experience of 15-year-old Peter Harris, son of a member of Veniard's staff, who, whilst fishing a large reservoir in the Midlands, hooked and landed a 9 lb. pike on a "Black & Silver" streamer type lure. That he was fishing for trout at the time does not detract from the achievement of landing a fish of these proportions, and emphasizes the possibilities of what could be achieved by more deliberate fly-fishing in waters where this method has hitherto been neglected.

The other story which deals with deliberate fly fishing for pike was described in an article by Peter Wheat in the May 1970 edition of *Angling* magazine. He landed

two fish using orthodox reservoir fly fishing tackle, a 5-in. deer hair and feather streamer with a built-in monofil tippet of 30 lb. (for protection against the pike's teeth), attached by a whipped eye to a cast tapering down from 40 lb. through to 10 lb. at the tip. The first fish weighed $17\frac{1}{2}$ lb. and the second $20\frac{1}{4}$ lb.

His general observations were that using ordinary reservoir gear and lures it was a first class sporting method of catching jack pike.

Secondly, that if the method was used when pike were fry-feeding it could result in specimen fish, using ordinary sized lures with extra strong tippets as mentioned earlier.

Thirdly, as a general-purpose method, combining big lures with spinning tackle as I have described earlier in this chapter, feather-lure fishing for pike could be a welcome development and addition to our angling interest.

CHAPTER SIXTEEN

FLIES FOR GRAYLING FISHING

THE FOLLOWING DRESSINGS OF FLIES for grayling are what is known as "fancy flies". Grayling will rise very freely to them, even when there are no natural flies on the water. If, however, there is a hatch on, it will be found that they are much less successful. The fisher for grayling should therefore be well equipped with a supply of imitations of natural flies, especially the duns and midges.

The fancy flies are very simple in construction, and nearly all of them have peacock herl or peacock quill bodies. Rarely are they winged, and a tag of red wool or floss, or the tip of a red feather, is to be recommended.

If fished dry, the flies should be fairly small (oo and o), but the wet patterns should be tied as large as 2 or 3, especially for winter fishing.

During the winter months the fish stay well down, and will rarely come to the surface for a fly. It is therefore a good idea to pad the shank of the hook with lead wire before the body is wound on. Big grayling can be expected during the winter, but only if the fly is fished deep.

Grayling Witch
TAG. Red floss.
BODY. Green peacock herl, ribbed silver wire.
HACKLE. Medium blue dun cock.

Rolts Witch
TAG. Red floss.
BODY. Green peacock herl, ribbed gold wire.
HACKLE. Honey dun hen.

Silver Witch
TAG. Red floss.
BODY. Green peacock herl, ribbed silver wire.
HACKLE. Badger cock.

White Witch
TAG. Red floss.
BODY. Green peacock herl, ribbed silver wire.
HACKLE. White cock tied palmer.

Dean's Fancy
TAG. Indian crow.
BODY. Magenta peacock herl, ribbed gold wire.
HACKLE. Speckled cock.

Burton Blue
BODY. Waxed yellow silk, ribbed gold wire.
HACKLE. Medium blue dun hen.
WINGS. Waterhen breast feathers.

Green Insect
BODY. Green peacock herl.
HACKLE. Pale blue, almost white cock.

Silver Twist
BODY. Mole fur ribbed round silver tinsel.
HACKLE. Blue dun hen from shoulder to tail.

Rough Bumble
BODY. Yellow floss, ribbed peacock herl and red silk.
HACKLE. Medium blue dun hen tied palmer.

Ruby Bumble
BODY. Claret floss ribbed peacock herl from eye.
HACKLE. Pale blue dun hen tied palmer.

Burton Gold Spinner
BODY. Waxed yellow silk, ribbed fine gold wire.
WINGS. Starling wing.
HACKLE. Ginger hen.

Brunton's Fancy
TAG. Indian crow.
BODY. Gold twist at tail end, remainder green peacock herl.
HACKLE. Badger cock.

Roger's Fancy
BODY. Blue heron herl, ribbed fine silver wire, red floss tag at head and tail.
HACKLE. Pale blue hen.

Silver Dun
BODY. Silver tinsel, with or without a red tag.
HACKLE. Blue dun hen.
WINGS. Starling wing.

Little Chap
BODY. Brown peacock herl from eye of feather.
HACKLE. Medium dun cock.

Jackie's Fancy
TAG. Red floss, tip of round tinsel silver under tag.
BODY. Peacock herl.
HACKLE. Yellowish white cock.

Kill Devil Spider
BODY. Peacock herl, tipped gold or silver round tinsel.
HACKLE. Bright medium blue cock, long in fibre.

CHAPTER SEVENTEEN

FLY FISHING FOR CHUB, DACE, ROACH AND RUDD

DRY FLY-FISHING FOR CHUB, roach and dace is becoming more popular every year and, except for chub, this method of catching these fish has been too long ignored.

There must be many coarse fishermen who have spent endless hours watching a useless float, while fish have been rising all round them. By a little variation in tackle, many a blank day can be turned into a memorable one. This is especially the case when the weather is very warm and the fish will only take baits in the early morning or late at night.

It is during the warm weather that dace and roach rise readily to the dry fly, and the fly-taking qualities of chub are too well known to require comment here.

There are also many trout streams that contain coarse fish, and although the latter do not fight so well as trout, a sizeable fish can give good sport on light tackle.

Roach and dace are not usually so particular as trout when it comes to choice of fly, although this applies in a lesser degree to dace. Size of fly, however, is more important and, for general purposes, numbers 15 (o) or 16 (oo) with a slight sneck are the most useful.

Chub flies can be tied on larger hooks, but should not exceed size 12 (3). The huge hackled monstrosities that one can purchase in the shops are quite unnecessary.

The fly and the line should be made to float well, care being taken to avoid preparations that leave a greasy film on the water.

It is not necessary for the angler to encumber himself with a multitude of dry-fly patterns, and the following list should fill all his requirements—

Wickham's Fancy.	Coachman.	Black Gnat.	Red Tag.
Brown Palmer.	Red Palmer.	Olive Quill.	Alder.

The dressings of these patterns are given elsewhere in this book in the section of Dry Fly Dressings. They are also listed in the index at the back for easy reference.

CHAPTER EIGHTEEN

MATERIALS—SALMON FLIES

A GENERAL SURVEY

THE RANGE OF MATERIALS REQUIRED by the salmon fly-tyer is fairly extensive, but once a good collection has been built up, it will be found that many items can be used for quite a number of flies.

This applies particularly to the materials used for bodies and wings, such as floss silks, tinsel, and the various feathers from which the "mixed" type of wings are built up. Some items, of course, can only be used once, such as single golden pheasant crest feathers that form the toppings and tails, and feathers which go to form sides and cheeks such as jungle cock, blue chatterer and Indian crow, etc.

It will also be found that a collection of wing materials will cover several different patterns, a factor which does much to offset the original outlay.

The tools and accessories are the same as those used by the trout fly-tyer. These can be classified as follows—

Vice—The five types shown on pages 20, 21 and 22 are all suitable for salmon fly-tying, as they have a good grip and are capable of taking very large hooks. The one on page 21 is particularly useful, as it was specially designed for the salmon fly-tyer.

Hooks—The range of salmon fly hooks is quite limited, and the four types shown on pages 21 and 27 should cover the most exacting requirements. All of them can be otained as "doubles" if they are required, except the "Wilson" hooks.

Other items required are hackle pliers (two pairs will be found an asset), a dubbing needle, and tweezers. These are described and illustrated on pages 17 and 18. Two useful additions to one's kit are the bobbin holder and whip finishing tool, described and illustrated on pages 18 and 19.

Tying Silks—Pearsall's "Naples" tying silk is invariably used for tying salmon flies, although "Gossamer" is better for the lightly dressed "Lower Water" type of fly. For a complete list of colours, *see* chapter III, page 29.

It is a good idea for the beginner to obtain materials for, say, two patterns of the flies he wishes to tie, and then build up as his experience increases.

The following list contains the materials that would be required for the patterns "Silver Doctor" and "Dusty Miller". Quantities would, of course, vary for the number of flies to be tied, but, as previously stated, it will be seen that many items used in one pattern are also used in the other. The dressings of these flies will be found on pages 212 and 216.

Silver Doctor—The items duplicated in the "Dusty Miller" are marked ★—

1. Round silver tinsel for the tag.★
2. Yellow floss, also for the tag.★
3. Small golden pheasant crest feather for the tail.★
4. Blue chatterer (or kingfisher) feather for the tail.
5. Scarlet wool for the butt.
6. Flat silver tinsel for the body.
7. Oval silver tinsel for the ribs.★
8. Pale blue hackles.
9. Widgeon feathers for the throat hackle.
10. Feathers for the wings as follows—

    Golden pheasant tippets.
    Scarlet★, blue, yellow★, swan or goose.
    Florican bustard.★
    Speckled bustard (or turkey substitute).
    Peacock wing feathers (or turkey substitute).
    Light mottled (grey) turkey tail.
    Teal flank feathers.★
    Barred summer duck or barred mandarin duck.★
    Brown mallard feathers.★

11. Golden pheasant crest feather for the topping.★
12. Scarlet wool or scarlet varnish for the head.

Dusty Miller—Items duplicated in the "Silver Doctor" have been omitted—

13. Indian crow feather for the tail.
14. Black ostrich herl for the butt.
15. Embossed silver tinsel for the body.
16. Orange floss silk for the body.
17. Golden olive hackles.
18. Speckled guinea fowl for throat hackles.
19. Feathers for wings as follows—

    Black/white-tipped turkey tails.
    Orange swan or goose.
    Golden pheasant tails.
    Pintail flank feathers.

20. Jungle cock feathers for the sides.
21. Black varnish for the head.

Horns of blue/yellow macaw tail fibres are sometimes added to the above, but, owing to the scarcity of these feathers, most patterns now omit them.

The illustrations in colour, facing page 170, will give the beginner an idea of what some of the materials look like, and the Index of Feathers on pages 173 and 174, together with the notes on their uses, will assist him in selecting his requirements for the particular patterns he wishes to tie.

An illustration of a salmon fly, showing its component parts, is given below. This should be regarded more as a "blue print" than an actual picture of what a fly should look like. Details of size and form in respect of salmon flies, is given on page 187.

To give some semblance of order to the long list of materials that go to make up the various patterns of salmon flies, I think it would be a good idea to tabulate them under the part of the fly for which they are used.

To simplify matters even further, the tabulations will follow the order in which the parts are tied in. Therefore, as the tying in of the tag is always the first operation when tying a fly, it will be the first item on our list.

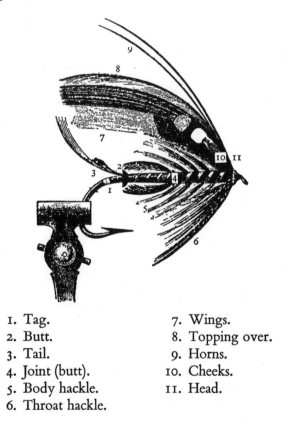

1. Tag.	7. Wings.
2. Butt.	8. Topping over.
3. Tail.	9. Horns.
4. Joint (butt).	10. Cheeks.
5. Body hackle.	11. Head.
6. Throat hackle.	

(*a*) T A G—This is invariably of round tinsel, followed by floss silk. Most patterns have tags of this kind, although some consist of silk or tinsel only. For the lightly dressed Low Water patterns plain drawn wire can be used.

A complete list of tinsels and their descriptions will be found in Chapter IV, page 33, and descriptions of the two kinds of floss silks used, together with a list of colours, will be found in Chapter III, pages 29 and 30.

(*b*) T A I L—The tails of practically all salmon flies are composed of a single golden pheasant crest feather. This is because of its natural shape and its golden yellow translucence which is an important factor in the attractiveness of the fly (illustrated, facing page 170). The words "golden pheasant crest" are usually abbreviated to "topping" in the dressings.

Other items are sometimes added to the golden pheasant crests. Those being most used are: Strands of golden pheasant tipped neck feathers, Indian crow breast feathers, red ibis, dyed swan or goose, barred teal flank, summer duck, toucan, cock o' the rock, and small jungle cock feathers.

(*c*) B U T T—This is invariably formed of a single herl from a black ostrich plume. Other colours of the same material are sometimes used and, in one or two instances, coloured wools are employed.

(*d*) B O D Y—There are three main items used for the bodies of salmon flies, and these are—

    1. Floss silk (*see* Chapter III, pages 29 and 30).
    2. Flat or embossed tinsel (*see* Chapter IV, page 33).
    3. Seal's fur.

Seal's fur is almost always used on patterns which call for fur bodies. In its natural state it is a light cream colour, and it is very easily dyed. The colours most used are black, bright orange, yellow, claret, green, golden olive, fiery brown, scarlet, purple and blue. When dyed silver grey it can be used as a substitute for silver monkey fur, which is very difficult to obtain.

About the only other fur used is that taken from the hare's poll.

Other body materials sometimes called for are silk chenille, mohair, wool, and peacock herls from the eye tail feathers.

(*e*) R I B—Oval tinsel is the most used for this item, although flat and twist tinsels are sometimes used on the larger sizes of some patterns. *See* page 33.

(*f*) B O D Y H A C K L E S—The finely fibred hackles of common poultry are generally used for body hackles, and more dyed shades are used than natural. For a list of the different kinds of natural hackles and their description. *See* page 38.

There is very little difficulty in obtaining hackles for salmon flies, owing to the fact that there are plenty of the larger sizes left after the smaller sizes have been extracted for trout fly-tying. This even applies to the rarer kinds such as badger, furnace (red/black), and grizzle.

Other feathers used for body hackles are heron (grey and black) for spey and dee strip wing flies, and the fluffy feathers from the thigh of the golden eagle, which are also used for some patterns of dee strip wing flies. The golden eagle hackles are very difficult to obtain, but a very good substitute is found in turkey marabou plumes dyed the required shades.

The scale given below will give the tyer some idea of the size of poultry hackles to be used on the different sizes of hooks. They are only approximate sizes of course, as the size of the hackle to be used is regulated not by its length, but by the length of the fibres on it.

Hook Numbers					Hackle Sizes (in.)
5	.	.	.	.	2
4	.	.	.	.	$2\frac{1}{4}$
3	.	.	.	.	$2\frac{1}{2}$
2	.	.	.	.	$2\frac{3}{4}$
1	.	.	.	.	3
$1\frac{1}{2}$	.	.	.	.	$3\frac{1}{4}$
1/0	.	.	.	.	$3\frac{1}{2}$
2/0	.	.	.	.	$3\frac{3}{4}$
3/0	.	.	.	.	4
4/0	.	.	.	.	$4\frac{1}{4}$
5/0	.	.	.	.	$4\frac{1}{2}$
6/0	.	.	.	.	5
7/0	.	.	.	.	$5\frac{1}{2}$
8/0	.	.	.	.	6

(g) THROAT HACKLE—The feathers used for throat hackles are usually much coarser fibred than those used for body hackles, although one or two patterns call for poultry hackles. The "Durham Ranger" is one of these patterns and calls for a light blue cock's hackle for the throat.

The coarse fibred hackles most in general use are—

Guinea fowl (gallena) spotted throat, breast and flank feathers.
Partridge brown back and grey breast feathers.
Grouse breast and rump.
Woodcock back and rump.
Teal breast feathers.
Widgeon neck feathers.
Golden pheasant red breast and yellow back feathers.
Jay, blue lesser wing coverts.

(*h*) WINGS—This is the most varied section of the salmon fly-tyers' materials, owing to the fact that some flies of the "mixed" or "built" wing type often require strips from half a dozen or more different feathers. The strips are very narrow, of course, varying in thickness from one to three fibres according to the size of fly being tied. This means, therefore, that strips for quite a large number of flies can be taken from each feather, and this does much to offset the original outlay on this part of one's collection.

Golden Pheasant Tippet Neck Feathers (illustrated, facing page 170)— These are orange with two black bars, and form the base of several salmon fly wings. They cannot be "married" with fibres from other feathers so tippet fibres are tied in before the rest of the wing.

Whole feathers of tippet are used back to back for the wings of such patterns as the "Durham Ranger" and "Orange Parson". These flies are illustrated, facing pages 212 and 236 respectively.

Golden Pheasant Crest Feathers (illustrated, facing page 170)—Although the main functions of these feathers is to form the tails and toppings of many patterns, there are one or two flies that have wings composed entirely of these feathers. They are a bright, translucent golden yellow. Regardless of the use to which they are put, golden pheasant crest feathers are usually referred to as "toppings", especially in the dressings.

Golden Pheasant Tail Feathers (illustrated, facing page 170)—These are black/brown mottled centre tail feathers, and their fibres "marry" well with fibres from other feathers.

They have to be purchased in pairs as there is no true centre tail on the golden pheasant. This means that the fibres on one side of each tail feather are shorter than those on the other side of the quill. The three feathers illustrated in Fig. 114 show the basic difference between a centre tail and two side tails.

Swan and Goose Shoulder Feathers (illustrated, facing page 170)—These can be obtained either white or dyed, the most usual colours being red, blue, yellow, green and orange. They are used in all mixed or built wing patterns.

The goose feathers are easier to obtain than the swan, but for the larger patterns the fly-tyer should always endeavour to get swan.

Amherst Pheasant Tail Feathers (illustrated, facing page 170)—There are not many British patterns that call for these feathers, but they are popular in Canada, Iceland and Norway. They are similar in shape to golden pheasant tails, but are larger and have black and silver markings instead of black and brown.

Speckled Bustard Wing Quills—These feathers are required for many patterns but, unfortunately, supplies are very limited. The grey speckled and oak brown speckled feathers from the wing of the turkey make excellent substitutes.

WHITE TIP DARK TURKEY TAIL

Base of wings of "Jock Scott" and "Red Sandy". Is also used in some of the larger patterns of trout flies requiring a white-tipped wing.

FLORICAN BUSTARD QUILL

Found in the wings of most "mixed wing" salmon flies, such as "Jock Scott", "Dusty Miller", etc.

GREY MOTTLED TURKEY TAIL

Wings of "Grey Eagle" and also an excellent substitute for peacock wing quill for "Black Dose", "Black Doctor", etc.

OAK SPECKLED TURKEY QUILL

Used as a substitute for speckled bustard, which is also found in the wings of most "mixed wing" salmon flies.

CINNAMON BROWN TURKEY TAIL

Wings of Dee strip-wing flies, "Akroyd", "Jock o' Dee", etc.

LIGHT SPECKLED TURKEY QUILL

Used in the smaller patterns of flies requiring grey mottled turkey tail.

BROWN MOTTLED TURKEY TAIL

Wings of the "Blue Charm", "Jimmie", "Dunkeld", "Helmsdale Doctor", "Mar Lodge", etc.

SWAN SHOULDER

Used in nearly all "mixed wing" salmon flies, dyed yellow, red, blue, green, orange, etc. Goose shoulders are used similarly.

AMHERST PHEASANT TAIL

Wings of "Lady Amherst" and Canadian patterns, etc.

GUINEA FOWL TAIL

Wings of "Sir Richard", "Butcher", etc.

GOLDEN PHEASANT TAIL

Wings of "Jock Scott", "Dusty Miller", "Torrish", etc. Found in the dressings of nearly all "mixed wing" salmon flies.

MACAW TAIL

Horns of salmon flies.

BROWN MALLARD

Wings of "Thunder and Lightning", "Fiery Brown", "Silver Grey", "Jennie", etc.

TEAL DUCK FLANK

Wings of "Blue Charm", "Black Doctor", "Green Highlander" "Jock Scott", "Silver Blue". Throat hackle of "Akroyd", etc.

JUNGLE COCK

Sides of salmon flies. Sometimes used in tails also (Mar Lodge), and veiling in "Jungle Hornet", etc.

GOLDEN PHEASANT CREST (TOPPING)

Found in nearly all salmon flies as a tail or "topping".

GOLDEN PHEASANT TIPPET

Tails of salmon flies and as whole feathers or strips in many wings. Whole in "Durham Ranger", "Popham", etc. Strips in "Silver Grey", etc. Hackle of "Tippet Grub".

The illustrations (facing page 170) are full size sections of the original feathers.

Florican Bustard Wing Quills (illustrated, facing page 170)—This is a "tiger-striped" quill, the stripes being of black and buff.

Guinea Fowl Wing and Tail Feathers (illustrated, facing page 170)—These are dark grey feathers with white spots. They are used in one or two patterns, but, owing to the shortness of their fibres, they cannot be used on very large hooks.

Hen Pheasant Tail Feathers (illustrated, facing page 170)—These are not used very often, one of the few patterns being the "March Brown". This is illustrated as a Low Water pattern, facing page 212. They are true centre tails, which means that pairs of wings can be made from single feathers.

Turkey Wing and Tail Feathers (illustrated, facing page 170)—The turkey supplies us with many feathers for salmon flies, the most useful being the tails, of which there are a large variety, namely—

Dark with white tip, for "Jock Scott" and "Dusty Miller", etc.
Grey mottled. "Silver Doctor" and "Yellow Eagle", etc.
Plain cinnamon brown. "Akroyd", etc.
Brown mottled. "Blue Charm", etc.
White and dyed. These are used as a substitute for swan, especially on very large patterns.

Grey Mallard Drake (Wild Duck) Flank Feathers—These are light grey feathers with slightly darker grey bars. They are sometimes used as a substitute for pintail flank feathers (illustrated, facing page 50).

Brown Mallard Drake Shoulder Feathers (illustrated, facing page 170)—These are brown speckled feathers, the fibres varying in colour from deep brown at the tips to grey at the roots. They are used on nearly all standard patterns, forming the roof of the wing before the topping is put on. Some patterns have wings that consist solely of two strips of these feathers, a well-known one being the "Thunder and Lightning" illustrated, facing page 188.

Barred Mandarin Duck and Barred Summer Duck Flank Feathers—These are buff speckled feathers with heavy black and white bars at their tips. They are incorporated in the wings of many patterns, and sometimes used as sides.

Peacock Wing Quills—There are several patterns that call for these feathers, but, owing to their scarcity, buff mottled turkey tails are used as a substitute.

Pintail Flank Feathers—These feathers have heavy black stripes on a pale grey background.

Teal Duck Flank Feathers (illustrated, facing page 170)—These have heavy black bars on a white background. They are also used as hackles, the "Akroyd" being one pattern that makes use of them for this purpose.

Widgeon Shoulder Feathers—Similar to the teal feathers but more finely marked. They are not quite so long in the fibre so are more suitable for small

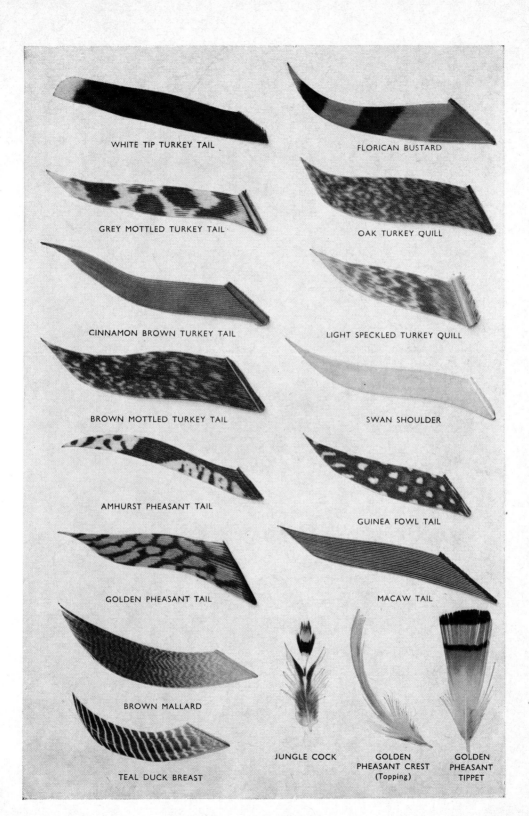

WHITE TIP TURKEY TAIL

FLORICAN BUSTARD

GREY MOTTLED TURKEY TAIL

OAK TURKEY QUILL

CINNAMON BROWN TURKEY TAIL

LIGHT SPECKLED TURKEY QUILL

BROWN MOTTLED TURKEY TAIL

SWAN SHOULDER

AMHURST PHEASANT TAIL

GUINEA FOWL TAIL

GOLDEN PHEASANT TAIL

MACAW TAIL

BROWN MALLARD

JUNGLE COCK

GOLDEN PHEASANT CREST (Topping)

GOLDEN PHEASANT TIPPET

TEAL DUCK BREAST

FEATHERS FOR SALMON FLIES

patterns, especially of the Low Water type such as the "Silver Blue" (illustrated, facing page 236).

Peacock "Sword" Tail Feathers (illustrated, page 45)—The herls from these tails are used in some wings, the "Jock Scott" requiring two or three. The "Alexandra" has wings that consist entirely of these herls.

Peacock "Eye" Tail Feathers (illustrated, page 45)—The herls from the "eye" part of these tails are used, the "Beauly Snow Fly" being the most well-known pattern that uses them. The herls from the lower part of the feather are often used for bodies.

(*i*) SIDES—Some of the feathers used for wings are also required as sides in some patterns. These are the pintail, teal, widgeon and barred mandarin duck or summer duck. Not many more are required, and the following list should cover all general requirements—

Blue chatterer (or blue kingfisher as a substitute).
Indian (red) crow feathers.
Toucan breast feathers.
Jungle cock feathers (illustrated, facing page 170).
Cock o' the rock feathers.

(*j*) CHEEKS—Smaller sizes of the above feathers are used as cheeks, the most used being the blue chatterer and Indian crow.

(*k*) TOPPING—With very few exceptions this is always a golden pheasant crest feather, two exceptions being amherst pheasant crests and peacock "sword" herls. The function of the topping is not only to add to the attractiveness of the fly, but also to keep the wing in good shape. They are difficult feathers to tie in, and details of the best methods of handling them will be found on page 185 (illustrated, facing page 170).

(*l*) HORNS—It is a modern tendency to omit these from the dressings, but if they are used they are obtained from the tail feathers of the macaw. These feathers are usually blue on the outer face and either red or yellow underneath. They are difficult to obtain, which is the main reason for their not being used very much (illustrated, facing page 170).

(*m*) HEAD—The heads of nearly all salmon flies are finished off with black varnish, red being about the only other colour used. Some patterns call for wool or peacock herl heads, but their number is very small.

(*n*) VARNISHES AND WAXES—In addition to the varnishes required for heads, a thin clear celluloid varnish is sometimes used to strengthen the turns of tying silk during the actual tying of the fly. It is often applied to the turns of silk on which the wing is bedded down.

When silk bodies are used for salmon flies, a couple of coats of celluloid varnish will lengthen the life of the fly by fortifying it against the teeth of kelts.

This idea was suggested by Mr. A. S. Rooke, of Claremorris, County Mayo.

A good solid wax is most essential for waxing the tying silk so that the silk does not slip or unravel during the tying operations. If a fur body is called for, heavy waxing of the silk is even more important. The application of a little liquid wax to that portion of the silk on which the fur is dubbed, will simplify the forming of the dubbing body. Details of how best to do this will be found on page 53.

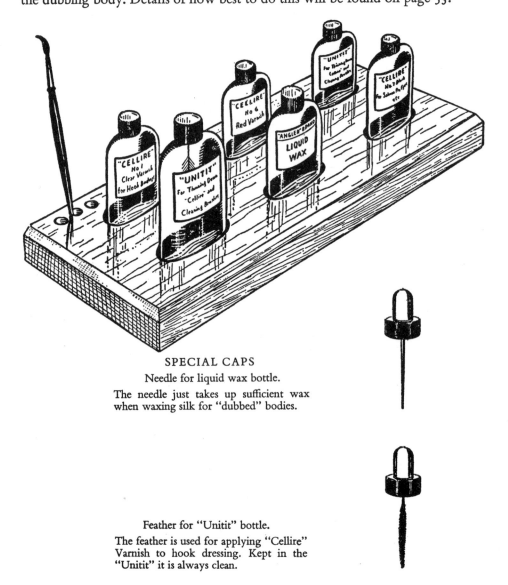

SPECIAL CAPS

Needle for liquid wax bottle.

The needle just takes up sufficient wax when waxing silk for "dubbed" bodies.

Feather for "Unitit" bottle.

The feather is used for applying "Cellire" Varnish to hook dressing. Kept in the "Unitit" it is always clean.

Varnishes, their thinners, and liquid wax are usually purchased in small two-ounce bottles, and if one of these is knocked over while it is being used the results can be disastrous. To avoid this a neat bottle stand was designed by Mr. Peter Deane, the well-known fly-tyer, and an illustration of this is given below. Special caps which can be obtained for the bottles are also illustrated.

INDEX OF FEATHERS FOR SALMON FLIES

BIRD	FEATHER	USE IN FLY-TYING
Amherst Pheasant	Tail	Wings
,, ,,	Head (topping crest and tippet collar)	Tails and wings
Bustard florican	Wing	Wings
Bustard (speckled)	Wing	Wings
Bustard, white	Shoulder	Wings
Chatterer (blue)	Breast or back	Sides and cheeks.
Cock o' the rock	Breast	Sides, tails, and veiling
Eagle	Leg	Hackles ("Yellow Eagle", etc.)
Golden Pheasant	Flank (red)	Hackles ("Brown Fairy", etc.)
,, ,,	Rump (yellow)	,,
,, ,,	Head (topping crest)	Tails and wings
,, ,,	Neck (tippet collar)	,, ,, ,,
,, ,,	Tail	Wings
Goose	Shoulder (soft)	,,
Guinea Fowl (gallena)	Breast and flank (spotted)	Throat hackles
,, ,,	Wing	Wings
,, ,,	Tail	,,
Hen Pheasant	Tail	Wings
Heron	Breast (grey)	Hackles ("Grey Heron", etc.)
,,	Crest (black)	Hackles ("Akroyd", etc.)
Ibis	Breast	Tails
Indian Crow	Breast	Tails and cheeks
Jay	Lesser coverts (blue)	Throat hackles ("Thunder and Lightning", etc.)
Jungle Cock	Neck	Sides

BIRD	FEATHER	USE IN FLY-TYING
Kingfisher (substitute for blue chatterer)	Back (blue)	Cheeks and sides
Macaw	Tail	Horns
Mallard Duck (drake)	Grey Flank (large)	Wings
,, ,, ,,	Brown Shoulder	Wings
Mandarin Duck	Flank (barred)	Wings and sides
,, ,,	Wing (brown with white tip)	Wings ("Akroyd", etc.)
Ostrich	Wing	Butts
Peacock	"Sword" tail	Wings
,,	"Eye" tail	Wings and bodies
,,	Wing	Wings
Partridge	Back (brown)	Hackle ("March Brown")
Pintail Duck	Flank	Wings
Poultry (chicken) cock	Neck hackles	Hackles
Summer Duck	Flank (barred)	Wings and sides
Swan	Shoulder (soft)	Wings
Teal Duck	Flank	Wings and sides
Toucan	Breast	Sides, tails and "Veiling"
Turkey	Quill (grey speckled)	Wings
Turkey (substitute for speckled bustard)	Quill (oak brown)	Wings
Turkey	Rumps (white tip)	Wings
Turkey	Rumps (cinnamon)	Wings
Turkey (substitute for Peacock Wing)	Tail (buff mottled)	Wings
Turkey	Tail (white tip)	Wings
Turkey	Tail (cinnamon)	Wings
Turkey	Tail (brown mottled)	Wings
Vulturine Gallena	Breast (striped)	Wings ("Elver Fly")
,, ,,	Back (blue)	Hackle ("Elver Fly")
Widgeon Duck	Shoulder	Wings, sides and hackles
,, ,,	Neck	Hackles
Wood-Duck (*See* Summer Duck)		

CHAPTER NINETEEN

DRESSING FLIES FOR SALMON FISHING

A GENERAL SURVEY

BECAUSE OF THE NUMBER OF MATERIALS that go into the forming of some salmon fly patterns, many would-be fly-tyers are deterred by the idea that the actual tying of salmon flies is difficult. In fact, some of them are much easier to tie than trout flies. They take longer, of course, which is to be expected of some patterns which can consist of two dozen or more different items, but the actual manipulation of the materials is simpler than if one were tying a small double split-wing dry fly.

In my opinion, anyone who can make a reasonable job of a trout fly, can also tie a salmon fly. I have also found, when giving instruction, that it is easier to put across the technique of salmon fly-tying than it is trout fly-tying.

I do not wish by the foregoing to imply that salmon fly-tying is any less devoid of fascination than trout fly-tying. In fact, the reverse applies. Because of the variations of colours and materials, many artistic creations can be produced, and I know many enthusiastic fly-tyers, although they are also keen fishermen, who would consider it sacrilege if some of their creations ever got wet.

A perfectly tied salmon fly, correct in every detail as to shape and colour, is without doubt a thing of beauty. It is, therefore, little wonder that salmon fly-tying has developed from its original utilitarian purpose (catching fish), to an art form in its own right.

In the following pages I can only hope to impart some of the technical details necessary for the making of the several different types of salmon flies. Standards of perfection must be left entirely to the fly-tyer himself, and I hope that the instructions I give will enable him to derive the full pleasure and satisfaction that can be obtained from this fascinating offshoot of salmon fishing.

The most complex part of practically all salmon flies is their wings, and it is because of this complexity that we have come to classify a salmon fly according to the type of wing it carries—

(a) Simple strip wings such as the "Thunder and Lightning" and "Silver Blue".
(b) Whole feather wings, as the "Durham Ranger" and "Orange Parson".
(c) Mixed wings, as the "Gordon" and "Green Highlander".
(d) Built wings, as the "Butcher" and "Silver Wilkinson".
(e) Topping wings, as the "Canary".
(f) Herl wings, as the "Beauly Snow Fly" and "Alexandra".

The above types are usually classified under one main heading of "Standard patterns". The sub-titles are self explanatory, but further elucidation may be of assistance to the beginner.

(*a*) Simple strip wings are wings that are formed of single left and right strips of feathers.

(*b*) Whole feather wings are formed of a pair of feathers tied in back to back, usually golden pheasant tippets or jungle cock feathers.

(*c*) Mixed wings are similar to simple strip wings when they are tied in, the big difference being that, instead of being whole strips from left and right feathers, each wing is built up by "marrying" together the fibres of several different feathers. It cannot be stressed too often that all the fibres for a left-hand wing must come from the left-hand side of the feathers, and the fibres for the right-hand wing from the right-hand side. Not only is this important to get the wing to set properly, but it will be found impossible to marry fibres from opposite sides.

(*d*) Built wings are made up of mixed wings superimposed on simple strip wings or whole feather wings, and are the most difficult of all to tie. The modern trend towards lightly dressed flies is reducing the popularity of this type of wing, and a pattern that calls for a built wing is often dressed as a mixed wing. This is achieved by incorporating fibres of the under wing into the mixed wing.

(*e*) Topping wings are those formed of several golden pheasant toppings.

(*f*) Herl wings are formed of either green herls from the peacock "sword" tail, or the bronze herls from the peacock "eye" tail.

Following the standard patterns we have the Low Water series. Many of these are just lightly dressed standard patterns, but there are several that are recognised to be designed specially for summer fishing. The most well-known are the "Silver Blue", "Logie", and "Blue Charm".

The next two types of fly have local origins, as their names imply. They are the "Dee Strip Wings", and "Spey" flies. Both these types have characteristic wings.

The flies used in Ireland can also usually be recognised by the type of wings they carry. In nearly every case the wing is sheathed entirely by brown mallard strips, and the topping is not always evident. Another characteristic is that nearly every pattern has fibres of golden pheasant tippets as a base to the wing.

Hair wing flies are increasing in popularity every year, not only because of the lively action of the hair in the water, but also because of the extreme durability of wings made in this fashion. The "Garry" or "Yellow Dog" as it is sometimes called, is probably the most well-known in this country, but this type of fly has been popular in America and Canada for many years. (*See* illustrations, facing page 146.)

In addition to the foregoing classifications, we have grubs, shrimps, dry flies and lures. These are illustrated in the coloured plates, facing pages 212 and 236.

Details for dressing the different types of salmon flies will be found in the sections

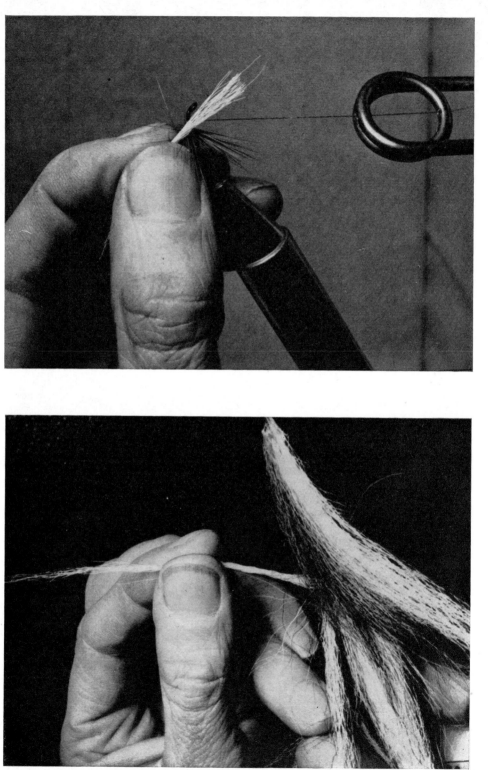

POSITION OF HAIR FIBRES BEFORE WINDING TYING SILK

SELECTING FIBRES FOR A HAIR WING

immediately following this general survey, but, before going on to these instructions, the beginner will probably find the next few pages helpful. I have extracted certain aspects of fly-tying procedure which are common to many types of flies, and which also present certain difficulties. I hope the clarification of these points, together with the instructions on tying, will enable the beginner to master the early stages with the minimum of trouble.

All hook sizes mentioned are old numbers, Redditch scale.

N.B.—The instructions on forming a dubbing body, and also tying wings on to the hook, are a repeat of the information given in the trout section of this book. I make no apology for this repetition as it is done for the convenience of the salmon fly-tyer, confining all the information he requires to one part of the book.

REVERSING SILK

At certain stages of tying salmon flies it will be found necessary to reverse the tying silk. The best way to do this is as follows—

Draw down a loop of the tying silk at the back of the hook (Fig. 103) and hold it in place with the point of the dubbing needle. The silk can now be wound in the reverse direction, and to the left, so as to bind down the ends of the loop (Fig. 104). The illustrations will no doubt be easier to understand than the written instructions.

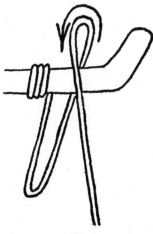

Fig. 103

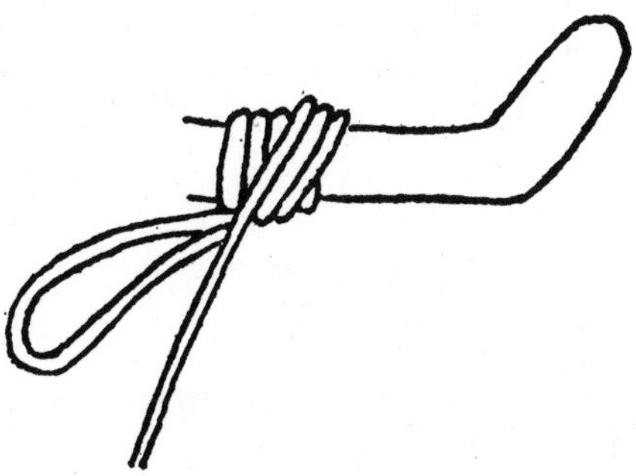

Fig. 104

HOW TO FORM A DUBBING BODY

The dressings in some of the following chapters call for fur bodies, so before we start on the actual fly-tying instructions, the procedure for spinning the fur on to the tying silk should be studied.

To wax the tying silk with solid wax, it is only necessary to draw the silk across the wax very rapidly. The friction caused by this action melts the wax immediately surrounding the silk, and it is only necessary to do this a couple of times. There should be no pause during the action, otherwise the wax sets immediately, and the silk sticks. This will either cause it to snap or strain it so that it snaps when being used during the tying.

The above should always be carried out before starting to tie a fly of any description, and will be found quite sufficient for small patterns with fur bodies. If larger flies are being tied, the addition of a little liquid wax to the silk will be found helpful.

A dubbing body consists of wool or fur spun on to the tying silk which is then wound round the shank of the hook from tail to shoulder.

The secret of successful dubbing lies in the use of very small quantities of fur, and ample waxing of the tying silk.

The procedure is as follows—

Hold the silk taut in the right hand, at a right angle to the hook shank, towards the body.

Select a minute pinch of the necessary fur and place it on the ball of the left forefinger. Bring the taut silk down on to the fur. Now lower the second finger down on to the ball of the thumb, and roll the silk and fur in a clockwise direction. This action will wrap the fur round the silk, and should be repeated with additional fur until a sufficient length of silk has been covered. The finger and thumb should be parted at the end of each "roll" when the silk will untwist without disturbing the "barrel" of fur that surrounds it. Roll in one direction only.

The silk is then wound to the shoulder, and the spacing judged to give the desired thickness and shape to the body. *See* opposite page for illustrations of the main stages of the operation, Figs. 105 to 108.

HOW TO FORM A DUBBING BODY

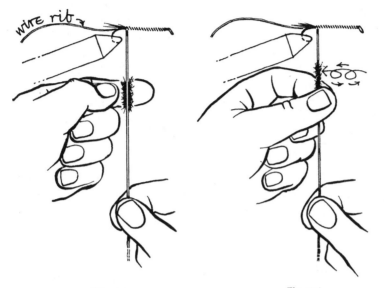

Fig. 105   Fig. 106

Fig. 107

Fig. 108

"DOUBLING" HACKLES

Hackles are "doubled" (which means giving them a "V" aspect instead of their being at right-angles to the quill) not only because this makes for easier entry into the water, but also because it improves the appearance of the fly. In fact a wet trout fly or a salmon fly which incorporates a well doubled hackle is the hall-mark of the expert fly tyer.

Hackle doubling is one of those fly-tying procedures which are always difficult until the proper "know-how" is acquired, and, as usual, the simplest method is always the best. Naturally, the method employed by professional tyers always falls into this category, and it was illustrated to me by Mr. Jimmy Younger, member of a Sutherland family which traces its fly-tying and fly-fishing associations back to the early nineteenth century.

Select the required hackle and place its stem in a pair of hackle pliers as Fig. 110. The tip of the hackle is then gripped in the thumb and forefinger of the left hand as shown in Fig. 111, or this can also be held in another pair of hackle pliers. The hackle pliers in the right hand should be held in the palm, thus leaving the finger and thumb free to draw down or "double" the hackle fibres as shown in Fig. 112.

The actual application of the hackle to the fly is also most important if we are to achieve the best effect from our doubling, so when it is wound on it must be ensured that all the fibres point to the rear at all times. If the stem of the hackle gets twisted, the fibres will go off in other directions and we would be worse off than if doubling had not been attempted.

If a doubled body hackle is being wound, the ribbing of the fly can be utilized to accentuate the doubling effect. This is done by winding the hackle stem close up to the left-hand side of the rib, thus ensuring that the doubled fibres are forced even more rearwards.

DOUBLING HACKLES

Fig. 109

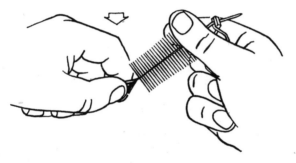

Fig. 110

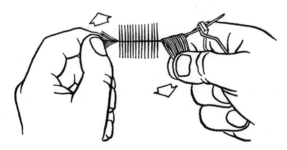

Fig. 111

PREPARING "MIXED" WINGS

Unlike trout flies most salmon fly wings are composite affairs, made up from fibres taken from an assortment of natural and dyed feathers.

The wings are formed by "marrying" the fibres. The fibres for the left hand wing (that is the wing furthest away when the hook is in the vice) are taken from the left hand side of the feathers. Which naturally brings us to the conclusion that the right-hand wing must come from the right-hand side.

Now this is not a hard and fast rule, but I have given this method here as it will be found that the natural curve of the fibres on, say, a goose feather, give the necessary downward sweep to the wing without a lot of "humping" being necessary.

It will be found, however, that if the wings are put on the opposite way, that is, left fibres forming the right wing, the fibres stay together better. Also, as the top part of the wing usually consists of strips of brown mallard, which must be put on left-hand strip for left-hand wing, this makes for a much neater and compact arrangement than if all the fibres curved downwards. If this method is used, it will be found necessary to "hump" the married fibres, and the way to do this is described later on in this section.

When golden pheasant tails are used as an under wing, they should always be tied in using the left-hand strip for the right-hand wing, as the fibres will nearly always fly apart if they are tied in the other way. If they sweep up too much after they are tied in, they can be made to lie more horizontal as follows: Grip the two strips where they are tied in, and with the left forefinger and thumb stroke them to the rear at the same time pulling them downwards. This will re-marry any fibres that have come adrift, and make them lie along the hook shank.

To decide which is the left- or right-hand side of a feather is quite simple.

Hold the feather so that you are looking at the "outside" face. The outside being the face that is outside when the feather is on the bird.

Those fibres now on the left-hand side of the quill are those we require for our left-hand wing (Figs. 112–114) showing a central feather (fibres of equal length each side of the quill) and two side feathers (usable fibres on one side of the quill only).

The best way to build up the wing is to start with one fibre (or two, if desired) as your base and marry the subsequent fibres until the required size is reached.

Marrying the fibres may seem a difficult operation, but if the following points are borne in mind, it soon becomes quite simple. A little practice will soon give one the required "knack". If we know what we are trying to do, we shall be saved a great deal of time, and do away with a lot of haphazard stroking.

The fibres of a feather do not remain aligned with their neighbours by chance, and it is up to us to take advantage of the devices used by nature to achieve this object. Along both edges of every fibre is a series of claws which look like very

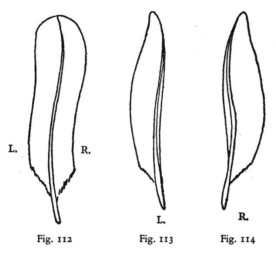

Fig. 112   Fig. 113   Fig. 114

small hairs. These claws grip their opposite numbers on the adjoining fibre in very much the same way as do the claws of a zip-fastener (*see* Fig. 115). If these claws become unhooked, the feather "splits", or, in our case, the wing splits. To rejoin or "marry" them, the procedure is as follows—

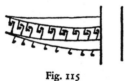

Fig. 115

Grasp the butts of the fibres in the tips of the forefinger and thumb of the right hand.

Grasp the extreme tips of the fibres in the forefinger and thumb of the left hand, and move the tips slightly up and down, at the same time pulling slightly to the left, Fig. 116. This will cause the claws to interlock, and by adding further fibres we can

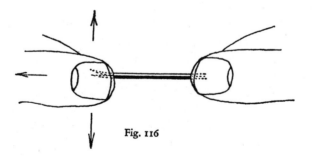

Fig. 116

build up our wings. A little stroking at the tips is all that should be necessary to make a neat job, and like everything else in fly-tying—practice is all that is required.

As our base we will take the fibre that will be at the bottom of the wing when it is tied in. Place the next fibre on top of it, between the finger and thumb of the right hand, projecting very slightly beyond the one underneath. "Marry" them and then place the next fibre on top of the other two, also extending it slightly (Fig. 117). Carry on in this fashion until the wing is completed and do exactly the same for the right-hand wing, using your right-handed fibres (Fig. 118).

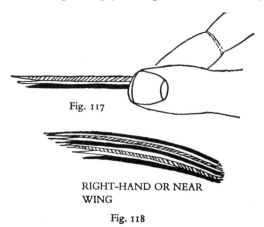

Fig. 117

RIGHT-HAND OR NEAR
WING

Fig. 118

If you mix right-hand fibres with left, you will find that they will not "marry", nor will they "set" right when the wing is tied in.

It will be found that some fibres marry better than others, and this is most noticeable when marrying fibres of different coloured goose or swan. When these fibres are placed together they lock almost automatically, and a little gentle stroking is all that is required to complete the operation. Other fibres that marry well are florican bustard, speckled bustard and turkey tails. More difficult ones are usually those from the wild fowl, such as brown mallard, teal, summer duck and pintail. When using these latter feathers it is better to leave a section of the quill adhering to them when cutting the fibres from the feather. This helps to keep the fibres together while they are being tied in. The fibres of other feathers can be cut straight from the quill.

When all the fibres are married the wing should be "humped" to form the shape it should have when the fly is finished. This is achieved by holding the butts of the fibres in the right hand and stroking them to the left, at the same time pulling downwards. This causes the wing to take a crescent shape.

To practice the operations of "marrying" fibres and "humping", the beginner is advised to practice with strips from single feathers. A strip of about ½-inch should be cut from its quill, and split into about six to eight smaller strips. The strips should then be re-married to form the original ½-inch. Any odd feather can be used for practice.

If several flies of one pattern are being tied, I find it is a good idea to make the wings first. The required number of pairs of wings can be stored between the pages of a book while the rest of the fly is being tied. This means that there is not a lot of material laying about to clutter up the work bench. After the wings are prepared, the wing materials can be returned to wherever they are stored, leaving the bench free for the comparatively few items required for bodies and tails, etc.

Another method of preparing mixed wings which is much simpler and produces quite a good effect, is as follows—

Cut single fibres from the left-hand side of all the feathers required for the fly being tied, and lay them all together with their tips level. Pick up the bundle of fibres and roll them between the finger and thumb. This will cause many of them to "marry" and a little stroking of the tips will assist this even further.

Carry out the same process with the fibres from the right-hand side feathers, and the pair of wings are now ready for tying in. They can be tied in together if it is a mixed wing pattern only, but if there is an under wing of any kind, they can be tied in one at a time, either side of the under wing. The left-hand fibres forming the far wing, and the right hand ones the near wing.

Wings tied in this fashion seem to lie much more closely along the body of the fly, and if a "roof" of brown mallard is put on over the top, they have quite an attractive appearance. The method of putting on the brown mallard I like best for this type of wing will be found on pages 213 and 214.

PREPARING TOPPINGS

These are not easy feathers to tie in, but if they are well prepared beforehand, many of the difficulties will be removed.

The first thing is to ensure that the feathers are well shaped and have the correct curve for the size of fly being tied. Owing to the way many of the crests lay on the skull of the golden pheasant, they become twisted, and no amount of careful tying in will eradicate this twist.

The best method of giving them the right curve is to moisten them and stick them inside a smooth tumbler or any other glass container. The sizes of the containers must vary according to the curve that is required. The crests must lie in the circumference of the glass and not sloping up or down. When they are dry they will fall to the bottom, retaining the curve imparted by the curve of the glass.

The fibres at the base of the crest should now be cut off (not torn) to a point where the crest will eventually be tied in.

The part of the stem where the fibres have been removed should also be drawn between the thumbnail and ball of a finger to flatten it and the point where it is to be tied in should be slightly nicked by the thumb nail. The prepared topping should now be as Fig. 119).

The above procedure should also be carried out on the crests that are used for tails, although it will be found that the smaller ones do not suffer from the same twisting as do the larger.

Fig. 119

PREPARING BLUE JAY WING COVERTS FOR HACKLING

These feathers are too stiff to be tied and wound as are other hackles. Only the blue/black barred side of the feather is used, and the grey side must be removed by splitting down the centre of the quill, Fig. 120. This is best done with a very sharp pair of scissors, trimming any edges that may remain. The pith should then be removed by scraping from the butt to the tip of the feather with a finger-nail.

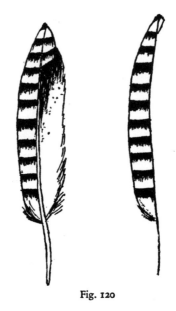

Fig. 120

Feathers from a right-hand wing have the barred markings on the right side, and therefore these must be wound round the hook shank in the opposite direction to those from a left-hand wing. When hackles are wound in a reverse direction, the tying silk must also be reversed (*see* page 177).

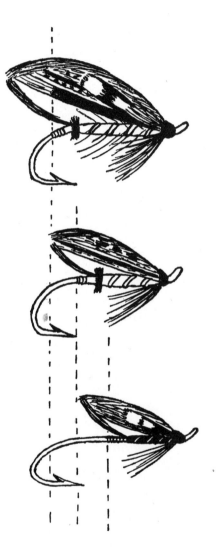

INTRODUCING STYLE

As well as becoming adept at tying in the various materials, the fly-tyer must also decide the style he wishes to introduce into his patterns.

Style is regulated by the amounts of materials that are used, the length of the wing in comparison with the hook, and the position of the tail section.

The modern trend towards more lightly dressed flies has resulted in several changes of style. Orthodox flies of earlier days had wings that projected well up to or beyond the bend of the hook, with a tail to match. Then came the theory that, if a fish snapped only at the brightly coloured tail section of the fly, there was a possibility of him missing the point of the hook altogether. If, however, the tail section was tied in further along the hook shank towards the eye, the hook would be that much further in the fish's mouth. This theory reaches its fullest conclusions in the Low Water series of flies, and the illustrations portray the difference between the three styles.

In the instructions that follow (with the exception of the Low Water patterns) the orthodox method of dressing is used. The final style is left to the fly-tyer.

CHAPTER TWENTY

DRESSING SALMON FLIES—STANDARD PATTERNS
TYING A SIMPLE STRIP WING FLY

The "Thunder and Lightning" (illustrated, facing page 188), tied by Mr. H. George.

Materials required—

Tag—Round silver tinsel and yellow floss.
Tail—Golden pheasant crest and Indian crow.
Butt—Black ostrich herl.
Body—Black floss.
Rib—Oval gold tinsel.
Hackle—Hot orange cock's hackle.
Throat—Blue jay wing feather, or speckled guinea fowl dyed blue.
Wings—Strips of brown mallard.
Sides—Jungle cock.
A golden pheasant crest over all (topping).

This is probably one of the best-known of the strip wing patterns and, although brown speckled turkey tail feathers are sometimes used as a substitute for the brown mallard wings, the latter are recognised to be the orthodox dressing.

The dyed blue speckled gallena is used on patterns that are too large for a jay hackle to be used.

Tied as a Low Water pattern the ostrich herl butt is omitted (*see* Illustration, facing page 236).

Place hook in vice, tie in silk about a $\frac{1}{4}$-inch from the eye, and spiral it until it is directly above the point of the hook. The butt and the tag should occupy an area of the shank of equal distance to the point and the tip of the barb (Fig. 121).

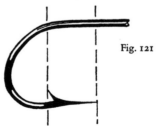

Fig. 121

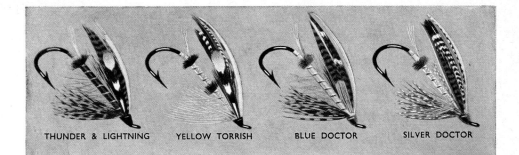

THUNDER & LIGHTNING   YELLOW TORRISH   BLUE DOCTOR   SILVER DOCTOR

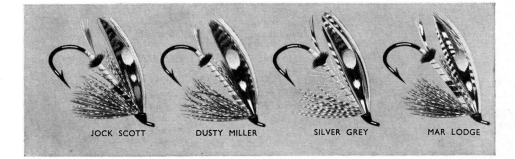

JOCK SCOTT   DUSTY MILLER   SILVER GREY   MAR LODGE

SALMON FLIES

Dressed by Mr. H. George

The silk must now be wound in close even turns to a point immediately above the tip of the barb. Tie in the round silver tinsel so that the short portion is to the right and underneath the shank. Wind the silk back to position midway between the barb and the point, still in close even turns. This is most important. Now wind the tinsel to the right five or six turns, making sure that the turns are very close and that no silk shows through. Before starting these turns one turn should be taken round the bare hook shank so that the silk that tied the tinsel in does not show. Finish the turns underneath the shank, tie in the tinsel and cut off the surplus.

Now continue winding the silk to the right until the point to be occupied by the butt is reached. Tie in a short length of the yellow floss silk on top of the hook with the short end to the left. This short end should not quite reach the last turn of tinsel. Now wind the floss to completely cover the turns of tying silk, first to the left and then back again. Tie in the floss with two turns of the tying silk, pulling it tight as you do so. Cut off the surplus floss and we are now ready to tie in the tail (Fig. 122).

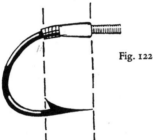

Fig. 122

Tie in the small golden pheasant crest feather (prepared as for toppings on page 185) so that it sweeps upwards, holding it in place on top of the hook shank as you do so. The instructions for tying in the wing, on page 192, should also be followed when tying in the tail. This will ensure that it is placed squarely on top of the hook shank. Now tie in the Indian crow feather, best side uppermost, and with the next turn of the silk, tie in the butt end of the ostrich herl. This part should be stripped of its flue, and the stripped part should lay to the right. Wind two or three turns of the silk to the right. Take one turn of the herl to the left so that it reaches the floss silk, and then cover this turn with two or three close turns to the right. This should conceal all the turns of tying silk used to tie in the tail and butt. Tie in the herl with a turn of the tying silk, pulling the herl tight as you do so. The tail section of the fly should now be as Fig. 123.

The oval silver tinsel for the rib should now be tied in, short end to the right and underneath the hook shank, and continue winding the tying silk to the right covering up the waste ends of the tail, herl and tinsel as you do so. The turns of silk should be close and even so that a well-shaped body can be wound over them.

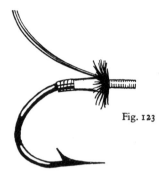

Fig. 123

Finish winding at a point where the throat hackle will be tied in, and tie in the length of black floss silk for the body, short end to the left, underneath the hook shank.

Wind the floss silk to the left in wide even turns, and before the butt is reached, tie in the tip of the orange body hackle with the floss. Continue winding until the butt is reached, and then back again to the starting point. Not touching the hackle, of course. The floss silk body should be smooth and even, and should have a gradual taper from butt to head, as Fig. 124.

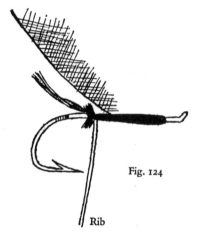

Fig. 124

Rib

Now wind the oval tinsel in an even spiral until the throat is reached. Tie in the tinsel underneath the hook shank and cut off the surplus.

The hackle is now wound to the same position, each turn being close up to a turn of the oval tinsel. The fibres should be stroked firmly to the rear if the hackle has not been "doubled" (the instruction for "doubling" will be found on page 180).

Make one complete turn of the hackle when the end of the body is reached, tie it in underneath the hook shank after stripping off any fibres that are left, and cut off the surplus. The fly should now be as Fig. 125.

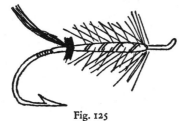

Fig. 125

If a blue jay wing feather is to be used as the throat hackle, this should be prepared as the instructions given on page 186. If a dyed blue guinea fowl hackle is to be used, the soft fibres should be stripped from the base, and one side completely stripped.

The tip of the throat hackle should be tied in close up to the body, and three close turns taken to the right. Finish underneath the hook shank tie in, and cut off the surplus. The fibres of the hackle should be stroked firmly to the left so that they point towards the bend of the hook (Fig. 126).

Fig. 126

We are now ready to tie in the wings, and to ensure a firm foundation for them, two or three turns of silk must be taken to the right, and then two or three back to the left until the throat hackle is reached. This should bring the layers of silk almost as high as any hump caused by the turns of the hackle. If any hump is allowed to remain the wings will be forced into a vertical position instead of laying along the body as they should.

We must now cut two strips from left and right brown mallard feathers, leaving the quill on (Fig. 127). The feathers should be selected so that, when the strips are tied in the turns of silk should be as near to the pieces of quill as possible. There is less likelihood of the fibres separating from each other when they are tied in by the roots (see Fig. 128).

For a downward sweep to the wings the slip from the left-hand feather will be the left hand or far wing, and the slip from the right-hand feather the right hand or near wing. The reverse applies if an upward sweep is required. This latter method is used for small and Low Water patterns. If the upward sweep is used, the wings are referred to in the dressings as being "set upright", If the downward sweep is used they are referred to as being "set horizontally".

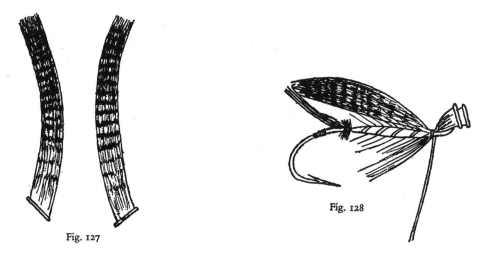

Fig. 127

Fig. 128

The procedure for tying in the wings is as follows—

Grasp them tightly in the thumb and forefinger of the left hand and place them on top of the hook shank, as Fig. 129. Bring the tying silk up between the thumb and rear side wing and take it down between the finger and far wing, forming a loop above the finger and thumb, as Fig. 130. Draw the silk down firmly so that all the fibres come down on top of one another, as Fig. 131. Do not allow the fibres to be pulled out of alignment, as Fig. 132, as this causes the fibres of the wing to split.

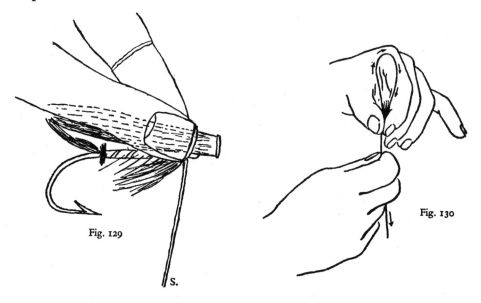

Fig. 129

S.

Fig. 130

HACKLE WING STREAMER FLY

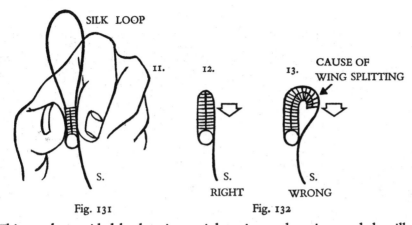

SILK LOOP

II.   12.   13.   CAUSE OF
                                WING SPLITTING

S.   S.   S.
             RIGHT   WRONG

Fig. 131   Fig. 132

This can be avoided by keeping a tight grip on the wings and the silk as the latter is being drawn down. Repeat this process two or three times, winding towards the right. The wings may now be released from the finger and thumb, but do not pull the silk tight after they are released or they might be pulled round the hook shank. If any more turns of silk are put round them, the wings should be held in position.

Strip off the soft fibres from the base of the jungle cock feathers and tie these in one on each side of the wings. As each one is tied in, pull it gently to the right so that a few of the fibres at the base are drawn under the turns of silk. This will ensure that the feathers lie flat against the wings.

The topping must now be tied in, after being prepared as the instructions given on page 185. Tie it in with even turns until the eye is reached, and cut off any surplus that projects beyond this point. Wind the silk back to the left and then back again to the right, and finish off the head with a whip finish.

The head can now be given a coat of black varnish. Two coats may be necessary to give a smooth finish as the first coat will soak into the silk, etc., and be uneven when it dries. The head can also be given a good coat of the "Cellire" varnish before the black varnish is put on. The varnishing not only improves the appearance of the fly, but ensures that the silk will not come unwound and that the materials are held in the position in which they were tied.

The illustration below shows the finished fly.

Amethyst
TAIL. Topping.
BODY. Quarter orange, quarter magenta, quarter green, quarter blue floss silk.
RIBS. Oval gold tinsel.
HACKLE. Black.
WINGS. Dark mottled turkey tail.
HEAD. Black varnish.

Badger
TAG. Round silver tinsel.
TAIL. Tippet strands, topping.
BODY. Crimson seal's fur.
RIBS. Oval silver tinsel.
THROAT. Silver badger hackle.
WINGS. Two strips of light mottled turkey tail.
HEAD. Black varnish.

Black Fairy
TAG. Round gold tinsel and yellow floss.
TAIL. Topping.
BUTT. Black ostrich herl.
BODY. Black seal's fur, ribbed gold tinsel.
THROAT. Black hackle.
WING. Brown mallard.
HEAD. Black varnish.

Black Spean
TAG. Round silver tinsel and lemon floss.
TAIL. A topping.
BODY. Black seal's fur (left smooth).
RIBS. Oval gold tinsel.
THROAT. Speckled gallina.
WINGS. Brown mallard strips (set horizontally).
HEAD. Black varnish.

Blue Charm
TAG. Round silver tinsel and golden yellow floss.
TAIL. A topping.
BUTT. Black herl.

BODY. Black floss.
RIBS. Oval silver tinsel.
THROAT. A deep blue hackle.
WINGS. Mottled brown turkey tail strips (set upright) and narrow strips of teal along the upper edge; a topping over.
HEAD. Black varnish.

Brown Turkey
TAIL. Topping.
BODY. Half yellow and half claret seal's fur, ribbed oval silver tinsel.
HACKLE. Brown.
WING. Piece of tippet with light cinnamon turkey over this.
HEAD. Black varnish.

Bumblebee
TAG. Round silver tinsel.
TAIL. A tuft of scarlet wool.
BODY. First third orange wool, remainder black wool.
RIB. Oval silver tinsel.
HACKLE. A Coch-y-bondhu hackle.
WINGS. Brown mallard (set horizontally).

Chalmers
TAG. Round silver tinsel, yellow floss silk.
TAIL. Topping.
BUTT. Black ostrich herl.
BODY. Magenta floss silk.
RIBS. Oval silver tinsel.
THROAT. Magenta hackle.
WINGS. Two strips dark mottled turkey tail, topping over.
SIDES. Jungle cock.
HEAD. Black varnish.

Cinnamon Turkey
TAG. Round silver tinsel, yellow floss.
TAIL. Topping and ibis.

BODY. One turn yellow and one turn of red, balance black seal's fur, ribbed flat silver tinsel.

THROAT. Dark blue hackle.

WINGS. Tippet, teal, veiled cinnamon turkey tail, topping over all.

HEAD. Black varnish.

Claret Alder

TAG. Silver thread and light orange floss.

TAIL. A tuft of claret wool.

BODY. Peacock herl.

RIBS. Fine oval gold tinsel.

HACKLE. A dark claret hackle.

WINGS. Brown mallard strips (set horizontally).

HEAD. Black varnish.

Claret and Yellow

TAG. Round silver tinsel and yellow floss.

TAIL. Topping, widgeon and ibis.

BUTT. Black ostrich herl.

BODY. Yellow 1st half and claret 2nd half, seal's fur, ribbed silver tinsel.

HACKLE. Claret over claret body.

THROAT. Guinea fowl dyed blue.

WING. Cinnamon turkey.

HEAD. Black varnish.

Dunwing

TAG. Round silver tinsel.

TAIL. Topping and tippet.

BUTT. Black ostrich herl.

BODY. Three sections yellow, claret and blue seal's fur, ribbed oval silver and black hackle.

WINGS. Grey (plain) with strip of teal each side.

HEAD. Black varnish.

Helmsdale

TAG. Round silver tinsel, orange floss silk.

TAIL. Topping.

BUTT. Black ostrich herl.

BODY. Two turns light yellow floss silk; remainder yellow seal fur.

RIBS. Oval silver tinsel.

HACKLE. Yellow.

THROAT. Light blue hackle.

WINGS. Brown mottled turkey tail.

HEAD. Black varnish.

Jeannie

TAG. Round silver tinsel.

TAIL. A topping.

BODY. First third lemon floss, remainder black floss.

RIBS. Oval silver tinsel.

THROAT. A (natural) black hackle.

WINGS. Brown mallard strips (set upright)

SIDES. Jungle cock.

HEAD. Black varnish.

Jimmie

TAG. Round silver tinsel.

TAIL. Topping.

BODY. In two equal halves; first half, bright orange floss; second half, black floss.

RIBS. Oval silver tinsel.

THROAT. A (natural) black hackle.

WINGS. Mottled brown turkey tail strips (set upright).

CHEEKS. Jungle cock.

HEAD. Black varnish.

Jockie

TAG. Round silver tinsel.

TAIL. A topping and Indian crow.

BODY. First third, gold yellow floss; remainder dark claret floss.

RIBS. Oval silver tinsel.

THROAT. A coch-y-bondhu hackle.

WINGS. Brown mallard strips (set upright).

SIDES. Jungle cock.

HEAD. Black varnish.

Killer Jock

TAG. Round silver tinsel, yellow floss.

BUTT. Black ostrich.

BODY. Black floss, ribbed flat gold tinsel and oval gold tinsel (fine) alternately.

HACKLE. (Throat only.) Golden pheasant topping and body feathers mixed.

WING. Yellow swan, sheathed with golden pheasant tail, topping over.

HEAD. Black varnish.

Lady Amherst

TAIL. Golden pheasant crest.

BUTT. Black ostrich herl.

BODY. Flat silver, ribbed oval silver tinsel.

HACKLE. Teal.

WINGS. Amherst pheasant centre tail, jungle cock either side, topping over.

CHEEKS. Blue chatterer.

HEAD. Black varnish.

March Brown

TAG. Round silver tinsel.

TAIL. A topping.

BODY. Fur from a hare's face (well picked out).

RIBS. Flat silver tinsel.

THROAT. Partridge back (or rump in the larger sizes).

WINGS. Hen pheasant tail strips.

HEAD. Black varnish.

Mignon

TAG. Round silver tinsel, yellow floss silk.

TAIL. Topping, teal.

BUTT. Black ostrich herl.

BODY. Claret chenille.

HACKLE. Claret.

THROAT. Grey heron and teal.

WINGS. Grey heron wing feathers.

HEAD. Black varnish.

Nigger

TAG. Round silver tinsel.

TAIL. Topping.

BODY. Black wool.

RIBS. Oval silver tinsel.

HACKLE. Black.

WINGS. Dark mottled turkey tail.

HEAD. Black varnish.

Night Hawk

(Canadian pattern tied by Mr. J. C. Arseneault, illustrated, facing page 236).

TAG. Silver tinsel, yellow floss.

TAIL. Golden pheasant crest and blue kingfisher.

BUTT. Red wool.

BODY. Flat silver tinsel, ribbed oval silver tinsel.

THROAT. Black hackle.

WINGS. Black turkey, topping over.

SIDES. Jungle cock.

CHEEKS. Blue kingfisher.

HEAD. Red varnish.

Sir Charles

TAG. Round silver tinsel.

TAIL. Golden pheasant crest.

BODY. Golden floss silk.

RIBS. Oval silver tinsel.

HACKLE. Pale blue cock.

WING. Two strands of peacock sword, with a strip wing of black/white teal flank over.

HEAD. Black varnish.

Skirmisher

TAG. Silver tinsel, light yellow floss silk.

TAIL. Toucan, ibis.

BUTT. Black ostrich herl.

BODY. Two turns light dirty orange floss silk, followed by orange seal fur.

THROAT. Badger hackle dyed brown.

WINGS. Golden pheasant tail, peacock herl.

SIDES. Teal, ibis.

HEAD. Black varnish.

Smoky Dun
TAG. Round silver tinsel.
TAIL. Peacock sword (green herl).
BODY. Rabbit fur.
RIBS. Oval silver tinsel.
THROAT. Blue dun hackle.
WINGS. Heron wing feather.
HEAD. Black varnish.

Stephen
TAG. Round gold tinsel, light blue floss silk.
TAIL. Topping.
BODY. Red floss silk.
RIBS. Oval gold tinsel.
HACKLE. Red.
WINGS. Golden pheasant red rump feather, brown mallard.
HEAD. Black varnish.

Thunder and Lightning
(Illustrated, facing page 188, tied by Mr. H. George).

TAG. Round gold tinsel, yellow floss silk.
TAIL. Topping.
BUTT. Black ostrich herl.
BODY. Black floss silk.
RIBS. Oval gold tinsel.
HACKLE. Orange.
THROAT. Blue jay or gallena dyed blue.
WINGS. Brown mallard and topping over.
SIDES. Jungle cock.
HEAD. Black varnish.

Trumpers Black
TAG. Round silver tinsel puce floss silk.
TAIL. Topping.
BUTT. Black ostrich herl.
BODY. Black floss silk.
BODY HACKLE. Orange.
THROAT HACKLE. Guinea fowl.
WING. Dark white tip turkey tail.
HEAD. Black varnish.

The "Beadles" Series—"Prismackle" Flies
Designed by C. G. HEYWOOD, Esq.

The bodies and hackles of this series of flies are all identical, and the arrangement is so designed that at least one of the three body hackles used will shine with a transmitted light against any background.

The term "Prismackle" is used to define the prismatic effect of this arrangement. Change of patterns is confined solely to the wing colourings.

The dressing of the basic bodies, tails, etc., is as follows—

Tag—Round silver tinsel.
Tail—Golden pheasant crest feather.
Body—Black floss silk ribbed with fairly fine oval silver tinsel.
Hackles (3)—Tail third of body—hot orange. Middle third of body—magenta. Front third of body—blue.
Head—Black varnish.

Six patterns were designed to cover the whole range of Standard Patterns, and these are as follows—

1. Brown "Beadle" . . . For the baron, blue charm, thunder and Lightning.
Wing—Two strips of golden pheasant centre tail.

2. Buff "Beadle" . . . . For the Logie and Wilkinson.
Wing—Two strips of cinnamon turkey tail.

3. Yellow "Beadle" . . . For the black goldfinch, blue limerick, Torrish, childers, or any fly that is normally used in peat or coloured waters.
Wing—Two strips of yellow turkey tail.

4. Red "Beadle" . . . . For use when a red fly is known to be attractive, Red ranger, Durham ranger, red Jock Scott, prawns.
Wing—Two strips of red turkey tail.

5. White "Beadle" . . . For use at night, or when a large fly is called for.
Wing—Two strips of white turkey tail.

6. Speckled "Beadle" . . . For the black and silver flies, such as the Mar Lodge, Silver Grey, etc.
Wing—Two strips of amherst pheasant centre tail.

The six patterns were redesigned for greased line fishing, and a description of them, together with the dressings, will be found in the chapter on Low Water flies on page 222.

TYING WHOLE FEATHER WING FLIES

The "Orange Parson" (Illustrated, facing page 236)

Materials required—

Tag—Round silver tinsel and lilac or light blue floss.
Tail—Golden pheasant crest and tippet in strands.
Body—Orange floss; orange, scarlet and fiery brown seal's fur in equal sections.

Ribs—Oval silver tinsel.
Body Hackle—Lemon yellow.
Throat Hackle—Orange.
Wings—A pair of tippets back to back with orange hackles either side.
Sides—Barred summer duck (or mandarin duck) feathers.
Cheeks—Blue chatterer (or kingfisher) feathers. Two or three golden pheasant crests (toppings) over all.
Head—Black varnish.

Tie in tying silk a short distance from the eye of the hook and spiral it down the shank until it is directly above the point of the hook. The tag and tail should now be tied in as described for the "Thunder and Lightning" on page 189. The only differences in this pattern are (*a*) golden pheasant tippet fibres are added to the tail instead of Indian crow, and (*b*) there is no Butt.

Now tie in the oval silver tinsel for the rib underneath the hook shank, close up to the last turn of the silk used for the tag.

Continue winding tying silk towards the eye until one-quarter of the shank is covered. Now tie in the orange floss silk, short end to the left, underneath the hook shank. Wind floss to the left, and with the first turn tie in the tip of the lemon yellow body hackle. Continue winding floss to left until the tag is reached, covering the ends of the tail and tinsel. Now wind floss back to its starting point, avoding the hackle. Tie in the floss with two turns of the tying silk, pulling it tight as you do so. Cut off the surplus and the fly should now be as Fig. 133.

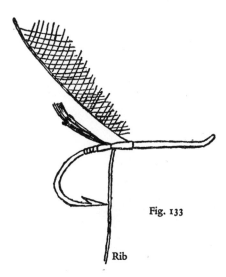

Fig. 133

Rib

Sufficient orange seal's fur for the next quarter of the shank should now be dubbed on to the tying silk as the instructions given on page 178. This is wound in tight even turns until its quarter is covered, and the same procedure is applied to the scarlet and fiery brown seal's fur.

The ribbing tinsel is now spiralled down the body until the end of the fiery brown seal's fur is reached. This should bring us to a point where the throat hackle will be tied in, leaving sufficient room for the wings, etc.

The hackle should now be wound to the same place, each turn close up to each turn of the tinsel rib. If the hackle has not been "doubled" as the instructions given on page 180, the fibres should be pressed to the rear during and after the winding. When the end of the body is reached, make one complete turn of the hackle, strip off any fibres that remain, and tie it in underneath the hook shank. Cut off the surplus and the fly should be as Fig. 134.

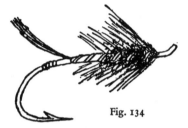

Fig. 134

The throat hackle is now tied in and wound two or three times and the surplus cut off. If it has not been doubled, the fibres must be pressed to the rear, but if possible it is better to use a doubled hackle at the throat. Another method for forcing the hackle fibres to the rear is to bring the forefinger and thumb up from underneath the hook, grasp all the fibres and bring them downwards, at the same time pulling them towards the rear. A couple of slanting turns of the tying silk are then made over the fibres as Fig. 135. The fly-tyer will no doubt form his own opinion as to which method he prefers, but it must always be borne in mind that as little hump as possible should be left after the throat is wound and tied in.

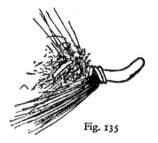

Fig. 135

The next step is to tie in the two tippet feathers back to back. Two feathers should be selected that will fit the length of hook without being too wide or too narrow. The base fibres are stripped off and the stems nicked slightly where they will be tied in. Place the feathers on the hook so that the bare stem starts immediately where the throat hackle finishes, and tie them in with two or three firm turns of the tying silk. This type of wing is much easier to put on than strip or mixed wings, but care is necessary to ensure that the two feathers stay absolutely flat together, and do not lean to either side.

The bases of the two orange hackles should now be stripped off so that, when they are tied in, one each side of the tippets, their tips should just project beyond the first black bars. Tie the hackles in and cut off the surplus stems.

Two strips of the barred summer duck (or mandarin duck) are now cut from these feathers, leaving the fibres adhering to the quill (Fig. 136). They should now be tied in, one on each side of the wing, occupying the centre section.

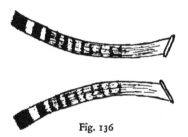

Fig. 136

The two blue chatterer (or kingfisher) feathers should now be prepared, as Fig. 137, and tied in each side of the barred summer duck. The base fibres should be cut off, as illustrated, and not torn off, as this makes them lie flat to the sides and less likely to be pulled out at any time.

Fig. 137

The golden pheasant crests for the toppings should now be prepared, as the instructions on page 185, and tied in one on top of the other. It is possible to tie them in all at once after a little practice, and moistening them in the mouth is helpful here.

The tying silk is now wound tightly and evenly towards the eye and, just before it is reached, the surplus stems of the toppings should be cut off. Continue winding the silk to the eye and then back to where the wings are tied in. Finish off the tying with a whip finish and the head is now ready for varnishing. The finished fly should be as Fig. 138.

Fig. 138

Avon Eagle
TAG. Round silver tinsel.
TAIL. A topping and the tip of a golden pheasant breast feather (best side under).
BODY. Lemon, bright orange, scarlet and fiery brown seal's fur in equal sections (dressed spare but picked out).
RIBS. Broad silver tinsel and twist.
HACKLE. An eagle's hackle (one side stripped) dyed yellow (or substitute).
THROAT. Widgeon.
WINGS. A pair of golden pheasant sword feathers.
SIDES. Jungle cock, three toppings over.
HEAD. Black varnish.

Black Dose
TAG. Round silver tinsel and light orange floss.
TAIL. A topping and "married" narrow strips of teal and scarlet swan (back to back).

BODY. Two or three turns of pale blue seal's fur, the rest black seal's fur (left smooth).
RIBS. Oval silver tinsel.
HACKLE. A black hackle.
THROAT. A light claret or fiery brown hackle.
WINGS. A pair of tippets (back to back) veiled with "married" strands of scarlet and green swan, light mottled turkey tail and golden pheasant tail, peacock herl in strands above.
HORNS. Blue and yellow macaw.
HEAD. Black varnish.

Black Ranger
TAG. Round silver tinsel and lemon floss.
TAIL. A topping and Indian crow.
BUTT. Black herl.
BODY. Black floss.
RIBS. Flat silver tinsel and twist.
HACKLE. A black hackle.

THROAT. A deep blue hackle.

WINGS. A pair of jungle cock feathers (back to back) covered for three-quarters of their length by two pairs of tippets (back to back), topping over.

SIDES. Jungle cock.

CHEEKS. Blue chatterer.

HORNS. Blue and yellow macaw.

HEAD. Black varnish.

Chatterer

TAG. Round silver tinsel, light orange floss silk.

TAIL. Two toppings.

BUTT. Black ostrich herl.

BODY. Two turns violet floss silk, making headway for numberless small blue chatterer feathers closely packed round the rest of the body.

THROAT. Guinea fowl.

WINGS. Four Indian crow feathers in pairs, first pair longer than the second, and having the points of blue jay feathers on each side, two-thirds length of Indian crow feathers, six toppings.

CHEEKS. Blue chatterer.

HEAD. Black varnish.

Dennison

TAG. One turn silver twist, one turn claret floss, one turn yellow floss.

TAIL. Golden pheasant crest and strands of wooduck.

BUTT. Black herl.

BODY. Half flat silver and half light blue floss.

RIBS. Oval silver tinsel.

HACKLE. Light blue down body, blue jay at shoulder.

WINGS. Two tippets (back to back) enveloping two extended jungle cock, veiled with two yellow golden pheasant rumps each side, topping over.

SIDES. Teal.

HEAD. Black herl.

Durham Ranger

(Illustrated, facing page 212.)

TAG. Round silver tinsel.

TAIL. A topping and Indian crow.

BUTT. Black herl.

BODY. Lemon floss, orange, fiery brown and black seal's fur in equal sections.

RIBS. Flat silver tinsel and twist.

HACKLE. A badger hackle dyed yellow.

THROAT. A light blue hackle.

WINGS. A pair of jungle cock feathers (back to back) covered for three-quarters of their length by two pairs of tippets (back to back), topping over.

SIDES. Jungle cock.

CHEEKS. Blue chatterer.

HORNS. Blue and yellow macaw.

HEAD. Black varnish.

Orange Parson

(Illustrated, facing page 236.)

TAG. Round silver tinsel and lilac floss.

TAIL. A topping and tippet in strands.

BODY. Orange floss, orange, scarlet and fiery brown seal's fur in equal sections (picked out).

HACKLE. A lemon hackle.

THROAT. An orange hackle.

WINGS. A pair of tippets (back to back) veiled with orange hackles.

SIDES. Barred summer duck strips.

CHEEKS. Blue chatterer, two or three toppings over.

HEAD. Black varnish.

Prosser's Black

TAG. Round silver tinsel and yellow floss.

TAIL. Topping and Indian crow.

BODY. Flat silver tinsel.

HACKLE. Black, at head only.

WINGS. Tippets faced with strips of dark white tip turkey tail.

HEAD. Black varnish.

Red Rover

TAG. Round silver tinsel, dark blue floss.

TAIL. Topping and Indian crow.

BUTT. Black ostrich.

BODY. Half red floss ribbed gold tinsel, half embossed gold tinsel ribbed oval gold tinsel, red hackle down body, dark blue hackle at shoulder.

WINGS. Two red hackles with two tippets up centre, yellow, blue, red and green swan, jungle cock and Indian crow cheeks, topping over all.

HEAD. Black varnish.

Sir Herbert

TAG. Round silver thread and pale orange floss.

TAIL. A topping and Indian crow.

BUTT. Peacock sword feather.

BODY. First three-fourths flat gold tinsel, remainder scarlet seal's fur.

RIBS. Fine oval silver tinsel.

HACKLE. A light orange hackle.

THROAT. A crimson hackle or golden pheasant breast feather.

WINGS. A pair of tippets (back to back) veiled with "married" strands of bustard, blue and crimson swan, light mottled turkey tail and golden pheasant tail,

strands of peacock herl above, topping over.

SIDES. Jungle cock.

HEAD. Peacock herl.

Silver Fairy

TAIL. Bunch of Amhurst pheasant small toppings.

BODY. Embossed silver tinsel, ribbed silver oval.

HACKLE. Front half of body, white.

WINGS. Amhurst pheasant tippets.

SIDES. Jungle cock.

HEAD. Black varnish.

Stevenson

TAG. Round silver tinsel and pale blue floss.

TAIL. A topping and Indian crow.

BUTT. Black herl.

BODY. First quarter orange floss; remainder, orange seal's fur of a deeper shade.

RIBS. Flat silver tinsel and silver twist.

HACKLE. A bright orange hackle.

THROAT. A pale blue hackle.

WINGS. A pair of jungle cock feathers (back to back) covered for three-quarters of their length by two pairs of tippets (back to back), a topping over.

SIDES. Jungle cock.

CHEEKS. Blue chatterer.

HEAD. Black varnish.

TYING MIXED WING FLIES

The "Silver Grey" (Illustrated, facing page 188, tied by Mr. H. George)

Materials required—

Tag—Round silver tinsel and yellow floss.

Tail—A golden pheasant crest and strands of barred summer duck (or mandarin duck).

Butt—Black ostrich herl.

Body—Flat silver tinsel.

Ribs—Oval silver tinsel.

Hackle—Badger.

Throat—Widgeon neck feather (small).

Wings—Tippet in strands; married strands of white, yellow, green swan (or goose), florican bustard, speckled bustard and golden pheasant tail; married strips of pintail and barred summer duck (or mandarin duck) each side. Brown mallard over, and a topping over all.

Cheeks—Jungle cock.

Head—Black varnish.

If it is preferred, the summer duck and teal feathers can be added to the mixed wing instead of put on separately as sides. If this method is used, the strands should take the centre section of the wing.

Tie in tying silk and spiral it until it is directly above the point of the hook. Form tag and tie in tail and butt as the instructions given for the "Thunder and Lightning", on page 189.

Now tie in the flat and oval tinsels for the body and ribbing. The flat tinsel should be cut to a tapering point where it is to be tied in and should be tied on to the hook shank, as Fig. 139. The tapering of the end permits it to be turned towards the eye for winding, without causing an unsightly hump. The ribbing tinsel should be tied in under the hook shank, short end to the right.

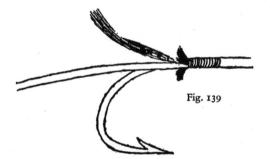

Fig. 139

Spiral the tying silk back to the starting point and tie in a short length of floss silk. This should be wound smoothly and evenly to the butt, covering the ends of the tinsel, and then back again. The purpose of the floss silk is to make a smooth even bed for the flat tinsel to lie on, as it is impossible to get the tinsel to lie evenly if there are any uneven patches on the hook shank. The thickness of the body can be varied by the amount of floss that is used. Floss silk is easily teased out to give different ticknesses.

The body hackle can be tied in at the rear with either the tying silk or floss silk.

The flat tinsel is now wound *tightly* to the shoulder, and each turn must lie close up to the preceeding one *but without any overlapping* (Fig. 140). Overlapping will ruin the appearance of the fly, and reduce the durability of the body. Tie in the tinsel with three turns of silk to the rear and then wind the ribbing tinsel to this point, pulling it tightly as you do so. The ribbing tinsel is now tied in with turns of silk to the right, covering the turns of silk that tie in the flat tinsel. The ribbing tinsel should finish underneath the hook. Cut off the surplus ribbing tinsel, but to remove the surplus flat tinsel it is better to bend it from side to side until it breaks. This will leave a small serrated edge that prevents the tinsel slipping through the turns of tying silk. The body hackle should now be wound to the shoulder, following closely the turns of the ribbing tinsel. One full turn should be made at the end and the surplus tied in and cut off.

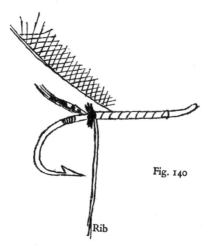

Fig. 140

Rib

Strip off one side of the widgeon feather and tie it in by the tip. It should be so tied in that when it is wound, the natural curve of the feather will point the fibres to the rear. Two turns of the hackle will suffice, and after stripping off any remaining fibres, the stem should be tied in underneath the shank.

Continue winding the silk to the right for two or three turns, and then back again to the left, so as to form a bed for the wings.

The wings should be prepared as the instructions on page 182, and tied in as the instructions on page 192. The sides of barred summer duck and teal should now be prepared as follows: Cut two sections of each from left and right feathers, leaving the quill adhering to the fibres. Before cutting, the sections should be pulled down as near as possible to right angles to the main stem. After the strips are married and "humped" they should appear as Fig. 141. Place the married sections each side of the wing and tie them in together.

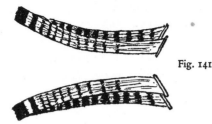

Fig. 141

To make the above operation a little easier, it is sometimes a good idea if the sides are tied in with the main wings. To do this a very small drop of very thin cellire varnish should be dropped on to the main wings, and the sides placed on to take up the centre section. If it is possible, the cellire should be put on to the *right* of where the wings will be tied in. This will ensure that there is no varnish on the wing after the waste ends have been cut off. Let the cellire dry before putting the wings on to the hook.

Two narrow strips of brown mallard should now be cut off, leaving the quill adhering. These are tied in left-hand strip for left-hand wing, and right-hand strip for right-hand wing. No "humping" is necessary with these strips, as the natural contour of the feather imparts the necessary curve (*see* Fig. 127).

Tie in the two strips of brown mallard, slightly overlapping the main wing. This is rather difficult to manage at first, but by pushing the waste ends upwards and stroking the strips over the main wing, it can be achieved with a little practice. *See also* page 213, for a very good method of putting on the brown mallard strips.

The next step is to tie in the jungle cock cheeks. Cut off the soft fibres at the base, and tie them in one at a time. Before cutting off the surplus stems pull these slightly to the right so that the fibres at the extreme base are drawn a little way under the turns of tying silk. This will keep the jungle cock feathers in place, and ensure that they remain flat against the wings.

Now cut off all the waste ends. To get a tapered head, lift the waste ends up and cut them off by placing the scissors flat on the hook shank.

Now tie in the topping after preparing it as the instructions on page 185. The tip of the topping should just reach the tip of the tail, forming that essential "halo" round the wing that is the hall-mark of a well-tied fly. Wind the silk to the right until the eye is nearly reached and cut off any surplus stem of the topping that remains. Wind the silk back to the base of the wing, and then back to cover all the previous turns. There should be no waste material showing after this is done.

Soak the head in cellire varnish and leave to dry. This can be either clear varnish or an undercoat of the black varnish that is used for the head. When it is dry give it a further coat of black varnish as this ensures that a smooth, glossy head is imparted.

A neat head is another sign of a well-tied fly, and the beginner will not always find it possible to achieve this at first. One important step in the right direction is judging the amount of room that must be left between the throat hackle and the eye, to take the wings, etc. Another is to keep the turns of silk down to a minimum. Each turn must be made to do its job, and not have three or four more to assist it. Sufficient waxing of the silk is essential for this. A short, round "bullet" head is better than a long, thin tapering one.

The finished fly, in its correct proportions, is as Fig. 142.

Fig. 142

Baron
TAG. Round silver tinsel, dark claret floss.
TAIL. Golden pheasant topping.
BUTT. Black ostrich herl.
BODY. Two parts. First half flat silver tinsel, ribbed oval silver tinsel, butted with Indian crow and ostrich herl. Second half black floss silk, ribbed oval silver tinsel, dark claret hackle over.
THROAT. Blue jay.
WINGS. Tippit, yellow swan, summer duck, golden pheasant tail, peacock wing, brown mallard, topping over.
SIDES. Jungle cock.
CHEEKS. Chatterer or kingfisher.
HEAD. Black varnish.

Black Doctor
TAG. Round silver tinsel and lemon floss.
TAIL. Topping and Indian crow.
BUTT. Scarlet wool.
BODY. Black floss.
RIBS. Oval silver tinsel.

HACKLE. Dark claret hackle.
THROAT. Speckled guinea fowl.
WINGS. Mixed—Tippet in strands with golden pheasant tail over, "married" strands of scarlet, blue and yellow goose, florican bustard, peacock wing and light mottled turkey tail, "married" narrow strips of teal and barred summer duck, narrow strips of brown mallard over, and a topping over all.
HEAD. Scarlet wool.

Black Dog
TAG. Round silver tinsel.
TAIL. Topping and red goose.
BUTT. Black ostrich herl.
BODY. Black floss ribbed with yellow floss, with flat silver tinsel either side of yellow floss.
HACKLE. Black heron (body and throat).
WINGS. Yellow goose, bustard, red goose, Amhurst pheasant pintail, topping over.
HEAD. Black varnish.

Black Dose

(Canadian pattern tied by Mr. J. C. Arseneault, illustrated, facing page 236.)

TAG. Round silver tinsel, yellow floss.

TAIL Golden pheasant crest.

BODY. Black floss, ribbed oval silver.

HACKLE. Black.

WINGS. Black turkey "married" strands of red, yellow, blue swan, grey mallard, golden pheasant tail, brown mallard over, a topping over all.

SIDES. Jungle cock.

HEAD. Black varnish.

Black Silk

TAG. Round silver tinsel.

BUTT. Yellow floss.

TAIL. Topping.

BODY. Black floss ribbed oval silver tinsel.

HACKLE. Claret.

THROAT HACKLE. Blue.

WINGS. Tippets in strands, mixed swan, red, yellow, blue, speckled turkey, with strips of black and white amhurst pheasant tippet each side.

HEAD. Black varnish.

Blue Doctor

(Illustrated, facing page 188, tied by Mr. H. George.)

TAG. Round silver tinsel and golden yellow floss.

TAIL. A topping and tippet in strands.

BUTT. Scarlet wool.

BODY. Pale blue floss.

RIBS. Oval silver tinsel.

HACKLE. Pale blue hackle.

THROAT. Blue jay.

WINGS. Mixed—tippet in strands with strip of golden pheasant tail over, "married" strands of scarlet blue, and yellow swan, florican bustard, peacock wing and light mottled turkey tail, "married" narrow strips of teal and barred summer duck, narrow strips of brown mallard over, a topping over all.

HEAD. Scarlet wool.

Bull Dog

TAG. Round silver tinsel and claret floss.

BUTT. Black ostrich.

BODY. First half flat silver tinsel, veiled with toucan, jointed with black ostrich. Second half light blue floss, ribbed with oval silver and light blue hackle.

THROAT. Guinea fowl hackle.

WINGS. Strips of yellow and black swan, golden pheasant tail, summer duck over (or teal), toppings over all.

CHEEKS. Jungle cock.

HEAD. Black ostrich.

Childers

TAG. Round silver tinsel and pale blue floss silk.

TAIL. A topping and Indian crow.

BUTT. Black herl.

BODY. Golden yellow floss, orange and fiery brown seal's fur in equal sections.

RIBS. Flat silver tinsel and twist.

HACKLE, A badger hackle dyed lemon.

THROAT. Golden pheasant breast feather followed by widgeon.

WINGS. Mixed—A pair of golden pheasant breast feathers (back to back) "married" strands of scarlet, blue, orange and yellow swan, bustard, florican, golden pheasant tail, cinnamon and mottled grey turkey tail, a topping over.

SIDES. Barred summer duck strips.

CHEEKS. Blue chatterer.

HEAD. Black varnish.

Coiner

TAG. Round silver tinsel, claret floss.

TAIL. Golden pheasant topping and Indian crow.

BUTT. Black ostrich herl.

BODY. One-third orange floss, covered by an orange hackle and fine gold tinsel; remainder silver monkey or grey seal's fur covered with grey hackle and silver tinsel of a thicker size than the other end.

THROAT. Claret hackle.

WINGS. Bustard, peacock wing, guinea fowl, red, blue and yellow swan, golden pheasant tail, topping over, in front of this, forming a head, a few strands of tippet.

HEAD. Black varnish.

Cound

TAG. Round silver tinsel.

TAIL. Topping.

BODY. Black floss, ribbed oval silver.

HACKLE. Yellow at head only.

WINGS. Mixed—Tippet in strands, yellow, blue and red swan, golden pheasant tail, brown mallard.

HEAD. Black varnish.

Dixon

TAG. Round gold tinsel, yellow floss silk.

TAIL. Topping.

BUTT. Black ostrich herl.

BODY. Two turns of light orange floss silk, followed by light orange wool.

RIBS. Oval gold tinsel and black floss silk.

HACKLE. Claret.

THROAT. Guinea fowl.

WINGS. Red-blue-yellow swan, bustard, peacock wing, golden pheasant tail, brown mallard, summer duck, guinea fowl, topping over all.

HEAD. Black varnish.

Dunkeld

TAG. Round silver tinsel and light orange floss.

TAIL. Topping, a pair of jungle cock feathers (back to back), veiled by a pair of Indian crow feathers (back to back).

BUTT. Black ostrich herl.

BODY. Flat gold tinsel.

RIBS. Fine oval silver tinsel.

HACKLE. Bright orange hackle.

THROAT. Blue jay.

WINGS. Mixed—Tippet in strands, "married" strands of scarlet, yellow, and blue swan, peacock wing, bustard, florican, golden pheasant tail and mottled brown turkey tail, strips of brown mallard over, a topping over all.

SIDES. Jungle cock.

CHEEKS. Blue chatterer.

HEAD. Black varnish.

Gordon

(Illustrated, facing page 212.)

TAG. Round silver tinsel.

TAIL. A topping and Indian crow.

BUTT. Black ostrich herl.

BODY. First quarter light orange and remainder red floss.

RIBS. Flat silver tinsel and twist.

HACKLE. Claret hackle.

THROAT. Light blue hackle.

WINGS. Mixed—A pair of bright red hackles (back to back) or golden pheasant sword feathers, strands of peacock herl "married" strands of orange, scarlet and blue swan, golden pheasant tail and bustard, a topping over.

CHEEKS. Tippet (small) and jungle cock over, topping over all.

HEAD. Black varnish.

Green Highlander

(Illustrated, facing page 236.)

TAG. Round silver tinsel.

TAIL. A topping and barred summer duck in strands.

BUTT. Black ostrich herl.

BODY. First quarter, golden yellow floss, remainder bright green floss or seal's fur.

RIBS. Oval silver tinsel.

HACKLE. A green hackle.

THROAT. A dyed lemon hackle.

WINGS. Mixed—Tippet in strands "married" strands of yellow, orange and green swan, florican, peacock wing, and golden pheasant tail, "married" narrow strips of teal and barred summer duck, narrow strips of brown mallard over, a topping over all.

SIDES. Jungle cock.

CHEEKS. Indian crow.

HEAD. Black varnish.

Mar Lodge

(Illustrated, facing page 188, tied by Mr. H. George.)

TAG. Bound silver tinsel.

TAIL. Topping, jungle cock.

BUTT. Black ostrich herl.

BODY. In three equal parts: Nos. 1 and 3 of embossed silver tinsel, No. 2 of black floss silk.

RIBS. Oval silver tinsel.

THROAT. Guinea fowl.

WINGS. Yellow-red-blue swan, strips of peacock wing, summer duck, grey mallard, dark mottled turkey tail, golden pheasant tail, topping over.

SIDES. Jungle cock.

HEAD. Black varnish.

Kate

TAG. Round silver tinsel, light yellow floss silk.

TAIL. Topping.

BUTT. Black ostrich herl.

BODY. Two turns of crimson floss silk, crimson seal fur.

RIBS. Oval silver tinsel.

HACKLE. Crimson.

THROAT. Light yellow hackle.

WINGS. Mixed—Tippet in strands, bustard, golden pheasant tail, yellow-crimson-light blue swan, brown mallard, topping over.

SIDES. Jungle cock.

HEAD. Black varnish.

Nansen

TAG. Round silver tinsel, yellow seal's fur.

TAIL. Topping and Indian crow.

BUTT. Black ostrich herl.

BODY. Four equal parts: red, orange, dark blue, claret seal's fur, ribbed silver oval tinsel.

HACKLE. Dark blue on dark blue seal's fur, and dark claret on claret part of the body.

THROAT. Guinea fowl.

WINGS. Extended red breast golden pheasant feathers, golden pheasant tail, light bustard and guinea fowl.

HEAD. Black varnish.

Popham

TAG. Round silver tinsel.

TAIL. Topping and Indian crow.

BUTT. Black ostrich herl.

BODY. In three equal sections: orange, lemon, yellow and pale blue floss respectively; first and second sections each butted with black herl, and all sections veiled above and below with Indian crow.

RIBS. Oval gold tinsel for first and second sections; oval silver tinsel for the third section.

THROAT. Blue jay.

WINGS. Mixed—Tippet in strands, "married" strands of bustard, florican, peacock wing, scarlet, blue, orange and yellow swan and golden pheasant tail, peacock sword over all.

SIDES. Barred summer duck, two or three toppings over all.

HEAD. Black varnish.

Rogue

TAIL. Orange and yellow swan or goose.

BODY. Orange and black seal's fur, ribbed silver oval tinsel.

HACKLE. Orange with blue jay in front.

WINGS. Yellow, blue, red swan or goose with teal over all.

HEAD. Black varnish.

Silver Doctor

(Illustrated, facing page 188.)

TAG. Round silver tinsel and golden yellow floss.

TAIL. A topping and blue chatterer.

BUTT. Scarlet wool.

BODY. Flat silver tinsel.

RIBS. Fine oval silver tinsel.

THROAT. A pale blue hackle, followed by widgeon.

WINGS. Mixed—Tippet in strands with strips of golden pheasant tail over, "married" strands of scarlet, blue and yellow swan or goose, florican, bustard, peacock wing and light mottled turkey tail, "married" narrow strips of teal and barred summer duck, narrow strips of brown mallard over, a topping over all.

HEAD. Scarlet wool.

Silver Grey

(Illustrated, facing page 188, tied by Mr. H. George.)

TAG. Silver thread and golden yellow floss.

TAIL. A topping and barred summer duck (in strands).

BUTT. Black ostrich herl.

BODY. Flat silver tinsel.

HACKLE. A badger hackle.

THROAT. Widgeon.

WINGS. Mixed—Tippet in strands, "married" strands of white, yellow and green swan or goose, bustard, florican and golden pheasant tail, "married" strips of pintail and barred summer duck, brown mallard strips over, a topping over all.

CHEEKS. Jungle cock.

HEAD. Black varnish.

Silver Wilkinson

(Illustrated, facing page 236.)

TAG. Round silver tinsel and golden yellow floss.

TAIL. A topping and blue chatterer (or kingfisher).

BUTT. Scarlet wool.

BODY. Flat silver tinsel.

RIBS. Fine oval silver tinsel.

WINGS. Tippet in strands with strips of golden pheasant tail over, "married" strands of scarlet, blue, yellow swan or goose, florican bustard, bustard (or substitute), light mottled turkey tail over, "married" narrow strips of teal and barred summer duck each side of the wings, and a topping over all.

THROAT HACKLE. A magenta hackle, followed by widgeon shoulder feather.

CHEEKS. Blue chatterer or kingfisher.

HEAD. Black varnish.

Tom Tickler

TAG. Round silver tinsel, blue floss silk.

TAIL. Topping.

BUTT. Black ostrich herl.

BODY. Orange floss silk.

RIBS. Oval gold tinsel.

HACKLE. Orange.

THROAT. Blue hackle and guinea fowl.

WINGS. Golden pheasant tail, red swan, bustard.

CHEEKS. Blue chatterer.

HEAD. Black varnish.

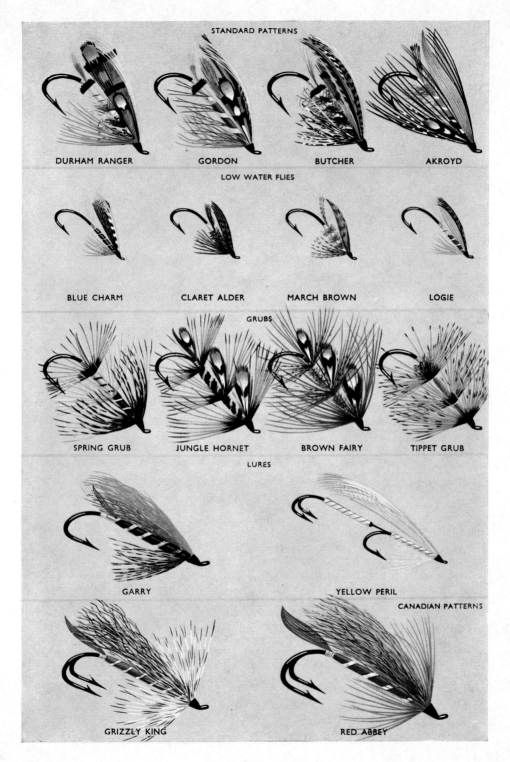

STANDARD PATTERNS

DURHAM RANGER   GORDON   BUTCHER   AKROYD

LOW WATER FLIES

BLUE CHARM   CLARET ALDER   MARCH BROWN   LOGIE

GRUBS

SPRING GRUB   JUNGLE HORNET   BROWN FAIRY   TIPPET GRUB

LURES

GARRY   YELLOW PERIL

CANADIAN PATTERNS

GRIZZLY KING   RED ABBEY

SALMON FLIES

TYING BUILT WING FLIES

"Jock Scott" (Illustrated, facing page 188)

Materials required—

Tag—Round silver tinsel.

Tail—A topping and Indian crow.

Butt—Black ostrich herl.

Body—In two equal parts: The first half yellow floss, veiled above and below with Toucan breast feathers. (Small golden pheasant crests may be used as a substitute.) Then another black ostrich herl butt and the remaining half of black floss.

Ribs—Fine oval silver tinsel over the first half, broader oval silver tinsel over the second half.

Body Hackle—Black—over the black floss only.

Throat—Speckled gallena (guinea fowl).

Wings—Two strips of dark, white-tipped turkey tails, back to back, then a mixed sheath, not entirely covering the turkey tails, of yellow, scarlet and blue swan (or goose), speckled bustard, florican bustard, golden pheasant tail, and two strands of peacock sword herl above; "married" narrow strips of teal and barred summer duck (or mandarin duck) each side, and brown mallard as the final sheath. A topping over all.

Sides—Jungle cock.

Cheeks—Blue chatterer (or kingfisher).

Head—Black varnish.

This is the most difficult type of wing to assemble, as the three main sections (a) the turkey tails, (b) the "mixed" wing, and (c) the brown mallard, should overlap each other somewhat like the tiles of a roof. It is well worth the trouble it entails, however, for a well tied "Jock Scott" is a beautiful object, besides being known the world over for its fish-taking qualities.

A very good method of putting on the brown mallard "roof" is as follows—

Cut two left and right strips from the feathers, leaving the quill adhering. Pull the fibres out at right-angles to the quill as much as possible. It will be found that the fibres retain a certain amount of their natural curve, but this is not important. Now place the two strips, one on top of the other, dark side uppermost. Pick the quill parts up in the right hand, and stroke the fibres as much into line as possible. It will be seen that one curves slightly to the left, and the other to the right, but again this is not very important. Now cut off quills.

Now place the two strips flat on top of the mixed wing, their tips in line with the tips of the mixed wing. Hold them in position with the right hand, and then with the thumb and forefinger of the left hand fold the strips down over the mixed wing. Keep them folded over with the thumb and forefinger of the left hand and tie them in in exactly the same way as any other wings (*see* pages 192 and 193).

It will be found that brown mallard wings tied in this fashion do not have the usual tendency to fly upwards from the main wing.

With the exception of the veiling on the first half of the body, the instructions up to the winging have already been dealt with in the three previous sections, so there is no point in my repeating them here.

The toucan feathers used in the veiling are very delicate and at least three are required above and below, and up to six may be used.

They should be prepared by cutting off the unnecessary fibres at the base, so that, when they are tied in, the remaining fibres should just overlap the rear butt.

They should be placed one on top of the other for tying in, and this will be helped if they are moistened first. Hold them in place firmly during the tying in, so that the stems are not displaced. The next step is to tie in and wind the middle butt, and this hides the turns of tying silk that hold the toucan feathers.

If golden pheasant crests are used as a substitute, only two of these will be required above and below, as they are much more substantial feathers. The stems at the base should be well flattened to simplify this operation.

After the body has been completed and the throat hackle tied in and wound, the next step is the winging.

The underwing of white-tipped turkey is the first stage, and two strips should be selected, left-hand strip for the left hand or far wing, and right-hand strip for the near wing. The natural curve imparted to the feathers when they are tied in in this fashion will make them lie low along the body. The fly should now be as Fig. 143

Fig. 143

Now the mixed sheaths are tied in either side of the turkey so that the base of the turkey can still be seen. The sheath formed of left-hand fibres should form the right-hand wing. Details of how the mixed sheaths are formed will be found on pages 182 to 185.

The strands of peacock sword herl should now be tied in over the top of the wings, their natural curve following the curve of the wings.

Next, the two "married" strips of teal and barred summer duck should be tied in, as described on pages 206 to 207.

The brown mallard strips are now tied in, overlapping the mixed wing, but not to hide it. In my opinion the "Jock Scott", illustrated, facing page 188, has brown mallard strips that are too wide. They should not obscure the rest of the wings quite so completely.

The jungle cock sides are now tied in and over them the blue chatterer or kingfisher cheeks. Then the topping, which should be prepared, as the instructions on page 185, and all that remains to be done is the varnishing of the head. The finished fly should now be as Fig. 144.

Fig. 144

Black Rover

TAG. Round silver tinsel, red floss.

TAIL. Topping and red crow.

BUTT. Bronze peacock herl.

BODY. First half yellow floss, hackle to match floss, silver tinsel ribbed. Second half black floss, black hackle, ribbed oval silver tinsel.

THROAT. Guinea fowl.

WINGS. Two strips of dark white-tipped turkey tail, golden pheasant centre tail, bustard, brown mallard, purple swan or goose, barred summer duck, topping over all.

HEAD. Black varnish.

Blue Jock

TAG. Round silver tinsel.

BUTT. Black ostrich herl.

BODY. In two equal halves. First half golden yellow floss butted with black herl and veiled above and below with six or more toucan feathers; second half blue floss.

RIBS. Fine oval silver tinsel over golden yellow floss, broader oval silver tinsel or flat silver tinsel and twist over the blue floss.

HACKLE. A blue hackle over the blue floss.

THROAT. Speckled gallena.

WINGS. A pair of black white-tipped turkey tail's strips (back to back) over these, but not entirely covering them; a mixed sheath of "married" strands of peacock wing, yellow, scarlet and blue swan or goose, bustard, florican and golden pheasant tail, two strands of peacock sword feather above "married" narrow strips of teal and barred summer duck at the sides, brown mallard over, a topping over all.

SIDES. Jungle cock.

CHEEKS. Blue chatterer.

HEAD. Black varnish.

Blue Rover

TAG. Round silver tinsel, magenta floss.

TAIL. Topping tippet and Indian crow.

BUTT. Black ostrich herl.

BODY. One-third blue floss, one-third silver tinsel, one-third blue floss; blue hackle down and ribbed silver oval, orange hackle and guinea fowl at shoulder.

WINGS. Two strips of white-tipped dark turkey tail, yellow, red and blue swan or goose, two red hackles, barred summer duck, topping over all.

SIDES. Jungle cock.

CHEEKS. Kingfisher.

HEAD. Black varnish.

Butcher

(Illustrated, facing page 212.)

TAG. Round silver tinsel and lemon floss.

TAIL. A topping and blue chatterer.

BUTT. Black herl.

BODY. Fiery brown, pale blue, claret and dark blue seal's fur in equal section (picked out).

RIBS. Flat silver tinsel and twist.

HACKLE. A dark claret or black hackle.

THROAT. Lemon hackle followed by speckled gallena.

WINGS. A pair of tippets (back to back) covered by a pair of golden pheasant breast feathers, and these by a pair of broad strips of teal, "married" narrow strips of yellow swan or goose and bustard, scarlet and blue swan or goose and orange swan or goose, golden pheasant tail, strips of brown mallard over (rather broad), a topping over all.

CHEEKS. Blue chatterer.

HEAD. Black varnish.

Dusty Miller

(Illustrated, facing page 188, tied by Mr. H. George.)

TAG. Silver thread and golden yellow floss.

TAIL. A topping and Indian crow.

BUTT. Black ostrich herl.

BODY. First two-thirds embossed silver tinsel, remainder orange floss.

RIBS. Fine oval silver tinsel.

HACKLE. Golden olive hackle over the orange floss only.

THROAT. Speckled gallena.

WINGS. A pair of black white-tipped turkey tail strips (back to back) over these, but not entirely hiding them; a mixed sheath of "married" strands of teal, yellow, scarlet and orange swan or goose, bustard, florican and golden pheasant tail, "married" narrow strips of pintail and barred summer duck, narrow strips of brown mallard over, a topping over all.

CHEEKS. Jungle cock.

HEAD. Black varnish.

Jock Scott

(Illustrated, facing page 188, tied by Mr. H. George.)

TAG. Round silver tinsel.

TAIL. Topping and Indian crow.

BUTT. Black ostrich herl.

BODY. In two equal halves. First half golden yellow floss, butted with black herl, and veiled above and below with six or more toucan feathers; second half black floss.

RIBS. Fine oval silver tinsel over golden yellow floss, broader oval silver tinsel or flat silver tinsel and twist over the black floss.

HACKLE. A black hackle over the black floss.

THROAT. Speckled gallena.

WINGS. A pair of black white-tipped turkey tail strips (back to back) over these, but not entirely covering them;

a mixed sheath of "married" strands of peacock wing, yellow, scarlet and blue swan or goose, bustard, florican, and golden pheasant tail, two strands of peacock sword feather above, "married" narrow strips of teal and barred summer duck at the sides, brown mallard over, a topping over all.

SIDES. Jungle cock feathers.

CHEEKS. Blue chatterer.

HEAD. Black varnish.

Red Drummond

TAG. Round silver tinsel, yellow floss.

TAIL. Topping and Indian crow.

BUTT. Black ostrich herl.

BODY. First half silver tinsel, ribbed oval silver tinsel. Second half red floss, ribbed oval silver tinsel.

HACKLE. Red hackle over red floss.

THROAT HACKLE. Guinea fowl.

WINGS. White tip turkey tail yellow, blue, red swan or goose, bustard, brown mallard and topping over.

SIDES. Jungle cock.

CHEEKS. Blue chatterer.

HEAD. Black varnish.

Red Sandy

TAG. Silver thread and golden yellow floss.

TAIL. A topping Indian crow and blue chatterer.

BUTT. Scarlet wool.

BODY. Flat silver tinsel.

RIBS. Fine oval silver tinsel.

HACKLE. A badger hackle dyed deep orange.

THROAT. Blue jay or speckled gallena dyed blue.

WINGS/SIDES/CHEEKS. As in Jock Scott, except that the blue swan or goose is omitted from the mixed sheath, and there is the addition of Indian crow under the blue chatterer cheeks.

HEAD. Scarlet wool.

Yellow Torrish

(Illustrated, facing page 188, tied by Mr. H. George.)

TAG. Round silver tinsel, yellow floss silk.

TAIL. Topping, ibis.

BUTT. Black ostrich herl.

BODY. In two equal parts of silver tinsel; first butted Indian crow and black ostrich herl.

THROAT, Yellow hackle.

WINGS. Two strips dark white-tipped turkey tail, bustard, peacock wing, guinea fowl, golden pheasant tail, red and blue swan, brown mallard, topping over.

CHEEKS. Jungle cock.

HEAD. Black varnish.

TYING TOPPING WING FLIES

The golden pheasant crests for these wings are prepared as the instructions on page 185.

The feathers should be selected so that the smallest forms the base. The rest should gradually increase in size until the largest on the top is reached.

All the stems must be tied one on top of the other, so it is most important that they be well flattened beforehand. It is better if they can all be tied in at once, but, if this proves difficult, they can be tied in singly or two at a time. It will be found helpful if they are moistened before tying in.

Black Prince

TAG. Round silver tinsel.

TAIL. Topping and jungle cock.

BUTT. Black herl.

BODY. Flat silver tinsel in three sections, each section butted with black herl and veiled above and below with small greenish bronze feathers from the head of English cock pheasant.

THROAT. A black hackle.

WINGS. Six golden pheasant toppings.

HEAD. Black varnish.

Blue Boyne

TAG. Round silver tinsel.

TAIL. Two Indian crow feathers.

BUTT. Black ostrich herl.

BODY. Four sections of silver with four points of blue chatterer above and below.

WINGS. Two golden pheasant toppings and two strands of blue macaw.

HEAD. Black varnish.

Canary

TAG. Round gold tinsel.

TAIL. A topping and Indian crow.

BODY. Flat silver tinsel in two sections and each section butted with black herl and veiled above and below with three or more toucan feathers.

THROAT. Orange hackle.

WINGS. Six golden pheasant toppings.

HEAD. Black varnish.

Variegated Sun Fly

TAG. Round silver tinsel and pale blue floss silk.

TAIL. A topping and strands of orange hackle.

BODY. Black, yellow and orange wool wound round together.

THROAT. Black hackle.

WINGS. Six golden pheasant toppings.

HEAD. Black varnish.

TYING HERL WING FLIES

The strands of herl for these flies come from the tail of the peacock; either the green "sword" tails or the bronze "eye" tails.

Those for the "Alexandra" (Fig. 145), which in reality is only a larger version of the lake trout fly of that name, come from the "sword" tail.

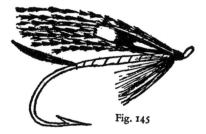

Fig. 145

As these feathers have the herl on one side only, a left and a right hand tail are required. The herls should not be stripped off the stem, but equal sections should be cut from the feathers, leaving the quill adhering. The two sections should be tied in as are strip and mixed wings.

The peacock "eye" tails, as used for the "Beauly Snow Fly" (Fig. 146), have herls on both sides of the central quill, so that the two wings can be cut from the same quill. They can be tied in like strip wings or in a bunch. Care should be taken to ensure that these herls are complete, and not broken off at the tips, as this spoils the appearance of the fly.

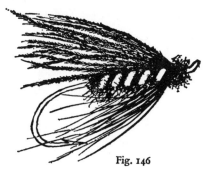

Fig. 146

Alexandra
TAIL. Scarlet ibis.
BODY. Flat silver tinsel, ribbed oval silver.
THROAT. A black or badger hackle.
WINGS. Peacock sword feather.
CHEEKS. Jungle cock.
HEAD. Black varnish.

Beauly Snow Fly
BODY. Pale blue seal's fur.
RIBS. Broad, flat, silver tinsel and gold twist.
HACKLE. A black heron's hackle from third turn of tinsel.
WINGS. Bronze peacock herl from "eye" tail in strands.
HEAD. Orange seal's fur, or a "collar" of cock o' the rock feathers.

Green Peacock
TAG. Round silver tinsel and golden yellow floss.
TAIL. A topping.
BODY. Pale blue floss.
RIBS. Oval silver tinsel.
THROAT. A pale blue hackle.
WINGS. Peacock sword feather.
HEAD. Black varnish.

Lovat
TAG. Round silver tinsel.
TAIL. Golden pheasant red breast feather.
BODY. Two turns of yellow wool, followed by blue wool.
HACKLE. Black.
WINGS. Bronze peacock herl from "eye" tail in strands.
HEAD. Yellow mohair picked out.

CHAPTER TWENTY-ONE

DRESSING SALMON FLIES
SMALL LOW WATER SUMMER PATTERNS

THERE ARE NOT really any specific patterns of Low Water flies as practically any standard pattern can be tied in this style. The "Logie", "Blue Charm", "Silver Blue", "Claret Alder" and "March Brown", shown in the illustrations facing pages 212 and 236, are usually tied as Low Water patterns, and they are included in the list of patterns given at the end of this chapter.

If "mixed" wing patterns are to be tied in this style, it is not possible to incorporate all the materials given in the dressings, and any omissions must be left to the discretion of the tyer. The "White Doctor", which is also illustrated, is an example of this.

The hooks used for these flies are the "Low Water" type illustrated on page 27.

The "Logie" (Illustrated, facing page 212)

Materials required—

Tag—Round silver tinsel, or silver wire.
Tail—Golden pheasant crest feather.
Body—First two-fifths pale primrose floss, remainder red floss.
Ribs—Finest oval silver tinsel.
Throat—Pale blue hackle.
Wings—Strips of yellow swan (or goose) set upright, brown mallard strips over.
Head—Black varnish.

The chief characteristics of this series of flies are the lightness of the dressing and the length of wing compared with the length of hook. They are used for greased line fishing during bright sunshine when the water is low and clear.

"Gossamer" tying silk should be used and the number of turns kept to a minimum.

"Marabou" floss should be used for the body, and this should be teased out to about one-third of its normal thickness. The completed body should be very little more in diameter than the hook shank itself.

One, or at the most two, turns of hackle at the throat is all that is required, and the fibres should be drawn downwards between the finger and thumb and sloped to the rear with a slanting turn of the tying silk, which goes over the top of the fibres only.

Two narrow strips of the yellow swan (or goose) are tied in to form a simple strip wing, sloping upwards. That is, right-hand strip to form left-hand wing and *vice versa* for the right-hand wing (Fig. 147).

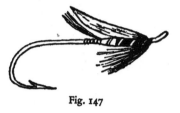

Fig. 147

Next, two narrow strips of brown mallard are tied in in the reverse way, so that they slope downwards over the yellow wing. No topping is required for this pattern, so all that remains is the varnishing of the head. The finished fly should be as Fig. 148.

Fig. 148

To complete the translucent effect required of these flies, the body can be given a coat of thin cellire varnish before the hackle and wings are tied in.

Blue Charm
TAG. Round silver tinsel.
TAIL. Golden pheasant crest (topping).
BODY. Black floss silk.
RIBS. Oval silver tinsel.
THROAT. Blue hackle.
WINGS. Brown mallard with narrow strips of teal over. Topping over all.
HEAD. Black varnish.

Claret Alder
TAG. Round silver tinsel and light orange floss.

TAIL. Claret wool.
BODY. Peacock herl.
RIBS. Oval gold tinsel.
THROAT. A dark claret hackle.
WINGS. Brown mallard.
HEAD. Black varnish.

Jeannie
TAG. Round silver tinsel or wire.
TAIL. Golden pheasant crest.
BODY. First third lemon floss, remainder black floss.
RIBS. Oval silver tinsel.

THROAT. Black hackle.
WINGS. Brown mallard.
SIDES. Jungle cock.
HEAD. Black varnish.

Logie
TAG. Silver tinsel.
TAIL. Golden pheasant crest.
BODY. First two-fifths pale primrose floss, remainder ruby red floss.
RIBS. Oval silver tinsel.
THROAT. Pale blue hackle.
WINGS. Strips of yellow goose set upright, covered by strips of brown mallard.
HEAD. Black varnish.

March Brown
TAG. Round silver tinsel.
TAIL. Unbarred summer duck or brown mallard.
BODY, Fur from hare's face, well picked out.
RIBS. Flat silver tinsel.
THROAT. Partridge brown back feathers.
WINGS. Hen pheasant tail strips.
HEAD. Black varnish.

Silver Blue
TAG. Silver tinsel.
TAIL. Golden pheasant crest.

BODY. Flat silver tinsel.
RIBS. Oval silver tinsel.
THROAT. Blue hackle.
WINGS. Two strips of teal breast feathers.
HEAD. Black varnish.

Thunder and Lightning
TAG. Round gold tinsel, yellow floss silk.
TAIL. Golden pheasant crest.
BODY. Black floss silk.
RIBS. Oval gold tinsel.
HACKLE. Orange.
THROAT. Blue jay.
WINGS. Brown mallard, topping over.
SIDES. Jungle cock.
HEAD. Black varnish.

White Doctor
TAG. Silver tinsel, yellow floss silk.
TAIL. Golden pheasant crest.
BUTT. Scarlet wool.
BODY. White floss silk.
RIBS. Silver tinsel.
THROAT. Blue jay in front of a pale blue hackle.
WINGS. Mixed—"Married" fibres of yellow, red, blue, green swan, golden pheasant tail, topping over.
SIDES. Blue chatterer or kingfisher.
HEAD. Black varnish.

The "Skeleton Beadle" series

These are a development of the "Beadle" series described on page 197, and were designed for greased line fishing.

They have the same features of the original "Beadles" in that the bodies and hackles are the same for each pattern. They are dressed extremely lightly, the bodies being very little thicker than the hook shank. The hooks used are the Low Water type described on page 27.

The wings deserve special mention as they are of a quite distinctive design. This design was thought out by Mr. L. Kilroy, and consists of narrow V's cut from various feathers. It is important that the feathers have fibres of the same length on each side of the quill. An illustration of this type of wing, and also a completed fly, are shown in Figs. 149 and 150. They are called "Aero" wings, and the reason for this will be obvious.

The whole range of "Beadle" patterns was taken up by the well-known London fishing tackle firm of C. Farlow, and proved to be good killers both at home and in Canada.

The dressing of the basic body of the "Skeleton Beadle" is as follows—

Tag—Fine oval silver tinsel.

Tail—Golden pheasant crest feather.

Butt—Fine ostrich herl dyed buff.

Body—Tail half red floss silk, front half black floss silk, both very thin, ribbed with fine oval silver tinsel, and the whole then varnished with clear cellire varnish.

Hackle—Badger—at front only.

The wings for the six patterns are of different materials to those used for the original "Beadles", and are as follows—

1. Brown "Beadle" . . . V's cut from a large brown hackle and a speckled grouse body feather.

2. Buff "Beadle" . . . V's cut from a large brown hackle and a cock pheasant shoulder feather.

3. Yellow "Beadle" . . . V's cut from a large brown hackle and the tip of a dyed yellow swan feather.

4. Red "Beadle" . . . V's cut from a large brown hackle and a golden pheasant red breast feather.

5. White "Beadle" . . . V's cut from a large brown hackle and the tip of a white swan feather.

6. Speckled "Beadle" . . . V's cut from a large brown hackle and a teal flank feather.

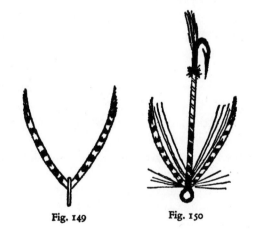

Fig. 149   Fig. 150

CHAPTER TWENTY-TWO

DRESSING SALMON FLIES

TYING DEE STRIP WING FLIES

The "Akroyd" (Illustrated, facing page 212)

Materials required—

Tag—Round silver tinsel.
Tail—A golden pheasant crest and strands of tippet.
Body—First half orange seal's fur, second half black floss.
Ribs—Oval silver over the first half, flat silver and round silver over the second half.
Hackle—A lemon hackle over the first half and a black heron hackle over the second half.
Throat—Teal flank.
Wings—A pair of cinnamon turkey tail strips.
Cheeks—Jungle cock, drooping.
Head—Black varnish.

Dee strip wing flies have several things in common with the spey flies discussed in the next chapter. They are lightly dressed, with mobile hackles and wings, and the method of dressing is also somewhat similar. They are usually tied on hooks with a slightly longer shank than those used for the standard patterns—namely, the "Low Water" type, illustrated on page 27.

They originated from the Aberdeenshire Dee, but their continual success over many years has extended their use to other rivers. They are used extensively during very cold weather, as the lightness of dressing allows them to sink very rapidly.

The tag and tail are formed in the usual way (*see* page 189) and then the oval silver tinsel for the rib of the first half of the body is tied in.

Now dub the orange seal's fur on to the tying silk, as described on page 178, and wind to the middle of the body. With the first turn of the tying silk and dubbing, tie in the tip of the lemon hackle.

The oval tinsel is now wound in even turns to the middle of the body, and then the hackle. This should follow closely the turns of the ribbing. Cut off the surplus ribbing and hackle stem, and the next stage is to tie in the flat silver and round silver tinsels that form the ribs of the second half of the body. The butt of the heron's hackle is also tied in at this point, and it should either be "doubled" or the fibres stripped from one side.

Continue winding the tying silk until the point where the throat hackle will be tied in is reached. Tie in a length of black floss, short end to the left, and wind it to the left until the orange seal's fur is reached, covering the ends of the tinsel and heron's hackle. Wind it back again to the throat; tie it in and cut off the surplus.

The flat silver is now wound in even turns to the throat, followed closely by the round tinsel. Tie both tinsels in and cut off the surplus. The heron's hackle is now wound to the same position, each turn being close up to a turn of the round tinsel. Finish off with one complete turn at the throat, tie in and cut off the surplus.

The teal feather for the throat must now either be "doubled" or the fibres stripped from one side. Tie it in by the tip, and two turns at the most is all that is required for this throat hackle. Cut off the waste stem, and continue winding the silk to the right and then back again to the left to form a "bed" for the wings. The fly should now be as Fig. 151.

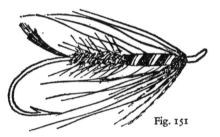

Fig. 151

For our wings we require two strips from either side of a cinnamon turkey *centre* tail, or a strip from each of a left and right feather. Assuming that the strips come from a centre tail, they should be cut from that feather with the quill still adhering to the fibres. The quill is then split down the centre, leaving the two strips as Fig. 152.

Fig. 152

When tied in they should lie horizontally and separated, and the best way to achieve this is as follows—

Place the right-hand strip against the hook shank, as Fig. 153, with the tying silk held vertically. This will ensure that the base of the wing is rightly positioned. Care should be taken to see that the tip of the wing does not project beyond the bend of the hook.

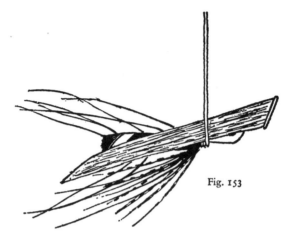

Fig. 153

Now take one or two turns at the most over the strip. This will take it over the top of the hook shank, so keeping the silk firmly in "catch", grasp the quill, and the fibres on the left of the tying silk, and draw all the fibres towards you until the top of the wing occupies a point exactly in the middle of the hook shank.

The same procedure must be followed with the far wing, the silk being reversed (*see* page 177) for this. Care must be taken to see that the top of the far wing lies exactly alongside the near wing on top of the hook shank. The reason for drawing the fibres closely together like this is the fact that the fibres of the turkey tail are particularly prone to splitting. Seen from above, the two strips should appear as Fig. 154.

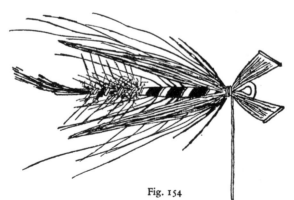

Fig. 154

Cut off the waste ends, as shown in Fig. 155, take two or three turns of silk to the right and then back again to the left. On no account go past the turns of silk holding the wings, otherwise they will immediately be thrown out of alignment, and the time spent seating them so carefully will have been wasted.

The jungle cock feathers are now tied in to flank the throat hackle, and not the wings, as is the usual custom. Tie them in firmly, cut off the surplus stems, and continue winding the silk to the right. Finish off with a whip finish, and the head is now ready for varnishing. The finished fly is illustrated in colour, facing page 212.

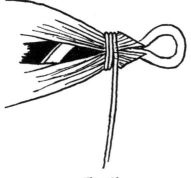

Fig. 155

Akroyd

(Illustrated, facing page 212.)

TAG. Round silver tinsel.

TAIL. A topping and tippet in strands.

BODY. First half light orange seal's fur, second half black floss.

RIBS. Oval silver tinsel over the orange seal's fur; flat silver tinsel and twist over black floss.

HACKLE. A lemon hackle over the orange seal's fur; a black heron's hackle over the black floss.

THROAT. Teal.

WINGS. A pair of cinnamon turkey tail strips (set flat). White turkey tail strips are often used, in which case the pattern is known as the white-winged Akroyd.

CHEEKS. Jungle cock (drooping).

HEAD. Black varnish.

Balmoral

TAG. Round silver tinsel.

TAIL. Topping and tippet.

BUTT. Black ostrich herl.

BODY. Equal halves of green and dark blue seal's fur, ribbed silver flat tinsel and silver lace.

BODY HACKLE. Black heron.

THROAT HACKLE. Widgeon.

WINGS. Two strips of plain cinnamon turkey tail.

SIDES. Jungle cock.

HEAD. Black varnish.

Black Eagle

TAG. Flat silver tinsel.

TAIL. Topping and Indian crow.

BODY. Black seal's fur, ribbed flat and oval silver.

HACKLE. Black down body and at head.

WINGS. Dark white tip turkey tail.

HEAD. Black varnish.

Glentana

TAG. Round silver tinsel and lemon floss.

TAIL. A topping and the tip of a golden pheasant's breast feather.

BODY. First third light orange seal's fur; remainder claret seal's fur (dressed thin, but well picked out).

RIBS. Flat silver tinsel and twist.

HACKLE. A black heron's hackle from third turn of tinsel.

THROAT. Widgeon.

WINGS. As in Akroyd.

HEAD. Black varnish.

Grey Eagle

TAG. Round silver tinsel.

TAIL. As in Glentana.

BODY. Light orange, deep orange, scarlet and pale blue seal's fur in equal sections (dressed thin, but well picked out).

RIBS. Flat silver tinsel and twist.

HACKLE. An eagle's hackle (one side stripped) from third turn of tinsel.

THROAT. Widgeon.

WINGS. A pair of light, mottled grey turkey tail strips (set flat), as in Akroyd.

HEAD. Black varnish.

Jock o'Dee

TAG. Round silver tinsel.

TAIL. A topping and Indian crow.

BODY. Two-fifths lemon floss; remainder black floss.

RIBS. Flat silver tinsel and twist.

HACKLE. A grey heron's hackle from third turn of tinsel.

THROAT. Widgeon.

WINGS. As in Akroyd.

HEAD. Black varnish.

Yellow Eagle

(Illustrated, facing page 236.)

TAG. Round silver tinsel.

TAIL. A topping and the tip of a golden pheasant breast feather.

BODY. Lemon, bright orange, scarlet and fiery brown seal's fur in equal sections. (Well picked out.)

RIBS. Broad flat silver tinsel and twist.

HACKLE. A marabou feather dyed yellow, one side stripped. (This is used as a substitute for an eagle's feather.)

THROAT HACKLE. Widgeon shoulder feather.

WINGS. A pair of light mottled grey turkey tail strips, set as in Akroyd.

HEAD. Black varnish.

CHAPTER TWENTY-THREE

DRESSING SALMON FLIES

TYING SPEY FLIES

The "Grey Heron"

Materials required—

Body—First third lemon wool, remainder black wool
Ribs—Flat silver tinsel, oval gold tinsel and fine oval silver tinsel.
Hackle—A grey heron feather.
Throat—Speckled gallena (guinea fowl).
Wings—Brown mallard strips.
Head—Black varnish.

These are very distinctive flies and, as their name implies, were designed for use in the strong currents of the river Spey. Their chief characteristics are the thin body, the long, flowing hackle, and the horizontal mallard wing. They are tied on hooks with a longer shank than the standard patterns, the "Low Water" type, illustrated on page 27, being the most popular.

Tie in the tying silk a short distance from the eye and spiral it until a position immediately above the point of the hook is reached.

Now tie in the lemon wool which is to form the first part of the body. Next the thin silver oval tinsel which will form the protecting rib of the hackle. Continue winding to the right and, with the next turn of the silk, tie in the heron hackle. By the stem, and not by the tip, as the longest fibres should be at the rear. The hackle should be doubled, or one side should be stripped completely. The stripped side of the stem should lie next to the body when the hackle is wound.

Now tie in the flat silver tinsel on the side of the hook shank, after tapering it to a point. Continue winding for several turns to the right and tie in the oval gold tinsel.

A few more turns to the right should bring you to the point where the lemon wool section of the body ends. Wind the lemon wool to the right until this point is reached, avoiding the other items as you do so. The reason for tying all the items in series to the right is to avoid an ugly lump at the tail end of the body.

Tie in the lemon wool with a turn of the silk, pulling it tight as you do so. Now tie in the black wool, right up against the lemon wool, and wind the silk back to the starting point. Wind the black wool to this position, tie it in and cut off the surplus.

The flat tinsel is now wound to the shoulder and then the oval gold tinsel. The spirals of these two tinsels should be equal in number, and the same distance apart all along the body.

The hackle is now wound to the shoulder, each turn to lie between the spirals of the tinsel, when the shoulder is reached, two complete turns of the hackle should be made before the tip is tied in and the surplus cut off.

The narrow silver oval is now wound to the shoulder in the opposite direction to the other two tinsels and the hackle. That is, if the other tinsels and hackle were wound clockwise, the oval silver must be wound anti-clockwise. The function of the oval silver tinsel is to secure and protect the turns of hackle, and each turn should cover one turn of the hackle.

In some instances it is the hackle that is wound the opposite way, and the oval silver then follows the same direction as the other two tinsels.

Care must be taken not to tie down any of the fibres of the hackle during this operation; the stem only is to be secured.

The fly should now be as Fig. 156, and this shows the protecting tinsel wound in the opposite direction to the other two tinsels and hackle.

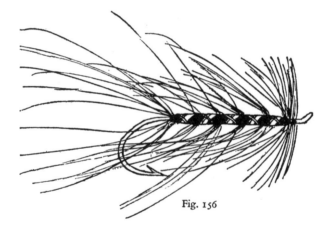

Fig. 156

The guinea fowl feather is now either doubled or stripped on one side, tied in and wound in the usual manner.

The next operation is the winging. The two strips from left and right brown mallard feathers should be selected so that, when their tips reach the bend of the hook (and no further), part of the grey roots near their stems will also be apparent when the wings are tied in.

The procedure for tying in this type of wing is rather different to anything we have dealt with previously.

All other wings, so far, have occupied a position as near as possible on top of the hook shank. The Spey wings should occupy the whole of the top half of the shank. The following two diagrams, Figs. 157 and 158, will probably illustrate this point more clearly.

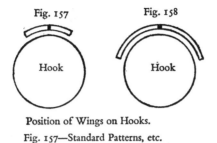

Position of Wings on Hooks.
Fig. 157—Standard Patterns, etc.
Fig. 158—Spey Flies

In this instance, as with dee flies, the wings are put on separately instead of in pairs, and the silk must be reversed before the far wing is put on (*see* page 177).

The two strips of brown mallard are cut from the main stems, and it is essential that the part of the quill to which the fibres adhere must be left on. The right-hand strip forms the right-hand or near wing, and the left-hand strip the far wing.

The near wing is placed alongside the hook shank, as Fig. 159, and one turn of

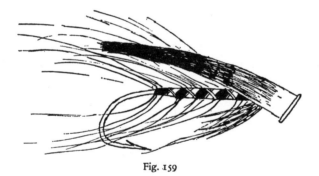

Fig. 159

silk taken round it immediately in front of the throat hackle. Doing this will no doubt take the top part of the strip too far over the hook shank, and it must be coaxed back to the middle by holding the wing each side of the tying silk and pulling it down. The silk must be firmly held in catch while this is being done. As soon as this is done, take two more turns of silk round the strip to the right. The wing should then be as Fig. 160.

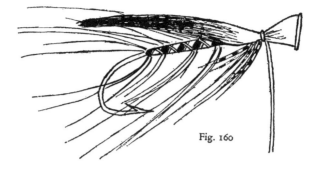

Fig. 160

To tie in the far wing it is now necessary to reverse the silk, and it is necessary also to complete this operation so that the silk is now where the first turn tied in the first strip, i.e., next to the throat hackle.

The silk can now be wound up and towards the tyer, instead of up and away. The far wing is now tied in the same way as the near wing and manipulated to occupy its half of the hook shank. It is possible to tie in this wing at the same time as the silk is reversed. This is achieved by holding a loop of silk in the middle finger of the left hand and winding the silk to the left in reverse over the far wing, which is held in place by the forefinger of the left hand. This may sound rather difficult when put into words, but soon becomes quite simple with a little practice.

The waste ends with the quill adhering are now cut off and the tying silk wound to the right to cover up any fibres left showing. The head must be kept as small as possible.

Finish off the tying silk with a whip finish, and the head is now ready for varnishing. The completed fly should now be as Fig. 161.

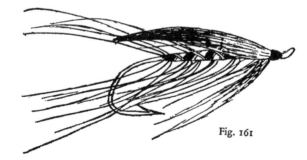

Fig. 161

Black King
BODY. Black floss.
RIBS. Flat and oval silver tinsels and silver thread.
HACKLE. A bronze-black spey cock's hackle.
THROAT. Teal.
WINGS. Brown mallard strips (short).
HEAD. Black varnish.

Carron
BODY. Orange wool.
RIBS. Flat silver tinsel, scarlet floss and silver thread.
HACKLE. A black heron's hackle (from the fourth turn of tinsel).
THROAT. Teal.
WINGS. As in Black King.
HEAD. Black varnish.

Gold Riach
BODY. First quarter orange wool; remainder black wool.
RIBS. Flat gold tinsel, oval gold tinsel and silver thread.
HACKLE. A reddish-brown spey cock's hackle.
THROAT. Widgeon.
WINGS. As in Black King.
HEAD. Black varnish.

Grey Heron
BODY. First third lemon wool; remainder black wool.
RIBS. Flat silver tinsel and oval silver and gold tinsels.
HACKLE. A grey heron hackle from one end of body tied in at the point.
THROAT. Speckled gallina.
WINGS. As in Black King.
HEAD. Black varnish.

Lady Caroline
TAIL. Golden pheasant breast feathers in strands.
BODY. Olive green and light brown wools wound together in the proportion of two strands of the latter to one of the former.
RIBS. Flat gold tinsel and oval silver and gold tinsels.
HACKLE. A grey heron hackle, as in the preceding pattern.
THROAT. Golden pheasant breast feather.
WINGS. As in Black King.
HEAD. Black varnish.

Red King
BODY. Red wool.
RIBS. Gold from far side, silver from near side, wound reverse way.
HACKLE. Spey cock wound from root instead of point.
THROAT. Teal.
WINGS. As in Black King.
HEAD. Black varnish.

CHAPTER TWENTY-FOUR

DRESSING SALMON FLIES

IRISH PATTERNS

IT IS NOT NECESSARY for me to give special tying instructions for these patterns as it is only in the matter of colouration that they differ from standard patterns.

As a general rule they are not as gaudy as the standard patterns, their more sombre hues being suitable for the peaty waters of Ireland.

Nearly every pattern is sheathed with brown mallard strips, and the use of toppings is not so general. Another feature is the popularity of golden pheasant tippet fibres as a base to the wings.

The method of dressing these flies is the same as for mixed and built wing patterns, as they usually consist of an underwing of mixed fibres and sheath of brown mallard.

The patterns illustrated, facing page 236, were tied by the well-known Dublin tackle firm of M. Garnett & Son.

Black Goldfinch
(Illustrated, facing page 236.)
TAG. Round silver tinsel and deep yellow silk.
TAIL. A topping.
BUTT. Black herl.
BODY. Black floss.
RIBS. Oval gold tinsel.
HACKLE. A claret hackle.
THROAT. Jay.
WINGS. Tippet in strands, covered by strips of deep yellow and red swan (set upright).
CHEEKS. Indian crow; two or three toppings over all.
HEAD. Black varnish.

Blue Palmer
TAG. Round gold tinsel.
TAIL. A topping and tippet in strands.

BUTT. Black herl.
BODY. Deep blue floss.
RIBS. Oval gold tinsel.
HACKLE. Jay.
THROAT. Jay.
WINGS. Mixed—Tippet in strands; "married" strands of scarlet, blue, yellow and orange swan, florican, bustard, golden pheasant tail, "married" narrow strips of teal (or pintail) and barred summer duck; strips of brown mallard over.
HEAD. Black varnish.

Blue Silk
TAIL. Strands of golden pheasant tippet, red ibis and peacock sword.
BODY. First quarter yellow, remaining three-quarters blue floss silk.
RIBBING. Silver twist or oval tinsel.

BODY HACKLE. A blood red hackle from the second turn of the ribbing tinsel to the throat.

THROAT. Dyed amber hackle.

WING. Strands of golden pheasant tippet, red goose, peacock sword, with brown mallard over all.

HEAD. Black varnish.

Claret Jay

TAG. Round silver tinsel and deep orange floss.

TAIL. A topping and tippet in strands.

BODY. First three-quarters deep claret seal's fur; remainder purple seal's fur.

RIBS. Oval gold tinsel.

BODY HACKLE. A deep claret hackle.

THROAT. Jay.

HEAD. Black varnish.

Fenian

TAG. Round silver tinsel.

TAIL. A topping and blue chatterer.

BODY. First quarter bright orange seal's fur; remainder bright green seal's fur.

RIBS. Oval gold tinsel.

HACKLE. A golden olive hackle over the green seal's fur.

THROAT. Jay.

WINGS. Mixed—Tippet in strands; "married" strands of green, yellow and orange swan, florican and golden pheasant tail; "married" narrow strips of pintail and barred summer duck, brown mallard strips over.

HEAD. Black varnish.

Fiery Brown

TAG. Round silver tinsel and golden yellow floss.

TAIL. A topping and tippet in strands.

BODY. First quarter bright orange seal's fur; second quarter light blue seal's fur; remainder fiery brown seal's fur.

RIBS. Oval silver tinsel.

HACKLE. A fiery brown hackle over the blue and fiery brown seal's fur.

THROAT. Jay.

WINGS. Mixed—Tippet in strands; "married" strands of scarlet, blue, yellow and orange swan, florican, bustard, golden pheasant tail; "married" narrow strips of teal (or pintail) and barred summer duck; strips (rather broad) of brown mallard over.

HEAD. Black varnish.

Gold Body

TAIL. Golden pheasant crest and strands of tippet.

BODY. Gold oval tinsel, or flat gold, ribbed with fine gold twist.

BODY HACKLE. Dyed blood red.

THROAT. Orange hackle.

WING. Strands of golden pheasant tippet, red goose, peacock sword, with dark mallard over all.

HEAD. Black varnish.

Goldfinch

This pattern is exactly similar to the Black Goldfinch except for the body, which is either of light orange floss or flat gold tinsel.

Golden Olive

(Illustrated, facing page 236.)

TAG. Round silver tinsel and golden yellow floss.

TAIL. A topping.

BODY. Light orange, bright orange, fiery brown and olive brown seal's fur in equal sections.

RIBS. Oval gold tinsel.

HACKLE. A golden olive hackle.

THROAT. Jay or dyed blue guinea fowl.

WING. Mixed—Tippet in strands; "married" strands of scarlet, blue, yellow and orange, and green swan, florican, bustard, golden pheasant tail, "married" narrow strips of teal (or pintail) and barred summer duck; strips (rather broad) of brown mallard over.

HEAD. Black varnish.

Green Silk

TAIL. Golden pheasant crest and strands of tippet.

BODY. Green floss silk.

RIBBING. Gold twist or oval tinsel.

THROAT HACKLE. Dyed yellow, followed by orange.

WING. Strands of tippet, peacock sword, with dark mallard over all.

HEAD. Black varnish.

Grouse and Green

TAG. Round silver tinsel.

TAIL. A topping.

BUTT. Black herl.

BODY. Grass-green floss.

RIBS. Oval silver tinsel.

HACKLE. A speckled feather from the rump of a cock grouse (one side stripped) from third turn of tinsel.

THROAT. Same as hackle.

WINGS. Mixed—Tippet in strands; "married" strands of yellow, green, scarlet and blue swan, florican and golden pheasant tail; strips of brown mallard over.

HEAD. Black varnish.

Grouse and Orange

TAG. Round silver tinsel.

TAIL. A topping and Indian crow.

BUTT. Black herl.

BODY. First quarter pale blue floss; remainder bright orange floss.

RIBS. Oval gold tinsel.

HACKLE. A speckled feather from the rump of a cock grouse (one side stripped) from third turn of tinsel.

THROAT. Same as hackle.

WINGS. Tippet in strands, veiled by golden pheasant breast feathers in strands; broad strips of speckled gallena wing; strips of brown mallard over.

HEAD. Black varnish.

Half Grey and Brown

TAG. Round silver tinsel and light orange floss.

TAIL. A topping and the tip of a golden pheasant's breast feather.

BODY. First half grey seal's fur (or grey squirrel); second half fiery brown seal's fur.

RIBS. Oval silver tinsel.

HACKLE. A grizzled hackle.

THROAT. A fiery brown hackle, followed by a lemon hackle.

WINGS. Mixed—Tippet in strands; "married" strands of orange, yellow, and scarlet swan, pintail and golden pheasant tail, brown mallard strips over.

HEAD. Black varnish.

Half Yellow and Black

TAG. Round silver tinsel.

TAIL. A topping and Indian crow.

BUTT. Black herl.

BODY. First half golden yellow floss; second half black floss.

RIBS. Oval gold tinsel.

HACKLE. A dark claret hackle over black floss.

THROAT. Jay.

WINGS. Mixed—Tippet in strands; "married" strands of scarlet, yellow and orange swan, bustard and golden pheasant tail; brown mallard strips over.

HEAD. Black varnish.

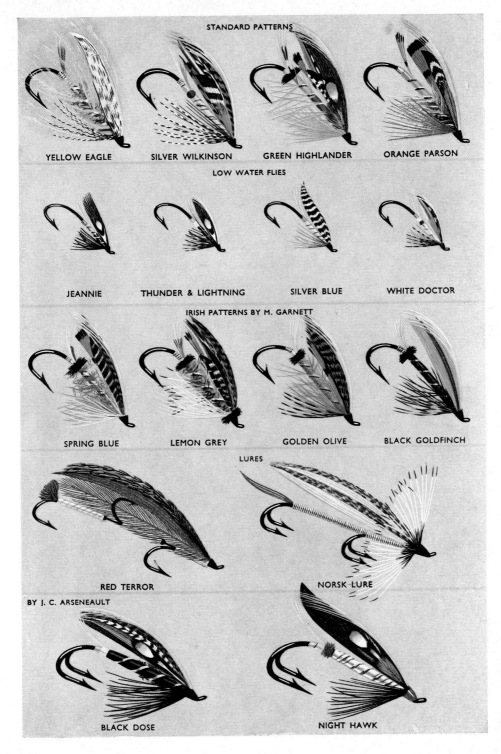

STANDARD PATTERNS

YELLOW EAGLE   SILVER WILKINSON   GREEN HIGHLANDER   ORANGE PARSON

LOW WATER FLIES

JEANNIE   THUNDER & LIGHTNING   SILVER BLUE   WHITE DOCTOR

IRISH PATTERNS BY M. GARNETT

SPRING BLUE   LEMON GREY   GOLDEN OLIVE   BLACK GOLDFINCH

LURES

RED TERROR   NORSK LURE

BY J. C. ARSENEAULT

BLACK DOSE   NIGHT HAWK

SALMON FLIES

Lemon Blue

TAG. Round silver tinsel and deep orange floss.

TAIL. A topping and tippet in strands.

BUTT. Black herl.

BODY. Deep blue seal's fur.

RIBS. Oval silver tinsel.

HACKLE. A blue hackle.

THROAT. A lemon hackle.

WINGS. Mixed—Tippet in strands; "married" strands of scarlet, blue, yellow and orange swan, florican, bustard, golden pheasant tail; "married" narrow strips of teal (or pintail) and barred summer duck; strips (rather broad) of brown mallard over.

HEAD. Black varnish.

Lemon Grey

(Illustrated, facing page 236.)

TAG. Round silver tinsel and golden yellow floss.

TAIL. A topping and Indian crow.

BUTT. Black herl.

BODY. Grey seal's fur.

RIBS. Oval silver tinsel.

HACKLE. A grizzled hackle.

THROAT. A lemon hackle.

WINGS. Mixed—Tippet in strands; "married" strands of green, yellow and orange swan, bustard, florican, golden pheasant tail; "married" narrow strands of teal and barred summer duck, brown mallard strips over.

HEAD. Black varnish, or peacock herl.

Spring Blue

(Illustrated opposite.)

TAG. Round silver tinsel and yellow floss.

TAIL. A topping and Indian crow.

BUTT. Black ostrich herl.

BODY. Blue seal's fur, ribbed silver tinsel.

BODY HACKLE. Blue

THROAT. Lemon yellow hackle.

WINGS. Tippet in strands, "married" strands of red, yellow, blue swan or goose, broad strips of teal at sides, brown mallard over; a topping over all.

HEAD. Black varnish.

CHAPTER TWENTY-FIVE

DRESSING SALMON FLIES
HAIR WING PATTERNS

"Jock Scott" (Illustrated, facing page 146)

Materials required—

Wings—Brown bear fur or bucktail, teal flank, two or three fibres of peacock sword and whisps of dyed scarlet, yellow and blue Polar bear or bucktail.

Shoulders—Jungle cock.

Cheeks—Blue chatterer (or kingfisher).

Head—Black varnish.

The tail, body, ribs, hackles, etc., are exactly the same as for the orthodox dressing of this fly and details will be found on page 213.

Hair-winged salmon flies are becoming increasingly popular in this country and, when their marked success becomes more widely publicised, they will be even more so.

Much of the popularity of the hair-winged fly is due to its extreme durability, an important item in these days of high prices, and also to the mobility of the fibres in fast water.

Most hair-winged patterns originated in the United States and Canada, but, by converting feathered colour schemes into terms of hair, it is possible to use all the well-established orthodox U.K. patterns. The "Jock Scott" discussed here is an instance of this, and no doubt the following simple conversion table will be found helpful—

For Dyed goose or swan	Dyed polar bear or bucktail.
Brown mallard	Brown bucktail.
Pintail, teal, etc.	Grey squirrel tail.
Brown mottled turkey	Brown squirrel tail.

One of the patterns originated in the U.K. is the "Garry", or "Yellow Dog", as it is sometimes called. The second name will give the reader some idea where the hair for this fly came from. Dyed bucktail is now generally used for this pattern.

The "Garry" was invented by the late John Wright, son of James Wright, the noted fly-tyer of Sprouston, Kelso-on-Tweed. It was named after the local

Minister's dog, who happened to walk into the shop when some black-bodied flies were being tied. A few hairs were cut from its tail, dyed yellow, and the result was the original of this pattern.

It is a very killing fly and, in fact, it killed three salmon the day following its origination. As all this happened twenty years ago, it is strange that the dressing of the fly is not more widely known.

Garry (or Yellow Dog)
(Illustrated, facing page 212.)
TAG. Gold or yellow floss and silver tinsel.
TAIL. Golden pheasant crest and ibis.
BODY. Black floss, silver oval rib.
HACKLE. Blue gallena.
WING. Yellow bear fur or bucktail, with a
few fibres of red at base.
HEAD. Black varnish.

The procedure for dressing hair wings will be found on pages 140–142, but it must be borne in mind that, as several different colours and types of hair are incorporated into each salmon fly wing, the quantities used must be much smaller.

The illustrations of the "Grizzly King" and "Red Abbey", facing page 212, show the type of fly that has been in use in Canada for many years. The use of the "collar" type of throat hackle should be noted, i.e., the hackle is left as wound and not drawn beneath the hook.

These patterns were tied by Mr. J. C. Arseneault, of Atholville, who is well-known on the Restigouche for his local patterns. The "Black Dose" and "Night Hawk" flies, illustrated, facing page 236, were also tied by Mr. Arseneault, and the dressings are given on pages 196 and 209.

Grizzly King
TAG. Round silver tinsel.
TAIL. Red ibis, swan or goose.
BODY. Green floss, ribbed oval silver tinsel.
WING. Mixed brown and white bucktail.
HACKLE. Grizzle.
HEAD. Black varnish.

Red Abbey
TAG. Round silver tinsel.
TAIL. Red ibis, goose or swan.
BODY. Red floss, ribbed flat silver tinsel.
WING. Light brown squirrel.
HACKLE. Light brown.
HEAD. Black varnish.

See also dressing hair wing "Silver Doctor" on page 146, illustrated, facing page 146.

CHAPTER TWENTY-SIX

DRESSING SALMON FLIES
GRUBS AND DRY FLY PATTERNS

With one or two exceptions there are no established patterns for grubs and dry flies. Both these types of fly are fairly simple to dress, as they are only elaborated "Palmer" flies. Those illustrated in colour, facing page 212, are quite well known, and are the type that are fished during summer weather when the water is low.

As to the dressing of them, they consist only of a salmon fly body with a hackle at the tail, middle and shoulder, with sometimes a pair of jungle cock feathers tied in back to back at each of these three points. They are excellent for practicing the tying in of tails, doubling of hackles, and forming of bodies, and tying one or two of them will give the beginner confidence in the handling of materials. This method of dressing the grubs is very similar to that used for tying some types of shrimp or prawn flies, which are discussed in the next chapter, *see* page 244.

Dry salmon flies are similar to the grubs, but they are usually tied on light hooks of sizes ranging from 10 to 7, *see* p. 27. Large, stiff cock hackles must be used and they are tied "Palmer" fashion, as described on page 72. The "Palmering" must be very heavy, so more than one hackle should be used.

Brown Fairy Grub
(Illustrated, facing page 212.)
TAG. Round gold tinsel.
TAIL. Tip of a golden pheasant red breast feather and pair of jungle cock feathers back to back.
TAIL HACKLE. Golden pheasant red breast feather, followed by a brown partridge back feather tied as hackles.
BODY. In two equal halves, fur from hare's face butted in the middle with same feathers as used for tail hackles.
THROAT. Same as the two tail hackles.
HEAD. Black varnish.

Glow Worm-Grub
TAG. Round silver tinsel.
TAIL. A tuft of scarlet wool.
TAIL HACKLE. A cock-y-bondhu hackle.

BODY. In two equal halves of oval gold tinsel, tightly twisted round before being wound on, butted at the joint with a cock-y-bondhu hackle, somewhat longer in the fibre than the previous hackle.
THROAT. A cock-y-bondhu hackle— longer still in the fibre.
HEAD. Black varnish.

Grey Palmer Grub
TAG. Round silver tinsel.
BODY. Peacock herl.
RIBS. Flat silver tinsel, comparatively broad.
HACKLE. A grizzled hackle from a Plymouth Rock hen, from the first turn of tinsel.
HEAD. Black varnish.

Jungle Hornet Grub

(Illustrated, facing page 212.)

TAG. Round silver tinsel.

TAIL. Scarlet ibis, and a pair of jungle cock feathers back to back.

TAIL HACKLE. A cock-y-bondhu hackle.

BODY. In two equal halves, each of turns of yellow and black wool wound together, and each butted at the joint with a cock-y-bondhu hackle and a pair of jungle cock feathers back to back.

THROAT. A cock-y-bondhu hackle. (The hackles on all the grubs should get larger as they near the head of the fly.

HEAD. Black varnish.

Spring Grub

(Illustrated, facing page 212.)

TAG. Round silver tinsel and pale blue floss.

TAIL. "Married" narrow strips of scarlet ibis and blue and yellow macaw (back to back).

TAIL HACKLE. A badger hackle dyed orange.

BODY. In two equal halves; first half golden yellow floss; second half black floss, butted at the joint with pale blue game hen's hackle or a natural blue gallena hackle.

RIBS. Black wool over the yellow floss, oval silver tinsel over the black floss.

THROAT. A coch-y-bondhu hackle, followed by a richly-coloured speckled grouse hackle.

HEAD. Black varnish.

Tippet Grub

(Illustrated, facing page 212.)

TAG. Round gold tinsel and scarlet seal's fur.

TAIL HACKLE. A tippet (wound as a hackle), followed by a furnace hackle.

BODY. In two equal halves, each beginning with three turns of silver thread, followed by green wool, butted at the joint with similar feathers and in the same way as for the butt.

THROAT. As for the butts (larger fibred feathers).

HEAD. Round silver tinsel.

Colonel Monell Palmer Dry Fly

TAIL. Fibres of grizzle cock's hackle.

BODY. Peacock herl ribbed red floss silk.

HACKLE. Grizzle cock hackle, tied palmer.

Soldier Palmer Dry Fly

TAIL. Fibres of natural red cock hackle.

BODY. Red seal's fur, ribbed gold tinsel.

HACKLE. Natural red.

Mole Palmer Dry Fly

TAIL. Fibres of mixed natural red, and grey cock's hackles.

BODY. Brown seal's fur.

HACKLE. Natural red, with grey at shoulder, tied palmer.

Pink Lady Palmer Dry Fly

TAIL. Fibres of ginger cock hackle.

BODY. Light pink silk, ribbed gold tinsel.

HACKLE. Ginger cock, with one or two turns of yellow at head, tied palmer.

The body dressing of these flies should be very light, and the "palmering" of the hackle very full.

See page 145 and 146 for hair-wing dressings of dry flies for salmon.

CHAPTER TWENTY-SEVEN

DRESSING SALMON FLIES
SHRIMPS AND PRAWNS

IT IS A WELL KNOWN FACT that when salmon will not look at the fly or spinner, fish can be taken on the shrimp or prawn. As supplies of the natural bait are not always available at times like this, a well-tied artificial may prove a satisfactory "killer".

In spite of this, really well-known imitations are of modern concept, two of the best I know being Mr. Pat Curry's golden and red shrimps. The dressings of these, together with an illustration, are given on page 244.

About the year 1953 Col. Esmond Drury produced his now famous "General Practitioner", so called because G. and P. were the initial letters of the feathers that formed most of the dressing—golden pheasant. On its first trial in the Test at Romsey, one hour's fishing resulted in three salmon and one lost!

It is a rather tricky fly to tie, but I hope the following instructions—with the illustration, will suffice.

1. Tie in at tail end four or five long fibres of red macaw. These are the long feelers.

2. Now wind a hackle of golden pheasant breast at the same place where the macaw is tied in. The fibres will form the shorter feelers or whiskers.

3. On top of this is tied a small orangy-red golden pheasant neck feather to form the lower part of the head. Concave side up.

4. Tie in a golden pheasant tippet to lie directly on top of No. 3.

5. Now tie in another orangy-red feather CONVEX side up, to lie directly on top of No. 4.

This completes the head of the prawn.

6. Tie in a very long hot orange cock's hackle, a strip of gold tinsel and dub the silk with a liberal quantity of pinkish-orange seal's fur. First wind the dubbed silk to A and secure, then rib the tinsel to A and secure, finally rib between the tinsel ribs with the hackle, and secure this at A.

Now cut away all hackle from the top side of the fly. This allows the other feathers to lie flat as they are tied in.

7. Tie in, convex side upwards, another orange-red golden pheasant breast feather long enough to partly overlap feathers 3, 4 and 5. Tie this down to lie flat.

8. Tie in tippet to lie flat on No. 7.

9. Dub a further length of silk as for operation 6 and wind dubbed silk tinsel and hackle as before, to B. Secure and cut away top side of hackle.

10 and 11. Repeat 7 and 8.

12. Repeat 9.

13. Repeat 7.

14. Finish head of fly and varnish red.

When the fly is complete, the feathers should be stroked backwards so that they lie snug to the body, this gives the effect of the scales of the prawn.

The dressing Col. Drury gives is for a fly to be tied on a large 3/0 to 5/0 hook, and may require to be modified on smaller hooks, by leaving out one of the body segments.

This fly can also be tied on tubes if required.

The foregoing dressing and the illustrations were first given in the *Fishing Gazette* of 9th January, 1960, and I am obliged to both Miss Marston, the editor, and Col. Drury himself, for their permission to include them in my book.

The complete list of materials is as follows—

Feelers (long)—Red macaw fibres.

Feelers (short)—Red golden pheasant breast.

Body—Pinkish-orange seal fur.

Hackle—Hot orange.

Rib—Oval gold tinsel.

Body Segments—Alternate golden pheasant orangy/red neck feathers and tippet feathers.

Head—Red varnish.

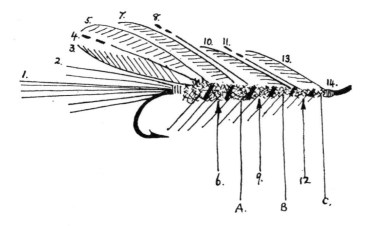

Two flies which have been found to be most successful are patterns produced by Mr. Pat Curry, the well-known fly dresser of Coleraine, and the dressings are given below—

Curry's Golden Shrimp

TAG. Flat silver tinsel.

TAIL HACKLE. Yellow golden pheasant body feather.

BODY. Two equal halves—embossed silver tinsel ribbed with oval silver tinsel. Both halves veiled with orange Toucan or substitute.

MIDDLE HACKLE. Orange.

WINGS. Two Jungle Cock feathers back to back, reaching to the end of the body.

FRONT HACKLE. Orange—longer in the fibre.

HEAD. Red varnish.

Curry's Red Shrimp

TAG. Flat silver tinsel.

TAIL HACKLE. Red golden pheasant body feather.

BODY. Two equal halves—tail half red floss ribbed fine oval silver tinsel, front half black floss ribbed thicker oval silver. Both halves veiled with Indian Crow or substitute.

MIDDLE HACKLE. Badger.

WINGS. Two Jungle Cock feathers back to back, reaching to end of body.

FRONT HACKLE. Badger—longer in the fibre.

HEAD. Red varnish.

Usk Grub

TAG. Fine round tinsel.

TAIL. Fibres from a red golden pheasant body feather.

BODY. (2 Halves) Tail half orange wool or seal fur, front half black do.

RIB. Fine oval silver tinsel.

CENTRE HACKLES. A white hackle superimposed by a hot orange hackle, tied in and wound where the two halves of the body meet.

FRONT HACKLE. Coch-y-bonddu, longer in fibre than the centre ones.

WINGS. A pair of Jungle cock feathers back to back, tied high.

HEAD. Red varnish.

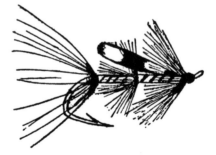

CHAPTER TWENTY-EIGHT

DRESSING SALMON FLIES

LURES

Lures similar to those used for sea trout are often used for salmon, and some of these are shown in the coloured plates facing pages 208 and 232. They are usually elongated strip and mixed wing patterns tied on tandem hooks.

The "Norsk" lure is an example of a strip-winged pattern, and any type of standard pattern can be tied on this system of hooks.

Norsk Lure
(Illustrated, facing page 236.)

Two double hooks whipped to a length of wire or gut.

TAIL. Scarlet ibis.

BODY. Oval silver tinsel wound without interruption from tail to throat.

WINGS. Alternate strips of white swan or goose and speckled bustard.

THROAT. A large badger hackle wound in front of the wings.

HEAD. Black varnish.

Red Terror
(Illustrated, facing page 232.)

Three hooks whipped to a length of gut or wire, the centre hook to be above, the first and last to be underneath.

TAIL. A tuft of red wool.

BODY. (All three hooks) fit silver tinsel.

WINGS. Two red hackles, covered by two strips of red swan or goose. Several strands of green peacock herl over.

HEAD. Black varnish.

Yellow Peril
(Illustrated, facing page 212.)

Two hooks in tandem, joined by whipping a tapered hook (rear) to an eyed hook on a length of wire or gut.

BODY. (Both hooks) flat silver tinsel.

THROAT. A yellow hackle.

WINGS. Two strips of yellow swan or goose with several toppings over.

HEAD. Black varnish.

The "Elver" Fly

This fly was mentioned in a radio broadcast given by Mr. A. Ransome. Its method of dressing brings it into the "Streamer" class of fly, but it is given here because it is a recognised salmon lure.

Hook—6–4.
Body—Black floss silk ribbed with flat silver tinsel.
Wings—(Back to back and parallel with the shank of the hook, completely

enclosing it): Blue vulturine guinea fowl feathers (2). This is a blue feather with a white central stripe, and the feathers used should be 2½ in. for the size of hooks given.

Hackle—Plain blue vulturine guinea fowl.

The feathers come from the African guinea fowl, and supplies are not plentiful.

CHAPTER TWENTY-NINE

DRESSING SALMON FLIES

TUBE FLIES

The years 1955 to 1960 brought the tube fly or lure to real prominence, but it was not until 1959 that the first instructional literature and lists of dressings were produced, by myself incidently, in the columns of the *Fishing Gazette*.

The dressings are my own idea of what can be done, and I hope they will form a basic guide to what the individual tyer can produce. As one can see, they are very easily adaptable. The "Blue Charm" for instance, has the normal black floss body and silver rib, while the effect of the usual barred teal feather of the original wing, is obtained by using fibres from a grey squirrel tail. The blue hackle in front can be added in "collar" fashion, or omitted altogether.

For the uninitiated, the tube fly, as its name denotes, consists of a length of polythene or metal tubing, round which are whipped hair fibres from the tails of different animals. Orthodox salmon fly bodies are sometimes added to the tubes, and long fibred hackles may be used in conjunction with the hair fibres or even in place of them. Heron and guinea fowl hackles are good examples of feathers which may be used for this purpose.

The tubes are fished in conjunction with a treble hook which is attached to the end of the cast. The tube is slid down the cast tail first until it is stopped by the eye of the hook. For colour variations or increase in size, two tubes can be used instead of one as per illustration.

Ordinary fly-tying implements are all that are required to make tube flies, plus two or three sizes of tapered (no eye) salmon hooks on which the tubes can be slid to facilitate the tying. I would suggest sizes 4, 2, 1/0 and 3/0.

The tube is slid on to the tapered hook firmly enough to hold it well, but not hard as to split or damage the end of it. A couple of turns of loose tying silk round the tail end of the tube and the hook will prevent it slipping round.

A body and rib, if required, are wound in the usual way as per the second illustration, bringing us to the stage where the hair fibres have to be tied in. The same principle is used as described in the chapter on hair wing flies, pages 140–143, except that several "wings" have to be tied on. The tube must be rotated on the hook shank for each "wing" of fibres to be tied on top, until the entire circumference of the tube is covered. Only small amounts of hair should be used each time otherwise the head will be very bulky. See illustration, page 249.

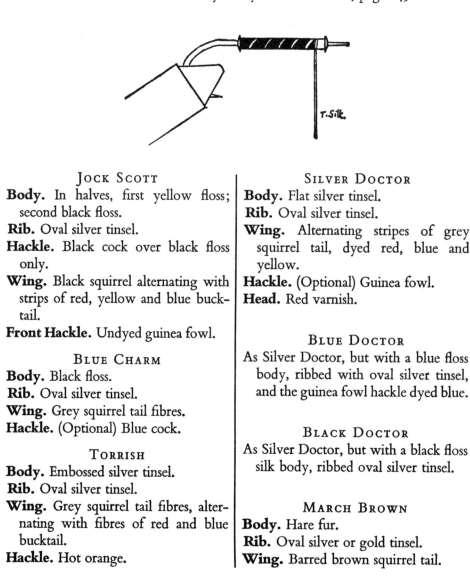

JOCK SCOTT
Body. In halves, first yellow floss; second black floss.
Rib. Oval silver tinsel.
Hackle. Black cock over black floss only.
Wing. Black squirrel alternating with strips of red, yellow and blue bucktail.
Front Hackle. Undyed guinea fowl.

BLUE CHARM
Body. Black floss.
Rib. Oval silver tinsel.
Wing. Grey squirrel tail fibres.
Hackle. (Optional) Blue cock.

TORRISH
Body. Embossed silver tinsel.
Rib. Oval silver tinsel.
Wing. Grey squirrel tail fibres, alternating with fibres of red and blue bucktail.
Hackle. Hot orange.

SILVER DOCTOR
Body. Flat silver tinsel.
Rib. Oval silver tinsel.
Wing. Alternating stripes of grey squirrel tail, dyed red, blue and yellow.
Hackle. (Optional) Guinea fowl.
Head. Red varnish.

BLUE DOCTOR
As Silver Doctor, but with a blue floss body, ribbed with oval silver tinsel, and the guinea fowl hackle dyed blue.

BLACK DOCTOR
As Silver Doctor, but with a black floss silk body, ribbed oval silver tinsel.

MARCH BROWN
Body. Hare fur.
Rib. Oval silver or gold tinsel.
Wing. Barred brown squirrel tail.

HAIRY MARY

Body. Black floss silk.

Rib. Oval silver or gold.

Wing. Brown part of bucktail. (Brown barred squirrel tail could be used as an alternative on small flies.)

STOAT TAIL

Body and Rib. As desired, or just the bare tube.

Wing. Fibres from a stoat's tail.

SILVER STOAT TAIL

Body. Embossed silver tinsel.

Rib. Oval silver tinsel.

Wing. Stoat tail fibres.

THUNDER AND LIGHTNING

Body. Black floss.

Rib. Oval gold tinsel.

Body Hackle. Hot orange.

Front Hackle. Black heron, with dyed blue guinea fowl in front.

TEAL BLUE AND SILVER

Body. Flat or embossed silver tinsel.

Rib. Oval silver tinsel.

Wing. Grey squirrel tail fibres.

Hackle. Blue cock or hen.

SHRIMP

Body. Tail half red floss, front half black floss.

Rib. Oval silver tinsel.

Middle Hackle. Hot orange or badger.

Wing. Dyed red bucktail, very long in fibre. (Long fibred feathers from golden pheasant breast could be used on smaller flies.)

Head. Red varnish.

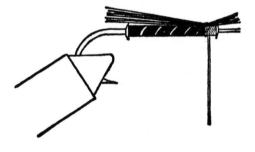

INDEX 1

Fly Tying and Materials

INDEX 2

Fly Patterns

Abbreviations: A—American flies; A/NZ—Australian and New Zealand flies; HW—Hair Wing flies; LW—Low Water Salmon flies; Str—Streamer flies; T—Tube flies; Tan—Tandem flies.

Patterns in **bold** *type are illustrated in colour*

252